Victory On the Battlefield

VAUGHN ALLEN

Delivered from Demon Possesion, 1981
More Than a Match, 1983
The War Is Real, 1988

*The Gospel Commission:
Its Nature, Restoration,
and Authority*

Distributed by Anchor Ministries
PO Box 39, Days Creek, OR 97427
(541) 839-6763

Unless otherwise indicated, Scripture quotations are taken from the King James Version.

All persons referred to in this book are real live people. Names have been changed to protect privacy.

VICTORY ON THE BATTLEFIELD

Edited and Produced by Masterbook Publishers
Cover illustrations by Bonnie Siebert
BGS Graphics
Typeset: Adobe Postscript Palatino 10/12
ISBN: 0-945383-52-5

Published by:

TEACH Services
Route 1, Box 182
Brushton, New York 12916
1(800) 367-1844
1(518) 358-2125

THE BATTLEFIELD

"This fallen world is the battlefield for the greatest conflict the heavenly universe and earthly powers have ever witnessed. It was appointed as the theater on which would be fought out the grand struggle between good and evil, between heaven and hell. Every human being acts a part in this conflict. No one can stand on neutral ground. Men must either accept or reject the world's Redeemer. All are witnesses either for or against Christ. Christ calls upon those who stand under His banner to engage in the conflict with Him as faithful soldiers, that they may inherit the crown of life...The Lord Jesus Christ has summoned the world to hear. 'He that hath ears to hear let him hear' " (LHU 253).

Acknowledgments

There are several persons without whose cooperation this book could not have been written, and it is appropriate that I acknowledge here my indebtedness to each one of them.

To my wife I am indebted for her sympathetic understanding and encouragement, for the times she joined me in spiritual warfare, and for the many hours she has spent alone while I was working on the manuscript which eventually became this book. Her support has been invaluable in ways too numerous to mention.

I am much indebted to the several hundred persons with whom it has been my privilege to engage in spiritual warfare during the past fifteen years. The experiences alluded to on these pages were all very real. Without these people allowing me to be involved in their life crisis, this book would not have been written. I thank God and praise Him for allowing me to be of service to Him and to them.

To my publisher, Masterbook Publishers, I am deeply indebted for their encouragement, their many helpful suggestions and their patience!

But, more than to anyone else, I am indebted to our Lord and Savior, Jesus Christ, whose victorious life on the battlefield of this "fallen world" makes it possible for us—every one of us—to know the joy of being set free by Him Who is the great Liberator.

That all who read these pages may experience the glorious freedom that our Lord died to provide is my constant hope and prayer. And if what you read on these pages contributes, even in the smallest way, to the joy of Christian freedom, I shall always be very thankful.

Vaughn Allen

AUTHOR'S ALERT

My book seriously considers the need to restore a proper Deliverance Ministry. I say "proper" because this ministry must always be kept in balance. It is not—and never should become—the main thrust or work of the church. Preaching the gospel should always receive primacy. Proclaiming the Three Angels' Message is still our God-assigned task and privilege.

But we must always be mindful that the Lord did not intend that preaching should stand alone. In harmony with His final commission, the disciples "went forth, and preached everywhere, the Lord working with them, and confirming with signs following." (Mark 16:20).

> "In sending out the twelve, Christ sent none alone. They were to go forth two and two, invested with power from himself to heal the sick and rebuke Satanic agencies *as proof of their mission*" (RH 3/23/97).

At this point, I must make a disclaimer. In popular religious circles there is much so-called "Deliverance and Healing" that leaves me terrified - especially what I see occasionally on television. There is much evidence of demonic "show business." This may fulfill the Lord's warning of Matthew 7:21-23. However, I feel that we must take extreme care, lest in exposing the false, we may over-react and reject the true ministry of the Lord's appointment.

I must repeat the question asked by God's servant years ago: "The gospel still possesses the same power, and why should we not today witness the same results?" (DA 823) It is my conviction that this question is purely rhetorical, and that its answer is obvious: The church today *should* witness the power of God the same as the early church did for three hundred years (see Appendix H). I believe this confirming power of God will return to His saints in the final movements.

> "By thousands of voices all over the world, the warning will be given. Miracles will be wrought, the sick will be healed, and signs and wonders will follow the believers" (GC 612)

May God grant that this may soon come to pass and that when it does, our spiritual eyes may be open to recognize it for what it is—a part of the final work of the Spirit of God.

Vaughn Allen

Abbreviations of Sources

AA — Acts of the Apostles
AH — The Adventist Home
BC — Adventist Bible Commentary, volume and page
Biog. — Biography of Ellen White, volume and page.
CD — Counsels on Diet and Foods
CG — Child Guidance
COL — Christ's Object Lessons
CT — Counsels to Parents, Teachers, and Students
Conf. — Confrontation
DA — Desire of Ages
Ed. — Education
EW — Early Writings of Mrs. E. G. White
FE — Fundamentals of Christian Education
GC — The Great Controversy
GW — Gospel Workers
Let. — Letters written by Mrs. E.G .White
LHU — Lift Him Up
LS — Life Sketches of Mrs. E. G. White
MCP — Mind, Character and Personality
MH — Ministry of Healing
MLT — My Life Today
MS — Manuscript, with number and year
MYP — Messages to Young People
OHC — Our High Calling
PK — Prophets and Kings
PP — Patriarchs and Prophets
RC — Reflecting Christ
RH — The Review and Herald (a magazine)
SC — Steps to Christ (paging varies with editions)
SD — Sons and Daughters of God
SG — Spiritual Gifts, with volume and page
SL — The Sanctified Life
SM — Selected Messages, with volume and page
SP — Spirit of Prophecy, with volume and page
SP-M — Spaulding-Magan Collection
ST — Signs of The Times (a magazine)
T — Testimonies for the Church, volume and page
TDWG — This Day With God
Te. — Temperance
TM — Testimonies to Ministers
UL — The Upward Look
YI — The Youth's Instructor (a magazine)

CAUTION

This book is an appeal for balance—a Gospel balance. The author and the publishers of this book do not wish to encourage a widespread, promiscuous activity in casting out demons. That would be fanaticism. We strongly caution against experimentation. However, we wish to inform and to alert. The unseen battle daily becomes more vicious.

Anyone reading the four gospels cannot help being impressed by the many highly descriptive narrations of Jesus in direct conflict with unclean spirits. Multitudes of oppressed people came to Him and were set free. We are told: "God's messengers are commissioned to take up the very work that Christ did while on this earth. They are to give themselves to *every line of ministry that He carried on*" (TDWG p. 30).

When Jesus outlined the ministry of His church, it was to be in three parts: Preach the Gospel, heal the sick, and cast out the devils (Mark 3:14-15). By this three-fold ministry all the needs of humanity were to be met - the mind, the body, the soul. This is the fullness of the Everlasting Gospel - the perfect plan of the Lord Jesus Christ for the complete redemption of mankind.

In our 20th Century church, we are pleased with good gospel preaching. We have no problem praying for the sick. However, the suggestion that anyone minister to individuals possessed by demons is almost always met with disapproval. This protest plays into the enemy's hands. The truth is that the enemy is playing havoc with many of our own people, with our homes, with your youth and even our churches. Tragedy after tragedy goes undetected as to its true cause. Mere token recognition of demonic working is non-Biblical, inadequate, and dangerous. Failure to detect his subtle working carries the high risk of eternal loss.

> "There is nothing that the great deceiver fears so much as that we shall become acquainted with his devices." (GC 516).

> "His deceptive powers have been sharpened by constant practice, and in the final crisis he will deceive to their own ruin those who do not now *seek to understand his methods of working*" (RH July 26, 1901)

> "I have seen that a fearful stupor is upon nearly all. It is almost impossible to arouse the very ones who should be awakened, so as to have any just sense of the power which Satan holds over minds" (2T 478).

The author of this book, a Seventh-day Adventist minister, unfolds his fifteen years experience in helping oppressed people. During this time he has found many physical, mental, emotional, and spiritual problems to be demonic in origin. He asks a serious question - have we allowed the devil to blind us to his many subtle workings? Has humanism colored our thinking?

Like the Gospel of Mark, this book is full of experiences of direct encounters with demonic force. These stories are not told to entertain, but to expose the wide variety of methods the devil is currently using to attack and destroy human beings. The author gives several cautions.

A FALSE VIEW: There are those who have thought Deliverance Ministry to be a quick and easy form of sanctification. This is not true, and never has been true. Ellen White wrote:

> "Do not think that God will work a miracle to save those weak souls who cherish evil, who practice sin; or that some supernatural element will be brought into their lives, lifting them out of self into a higher sphere where it will be comparatively *easy work,* without any crucifixion of self; because all who dally on Satan's ground for this to be done will perish with the evildoers. They will be suddenly destroyed, and that without remedy." TM 453

THE TRUE VIEW: Deliverance is an emancipation of the will. Those in a satanic bondage want to do what is right, but they cannot because their wills are captive of Satan. They have lost control.

> "He came to expel the demons that had controlled the will." DA 38

> "This powerful destroyer (Satan) considers them his lawful prey and exercises his power upon them, and that against their will. *When they wish to control themselves they cannot.* They yielded their minds to Satan, and he will not release his claims, but holds them captive. *No power can deliver the ensnared soul but the power of God in answer to the earnest prayers of His followers."* 1T 299

This book is a call to that kind of earnest prayer. There are multitudes of people oppressed by Satan who know not the cause of their distress. The good news must be proclaimed that the mighty One who delivered the man of Gadara and Mary Magdalene is alive and working today. Victory and freedom in Christ must be published far and wide.

This book issues a caution—We must never fall into the trap of an excessive and unhealthy interest in demons. We must not automatically ascribe every possible human flaw, struggle, disease, or misfortune to direct demonic oppression. On the other hand, to minimize the fact that the devil is very deeply involved in every aspect of individual human life is an equally dangerous distortion of Biblical truth.

This world is a battlefield, and until the Prince of Peace comes to give us final victory, we must fight the good fight of faith in our own behalf and in behalf of those we love. That this glorious victory may be yours is the prayer of

THE PUBLISHERS

Table of Contents

APPENDICES

CHAPTER
1
Those Seductive Voices

"There are, it may be, so many kinds of voices in the world, and none of them is without signification." 1 Cor. 14:10

When seven year old Kathy walked into the family garage, she found her father's body hanging by a rope from a rafter. He had taken his own life. This terrifying experience set in motion a series of events that plagued her for the next seven years. I want to tell you about them.

Soon after discovering her father's body, Kathy began to experience periods of deep depression. Then stranger things began to occur. What looked like a human figure began to appear in her bedroom during the night. The apparition dressed like her father, talked like her father, and acted like her father. It even sat on her bed and talked with Kathy just as her father used to do. Then it seductively began to urge Kathy—"Do what I did, so you can be with me." These suggestions became increasingly persuasive.

And then came another dreadful day. When her mother came home from work, she could not find Kathy until she went into the garage. To her horror, she discovered that Kathy had yielded to the apparition's deadly suggestions. She had finally attempted to do in the garage exactly what her father had done, but a kind Providence intervened. Kathy was rushed to the hospital where she was revived.

The following day Kathy's mother called me on the telephone. She asked me to visit Kathy in the mental health unit in one of our medical centers where she had been taken. Remember— seven years had passed since her father's death. She was now a personable, intelligent fourteen-year-old eighth-grader in one of our larger church-sponsored schools. Her first words to me were, "I feel very uncomfortable right now." She told me that "the voices" were warning her to have nothing to do with me. I assured Kathy that I was her friend, and that I would not hurt her in any way. It was only with much silent prayer and gentle encouragement that I succeeded in persuading her to stay in the same room with me.

1

"I've been in church school," Kathy said, when we were finally seated and were able to talk a bit. "I know what the Bible says about what happens when people die. I know it here," she said, pointing to her head. "But it's hard to believe it here"—and she placed her hand over her heart—"when you see your father sitting on your bed and you hear him talking about things that only he and I knew—then it gets hard."

Experiences similar to Kathy's are more common than most of us are aware. Satan frequently appears before people in the guise of their departed friends and relatives. He is able to produce a perfect counterfeit (GC 552). The familiar look, the words, even the tone of voice are reproduced with marvelous exactness. In this way Satan comforts his victim with the assurance that the loved one is enjoying the bliss of heaven. People like Kathy are innocently listening "to seducing spirits and doctrines of devils" (1 Tim. 4:1). Satan had exercised his bewitching influence upon Kathy's mind and had brought her under his subtle spell (See GC 552).

Once Satan gains access to a person's mind, he continues to hold him or her as his captives. Satan can exercise his control over such captives even against their wills (GC 558). It is impossible for such persons, in their own strength, to break away from Satan's alluring spell. Nothing but the power of God in answer to the earnest intercessory prayer of faith can deliver these ensnared souls (GC 558).

Satan had a powerful hold on Kathy's mind. I knew that prayer was the only solution to her problem. So I invited her to talk and pray with me in her hospital room. I knew very well why she felt uncomfortable and why "the voices" were telling her not to talk with me. And I also knew who "the voices" were. In my ministry I had heard them speak out of many of their victims on numerous occasions. They did not speak audibly out of Kathy, however; and I was glad for that.

The day came when Kathy and I could calmly discuss her experience. We talked about who had actually come into her room at night. We talked about how real Satan is. We discussed the reality of the war between Christ and Satan. We talked about how each of us can defeat the enemy through the power of Jesus living in us. I explained how Jesus had already won the decisive battle of the war at the Cross.

At the beginning of our times together, Kathy would not, or could not, pray. This did not annoy or astonish me. In the case of a strong bondage, it is not at all unusual that a person cannot pray. However, she did not object to my praying with her and for her. As we continued to talk and pray during my visits over the next couple of weeks, subtle changes took place. "I don't have any more urge to kill myself," she told me. Of course I thanked God for that. By now she was able to pray a beautiful prayer. Slowly but surely she was being set free. A few days after Kathy was discharged from the hospital, I phoned her mother. I rejoiced to learn that Kathy was doing well. She did not appear to have any problems. The Savior had set her free.

I am grateful to God that Kathy's story does not have a tragic ending. It had that strong possibility. But I am still filled with "righteous indignation" when I think about her experience. What kind of creature would resort to such "tricks" as those that were played on this child? Who would stoop to such cruel deceit? Only Satan, through his demonic powers, is capable of such actions. Just as God is the personification of love and kindness, so Satan is the personification of hate and cruelty. If Satan were permitted to do so, he would destroy the entire human race. He would wipe out every being made in the image of God (FE 299). He will stoop to any level, no matter how low; resort to any plan, no matter how cruel; and use any device, no matter how deceitful, in order to accomplish his goal. All of us are alive today only by the grace of God. In love He has made it possible for everyone of us to defeat the enemy.

Pedro

Let me tell you about Pedro. I saw him as a patient in a mental hospital. He, too, heard Satanic voices. As a result of listening, —a tragedy occurred. One day, at the command of the voices, he wrenched a piece of metal from his bed-spring and gouged out both of his eyes.

It makes me cringe to tell Pedro's story. I can almost feel the anguish and the pain. None of us has any idea of the hatred of these unseen evil forces. They are constantly working in an infinite variety of ways to destroy every one of us. They especially hate those who love God and His Son Jesus Christ. Pedro did not recognize the origin of these voices any more than Kathy did. The voices led him to do this terrible thing to himself. In spite of the medical treatment he had been given, the voices did not go away. In fact, they became louder, more insistent, and more persuasive.

"The voices told me they would kill my mother if I did not put out my eyes," Pedro said in relating the experience to me later. "I believed at the time that by blinding myself I was saving my mother's life."

In the many experiences the Lord has given me I have learned that the power of Satan is in his lies (Jn. 8:44). Pedro believed a lie. This belief led him to put out his own eyes. Jesus said, "The truth shall make you free"(Jn. 8:32). The price of not knowing and loving the truth is high. Truth is God's way of protecting us from the lies of Satan.

It is impossible for us who have never heard these voices to appreciate how devastatingly persuasive they can become in the minds of those unfortunate individuals who do hear them.

Marie

I must tell you about Marie. Her story has an entirely different twist. I am sure, however, if God had not intervened it would have worked out to her destruction. The powers of evil have only one purpose—destroy, destroy, destroy.

Briefly told, this is Marie's story as she related it to me: "When I became a Christian I joined a Pentecostal church. As we were taught to do, I prayed for the Holy Spirit. Soon after that I began to hear a voice which said such beautiful things. I was sure it was the Holy Spirit. I thanked God for answering my prayer. But a year or so later the voice was saying such ugly and blasphemous things that I knew it was not from God. The problem was that by that time I was "hooked" on the voice. I could not ignore it. Later I learned more Bible truth and became a Seventh-day Adventist. I know now that the voice I have been listening to all these years is from Satan. But it won't go away, even when I pray for it to leave. That's why I asked you to come and pray for me."

After gaining some understanding of Marie's problems, I assured her of God's power and promise to set Satan's captives free. Marie prayed, confessing her sins, claiming God's promise of forgiveness, and making a new commitment to Jesus Christ. Then

I began to pray a prayer of intercession for Marie. I had hardly begun to pray when the Holy Spirit began smashing Satan's strongholds (2 Cor.10:4, 5). A demonic voice began to speak through Marie.

Specific Work Assignments

"My name is Blasphemy," the voice said. "My assignment is to imitate the Holy Spirit."

From Marie's experience we have learned two valuable lessons. First, it is not unusual for these satanic "thought-voices" to pretend to be the Holy Spirit. Many Christians have fallen into this trap. A true Christian is dedicated to follow the Lord. If he believes this voice is truly from God he will instantly obey. This is why these deceptive voices are so dangerous. Marie is one of several persons I have prayed with who have been deceived on this very point. The devil frequently counterfeits the Holy Spirit.

Second, it is not unusual for demonic voices to refer to their work as an "assignment." This terminology may seem a bit strange until we remember that "Satan *assigns* to each of his angels a part to act" (EW 90, 264). Satan instructs some of his demons to imitate deceased human beings when it is to his advantage to do so (GC 552). Why should he not assign some of his agents to imitate the Holy Spirit? Be assured this really happens!

That voice was only the first of several which spoke out of Marie that day. This is not unusual. I have heard many different voices speak out of people who were deceived in much the same way as Marie was. These voices make the same false and deceptive claims.

The experiences of Kathy, Pedro, and Marie are more common than we realize. Each of these persons was a victim—a casualty, if you prefer—of the great controversy which the Bible teaches. Yet relatively few Adventists actually recognize how real the controversy is. Christians are intimately involved in this conflict. I must remind you that both Kathy and Marie are Seventh-day Adventists. They had no more desire to be deceived than you or I do. At the time of her "deliverance" Marie was in training as hospital chaplain. Remember none of us is immune from Satan's attacks. "There, but for the grace of God, go I."

Indeed, there are many kinds of voices in the world. Through these voices and in multitudes of other subtle ways, Satan is linking his mind with human minds. He imbues human minds with his thoughts. He does this in such a deceptive way that those who accept his suggestions do not know that they are listening to his voice. In this way Satan hopes to so confuse the minds of men and women, boys and girls that they will listen to no other voice but his. None of this should surprise us. We were told years ago that Satan's last exploits would be carried out with more power than ever before through "scientific scheming;" and that the enemy will use "every ingenious device" and take advantage of "every possible method" (TDWG 312).

Unconsciously, each of us hears these seductive voices. This is the way that many temptations come. All of us are living on a battlefield of devils playing "mind games"—each of us is under attack in our own individual way. These attacks are seen in fierce mental, emotional and spiritual assaults. This is why every thought must be brought into obedience to Christ. (2 Cor. 10:4,5) But if we will persevere in prayer we are certain of victory. The decisive battle of this war was gloriously won at Calvary two thousand years ago.

CHAPTER
2
So You Will Understand

"And he ordained twelve, that they should be with him, and that he might send them forth to preach, and to have power to heal sicknesses, and to cast out devils." Mark 3:14, 15.

It has been a decade and a half since my first experience with one who was "demon possessed." There was no plan on my part to become involved in "the Deliverance Ministry." Since that first experience took place, many other persons suffering from varying degrees of demonic harassment, control, and possession have come for help and have been delivered. For this we praise God, and to Him we give the glory.

In this book I shall refer to only a few of the several hundred confrontations we have experienced with demonic forces during these past few years. Some of you who read these pages may have difficulty believing that the experiences have actually taken place. But I assure you that every account is true and accurate. Only the names and places have been changed. And these experiences are not part of the dim past; they are happening today with an ever increasing frequency.

What The Bible Teaches

The reader will soon detect that I write with a personal conviction that the "Deliverance Ministry" or "Spiritual Warfare," is an essential but long-neglected aspect of the gospel ministry. In view of the plain teachings of the Bible and the Spirit of Prophecy, I do not see how we can come to any other conclusion. Consider the following scriptures:

"And he said unto them, Go ye into all the world, and preach the gospel to every creature. He that believeth and is baptized shall be saved; but he that believeth not shall be damned. And these signs shall follow them that believe; In my name shall they cast out devils; they shall speak with new tongues; they shall take up serpents; and if they drink any deadly thing, it shall not hurt them; they shall lay hands on the sick, and they shall recover" (Mk. 16:15-18).

7

"And when he had called unto him his twelve disciples, he gave them power against unclean spirits, to cast them out, and to heal all manner of sicknesses and all manner of diseases" (Matt. 10:1).

"Then he called his twelve disciples together, and gave them power and authority over all devils, and to cure disease" (Luke 9:1).

The Gospels are specific that the twelve were ordained to do three things—preach, heal the sick, and cast out the devils. These are the three component parts of the gospel commission. Jesus did all three—the Apostles were ordained to precisely follow His example.

"And He ordained twelve that they should be with him, and that he might send them forth to preach, and to have power to heal sicknesses, and to cast out devils" (Mk. 3:14-15).

No Evidence of Change

Take note that a little later He sent out seventy disciples with the same power and authority He had given the twelve.

"After these things the Lord appointed other seventy also, and sent them two and two before his face into every city and place, whither he himself would come... And the seventy returned again with joy, saying, Lord, even the devils are subject unto us through thy name. And he said unto them, I beheld Satan as lightning fall from heaven. *Behold, I give unto you power to tread on serpents and scorpions, and over all the power of the enemy: and nothing shall by any means hurt you*" (Luke 10:1, 17-19).

I find no scriptural evidence that the work of the church now should be any different from that of the Lord, the Twelve, or the Seventy. As a matter of fact, I believe that Deliverance Ministry is more needed now than at any time in world history. With Satan's attacks becoming more viscious and open, the need to restore this ministry is continuing to grow.

What The Spirit of Prophecy Teaches

The Spirit of Prophecy is in perfect agreement with the Scriptures on this matter. Ellen White indicated a unity in the gospel commission that must never be divided.

" The Lord's work is one, and His people are to be one. He has not directed that any one feature of the message should be carried on independently or become all absorbing. In all His labors He united the medical missionary work with the ministry of the word. He sent out the twelve apostles and afterward the seventy, to preach the gospel to the people, and *He gave them power also to heal the sick and to cast out devils in His name....Satan will invent every possible scheme to separate those whom God is seeking to make one. But we must not be misled by his devices.*"
(6 T 292).

God did not send the above warning through Ellen White without a cause. We were told that Satan would invent every possible scheme to separate the medical work from the ministry. Satan's scheme to separate Deliverance from the work of the ministry has been almost totally successful. I am sad to say that God's unified commission has been fragmented. The work of our pastors has been reduced to one of administrating, counseling, and preaching. They are not trained to recognize demonic oppression or to help the oppressed. We must not allow Satan's clever scheme to continue to succeed.

This book is an effort to expose a tragedy. We must act with prudence and caution. Fanaticism must be prevented, but we must never allow Satan to lead us into a policy of separating the three-fold commission. "Let not man put asunder."

A Word Picture from Ellen White

The following two paragraphs from her pen paint a perfect word picture of the Deliverance Ministry or Spiritual Warfare:

"They (Satan's captives) should entreat those who have had a religious experience, and who have faith in the promises of God to plead with the mighty Deliverer in their behalf. *It will be a close conflict.* Satan will reinforce his evil angels who have controlled these persons; but if the saints of God, with deep humility fast and pray, their prayers will prevail. Jesus will commission holy angels to resist Satan, and he will be driven back and his power (will be) broken from off the afflicted ones" (1T 344, 345).

"They have yielded their minds to Satan, and he will not release his claims, but holds them captive. *No power can deliver the ensnared soul but the power of God in answer to the earnest prayers of His faithful followers*" (1T 299).

Take special note of the words "plead; close conflict; fast and pray; prevail; will not release; earnest prayer." None of these expressions describe the quick victory which some have felt must always characterize a valid Deliverance Ministry. There is no quick and easy "fix."

In addition, the Spirit of Prophecy does not limit this ministry exclusively to Bible times. It was clearly the Lord's intention that the work of the church should be a positive and precise continuation of His own ministry. The church was to follow His example right up until His return.

"We are to feed the hungry, clothe the naked, and comfort the suffering and afflicted... Through His servants, God designs that the sick, the unfortunate and *those possessed of evil spirits* shall hear His voice through us. Through human agencies He desires to be a Comforter such as the world knows not" (MH 106).

Famine stalks many countries of our world. People need to be fed. We must do this. Naked bodies need to be clothed. This is our work. People possessed of evil spirits must hear His voice through us. This too is our work. May God help us to see it!

An Appeal for Investigation

As a people we have historically recognized our Christian obligation to "feed the hungry, clothe the naked, and comfort the suffering and afflicted," to use Ellen White's words. We have, within our church, organizations and institutions which are dedicated to fill these needs. But it appears that we have allowed the enemy to persuade us that there is no need to minister to "those possessed of evil spirits."

I find it strange that in a world that is becoming progressively more committed to doing evil there is so much resistance to restoring this part of the commission. If anyone mentions demonic activity, he is looked upon with suspicion by a large part of our church membership, including administrators and pastors.

Sealed Fountains to be Opened

I am urging a renewed study of the plain teaching of the Bible and the Spirit of Prophecy on this subject. I believe that it is time for Deliverance Ministry to be properly and sensibly restored. Hurting people are all around us. Ellen White speaks of sealed fountains being opened.

> "Souls possessed with evil spirits will present themselves before us. We must cultivate the spirit of earnest prayer, mingled with genuine faith to save them from ruin, and this will confirm our faith. God designs that the sick, the unfortunate, *those possessed with evil spirits, shall hear His voice through us...the sealed fountains of earnest, Christlike work are to be unsealed...* The time of need and of necessity makes plain our great need of a present, all powerful God, in Whom is everlasting strength and *in Whose power we may work*" (Spaulding-Magan 89).

Notice that Ellen White predicted a time when these "sealed fountains" would be opened. God wants us to work in His power, not in our weakness. Many needy people are already coming for help. Generally these persons do not understand the source of their distress. We praise God as we see the fountains being opened. God wants to help the oppressed. This is a vital part of what God wants done at this time.

However, I am very much aware that many people, whose sincerity I do not question, do not share my convictions. They find it difficult to accept the reality of demonization in today's Western culture. I have no quarrel with these people. Each of us must be guided by the light that God has given to him. I can write only from my own understanding and experience.

There is an ever growing number of Adventist pastors whose understanding and experience parallels mine. Many faithful ministers are now involved in Spiritual Warfare as the need arises. They are asking for divine guidance as they minister. I believe that this ministry will become increasingly important as we near the time when Jesus comes to destroy forever the works of the devil (1 Jn. 3:8).

Reconciliation

I must not close this introductory chapter without attempting to reconcile a seeming contradiction in the writings of Ellen White. The following paragraphs are self-explanatory.

1) "The way in which Christ worked was to preach the Word, and to relieve suffering by *miraculous works of healing. But I am instructed that we cannot now work in this way*, for Satan will exercise his power by working miracles. God's servants today could not work by means of miracles, because spurious works of healing, claiming to be divine, will be wrought" (2 SM 54).

2) "Servants of God, with their faces lighted up and shining with holy consecration, will hasten from place to place to proclaim the message from heaven. By thousands of voices all over the world, the warning will be given. Miracles will be wrought, *the sick will be healed*, and signs and wonders will follow the believers." (GC 612).

How can these statements be harmonized? We know that the Lord worked miracles to prepare the way for His teaching among the unconverted. The church is instructed not to use this approach to evangelism. We are not to make *public altar calls* for healing. However, this does not invalidate *individual and private healings.* (See James 5:17). Many times she herself was healed privately. *The difference lies between a public vs. a private ministry. There is no conflict here.* We do have

A Definite End-Time Warning

"Here we see that the church--the Lord's sanctuary--was the first to feel the stroke of the wrath of God. The ancient men, those to whom God had given great light and who had stood as guardians of the spiritual interests of the people, had betrayed their trust. *They had taken the position that we need not look for miracles and the marked manifestation of God's power as in former days*" (5T 211).

This is a prediction that end-time miracles would be opposed by the ancient men. The opposition would be vigorous. A sacred trust would be betrayed. In our anxiety to avoid being deceived by satanic miracles, there is danger of resisting an essential work of the Holy Spirit. This is a matter for earnest prayer. On this battlefield, we must to be on the right side in the conflict.

CHAPTER
3
Living on the Battlefield

"Be sober, be vigilant: because your adversary the devil as a roaring lion walketh about seeking whom he may devour."
1 Peter 5: 8.

"Pastor, I feel as though there is a devil in me."

"No, Paula, there can't be a devil in you, "I assured her, "You have just been baptized. You are a child of God. There isn't any devil in you. Satan must be harassing you with that idea. Get it out of your mind."

"But I am sure there is a devil in me. He has been there a long time."

We were in a hospital where Paula had been admitted as a patient a week earlier. Her chart said she was suffering from extreme fatigue although there was no detectable physical or medical reason for it.

Paula had studied the Bible with my wife and me on a weekly basis for several months, and I had baptized her only a few weeks before she was admitted to the hospital. I was surprised and a bit shocked at her suggesting that there was a devil in her. How could there be a devil in someone I had recently baptized? The whole idea was repulsive and unacceptable.

Besides, demons do not possess people in this twentieth century, especially in a sophisticated and civilized culture such as ours. Or do they? The Bible plainly teaches that devils, or demons, possessed people in Christ's day. The gospels record many examples of demonization, which we commonly call "demon possession." Let us look briefly at a few such cases.

Demonic Activity In The Gospels

"And when he (Christ) was come to the other side, unto the country of the Gergesenes, there met him two possessed with devils, coming out of the tombs, exceeding fierce, so that no man might pass by that way... And He said unto them, Go. And when they were come out, they went into the herd of swine..." (Matt 8:28-32).

Matthew 9:32 presents yet another case. "As they went out, they brought unto Him (Christ) a dumb man possessed with a devil. And when the devil was cast out, the dumb spoke."

Matthew tells of an unhappy man who suffered from a double affliction. "Then was brought unto him (Christ). one possessed with a devil, blind and dumb: and he healed him, insomuch that the blind and dumb both spoke and saw" (Matt. 12:22).

One of the better-known cases of demon possession is that of a boy whose father brought him to the apostles for healing. You will recall their failure to set the boy free.

> "And one of the multitude answered and said, Master, I have brought unto thee my son, which hath a dumb spirit; and wheresoever he taketh him, he teareth him: and he foameth, and gnasheth with his teeth, and pineth away: and I spoke to thy disciples that they should cast him out; and they could not...And He answered and said, 'Bring him unto me.' And they brought him unto him: and when he saw him, straitway the spirit tare him; and he fell on the ground, and wallowed, foaming. And he asked his father, How long is it ago since this came unto him? And he said, Of a child... Jesus said unto him, If thou canst believe, all things are possible to him that believeth.

> "And straightway the father of the child cried out, and said with tears, Lord, I believe; help thou mine unbelief. When Jesus saw that the people came running together, he rebuked the foul spirit, saying unto him, Thou dumb and deaf spirit, I charge thee, come out of him, and enter no more into him. And the spirit cried and rent him sore, and came out of him: and he was as one dead; insomuch that many said, He is dead. But Jesus took him by the hand, and lifted him up; and he arose" (Mark 9:17-27).

There was a demon who recognized the Messiahship of Jesus:

> "And there was in the synagogue a man with an unclean spirit; and he cried out, saying, Let us alone; what have we to do with thee, thou Jesus of Nazareth? Art thou come to destroy us? I know thee who thou art, the Holy One of God. And Jesus rebuked him, saying, Hold thy peace and come out of him. And when the unclean spirit had torn him, and cried with a loud voice, he came out of him"(Mark 1:23-26).

We remember Mary Magdalene by the fact that she was possessed by seven devils who apparently left her one at a time, at the command of Jesus (Mark 16:9; DA 568).

These and many other cases of demonization are recorded by the gospel writers, but these are only illustrations of many other such experiences whose details are not given. The Bible substantiates this idea by saying that "When evening was come, they brought unto him *many that were possessed with devils;* and he cast out the spirits with his word, and healed all that were sick "(Matt. 8:16).

One cannot read the gospels without recognizing that Jesus ministered to those who were demon possessed. I stand convicted that the same great need exists today. In our culture the need goes unrecognized.

The Apostles Continued This Ministry

Demon possession and its accompanying deliverances did not stop when Jesus ended His ministry and returned to heaven. In harmony with the gospel commission which Jesus had given, Philip, for instance, was used by God to free many people who had become captives of Satan.

> "Then Philip went down to the city of Samaria, and preached Christ unto them. And the people with one accord gave heed unto those things which Philip spake, hearing and seeing the miracles which he did. *For unclean spirits, crying with loud voice, came out of many that were possessed with them:* and many taken with palsies, and that were lame, were healed. And there was great joy in that city "(Acts 8:5-8).

We can't help noticing that in nearly every instance of deliverance recorded in the Bible, mention is made of the "loud voice" with which demons leave their victims. More times than I care to count, I have heard demons cry "with a loud voice" as they protested their having to leave the bodies of those whom they had possessed.

Demon-possession was not entirely unknown in Old Testament times. The experience of Saul, the first king of Israel, is a case in point. The record is that "the Spirit of the Lord departed from Saul, and an evil spirit from the Lord troubled him (1 Sam. 16:14).

"And the evil spirit from the Lord was upon Saul as he sat in his house with his javelin in his hand: and David played with his harp. And Saul sought to smite David even to the wall with the javelin; but he slipped away out of Saul's presence, and he smote the javelin into the wall: and David fled, and escaped that night "(1 Sam. 19: 9-10).

The evil spirit was "from the Lord" not in the sense that it came from God, but that God permitted it. Saul had grieved away the Holy Spirit which had "departed from Saul," and the evil spirit moved in to fill the void. It is not uncommon for the Bible to represent God as doing that which He does not choose to prevent. The facts are that Saul by his own consent gave the evil spirit legal rights; God does not deny legality.

The Gospel Commission

Demon-possession was a fact of life in Christ's time. There is no Biblical evidence that it would not continue to be a problem in our day. In His final words concerning the mission of the church He specifically implied that it would be an on-going plight of the human family till the end of time.

"And he said unto them, Go ye into all the world, and preach the gospel to every creature.... And these signs shall follow them that believe; in my name shall they cast out devils; they shall speak with new tongues; they shall take up serpents; and if they drink any deadly thing, it shall not hurt them; they shall lay hands on the sick, and they shall recover" (Mk. 16:15-18).

These words express not only the command to preach the gospel, but also the promise that certain signs or proofs would continue to accompany that preaching. In other words, wherever the gospel is preached, He intended that certain signs or proofs are to be seen. And among the signs—the first one given, in fact—is the casting out of devils.

But Jesus never commands His people to do anything without providing the power or ability to carry out the command. The inspired record makes clear that Jesus included power with the commission.

He "called unto him his twelve disciples, and gave them power against unclean spirits, to cast them out, and to heal all manner of sickness and all manner of disease" (Matt. 10:1).

Jesus also said, "This gospel of the kingdom shall be preached in all the world for a witness unto all nations; and then shall the end come" (Matt. 24:14). The gospel is to be preached right up to the second coming of Christ, or at least until probation closes just before Jesus returns. Since the gospel commission applies until the second advent, the signs that accompany the preaching must also apply until Christ comes. And among the signs and promises is the one that says devils will be cast out wherever the gospel is preached.

Yet many members of the Christian community who take seriously the gospel commission and who believe it applies today, find it difficult or impossible to accept the reality of demon-possession today. To believe that Satan or one of his demons can actually "possess" someone—that is, control that person's mind and body—seems to be totally incompatible with our sophisticated twentieth century thought.

In today's world, bizarre or violent behavior patterns are attributed to "natural" causes. Mass murderers who commit their heinous crimes in response to "voices "are considered to be the victims of mental or emotional problems or are declared to be insane. They are often considered to be the victims of a society. Society itself is made responsible for their offensive attitudes and behavior. Never is it thought that they might be under control of devils. Judges have been known to throw such a plea out of court. Do we do better?

Have We Ignored Supernatural Affliction?

There is no doubt that some persons suffer from mental or emotional problems which are due to "natural" causes. But we have been guilty of overlooking any and all supernatural causes. It might be wise to investigate whether drug or alcohol-related addiction may be demon-related. In the light of the Bible and the Writings we should not be so quick to rule out this possibility. We shall explore this idea in a later chapter when we discuss different kinds of demons and their work.

The Gospels present many accounts of people with serious physical problems of demonic origin. This may be true in some cases today. However, this point of view is completely foreign to modern thinking. Let us consider the Bible record:

"There was a woman which had a spirit of infirmity eighteen years, and she was bowed together, and could in no wise lift up herself" (Luke 13:11).

This woman's relatives and friends had depleted their resources in the hope of bringing her relief from this intense suffering. Her physician had tried his many skills in an effort to help her. Everyone assumed she was suffering from a disease from some "natural" cause. In their opinion it was a severe case of what we call arthritis or some other terrible disease which had attacked her spine and caused her to be "bowed together" so that she could not straighten herself up. But Jesus recognized the true cause of this unfortunate woman's suffering.

"And ought not this woman, being a daughter of Abraham, *whom Satan hath bound*, Lo, these eighteen years, be loosed from this bond on the Sabbath day?" (Luke 13:16).

Jesus spoke of the woman as one "whom Satan hath bound." He looked beyond the "natural" cause of her deformity and identified the woman's problem as being of supernatural or Satanic origin. He also called her a daughter of Abraham. In today's language we would say that she was a "Christian." The case of this woman shows that beyond reasonable doubt Christians, too, can come under attack.

Deaf, Dumb, and Blind

The gospels tell us of two demon-possessed men who suffered from physical disorders; One was blind and dumb. The other deaf and dumb. When Jesus healed them " the blind and dumb both spake and saw" (Matthew 12:22; Mark 9:25).

In both of these instances, when the devil was cast out, the person was "healed." The physical affliction which accompanied the demons' presence disappeared when the demons disappeared. When the demons left, the problem also left. It is obviously Bible doctrine that serious physical disabilities can be caused by the presence of a demon.

"The fact that men have been possessed with demons is clearly stated in the New Testament. The persons thus afflicted were *not merely suffering with disease from natural causes.* Christ had perfect understanding of that with which He was dealing, and *He recognized the direct presence and agency of evil spirits"* (GC 514).

The reading of the Gospels leaves no doubt that there were many people afflicted by demons. The people of New Testament times were well aware of its horrors. Many had relatives, neighbors, or friends who were its victims. They were all too familiar with these terrible manifestations. They were not the victims of ignorant superstition. Jesus dealt with these attacks as reality. Do they exist today? From our experience we believe that it is much worse now than then. Many of these attacks are tagged with a psychological or medical label. Like Jesus we need to learn to recognize the work and presence of evil spirits. We need a return to a biblical view of many human problems.

Possession and the Unpardonable Sin

In Christ's day, as in ours, there was considerable dispute about demon possession. But there was never a doubt about its existence. Demon possession was too common then to deny or doubt. But there was much contention, especially among the religious leaders, as to the power by which Christ cast out demons. Jesus' methods seemed to bother them. Matthew gives us a little glimpse of the dissension in these words:

"Then was brought unto him one possessed with a devil, blind and dumb: and he healed him, insomuch that the blind and dumb both spake and saw. And all the people were amazed, and said, Is this not the son of David? But when the Pharisees heard it, they said, This fellow doth not cast out devils, but by Beelzebub, the prince of the devils" (Matt. 12: 22-24).

Take notice that deliverance from demon possession, even when performed by Christ, was the subject of fierce controversy. His opponents could not dispute His results. They disputed the source of His power. They accused Him of casting out devils by the power of the devil. There are those today who make the same charge.

There is no questioning the fact that the strongest warning our Lord ever gave was this—He defined the unforgivable sin as crediting His Deliverance Ministry to Satan.

> "Wherefore I say unto you, All manner of sin and blasphemy shall be forgiven unto men: but the blasphemy against the Holy Ghost shall not be forgiven unto men. And whosoever speaketh a word against the Son of man, it shall be forgiven him: but whosoever speaketh against the Holy Ghost, it shall not be forgiven him, neither in this world, neither in the world to come" (Matt. 12:31-32).

In the light of the Savior's warning, I cringe whenever I hear anyone say (as I occasionally do) that the deliverance ministry is "the work of the devil." More about this in chapter 14.

Confirmation—A Strength to Faith

Mark's gospel carefully records the Lord's parting words to His church. This was no time to talk about the trivial and non-essential. Certainly He would repeat and emphasize only what He considered to be of ultimate importance. With this in mind, let us read anew His final words:

> "And He said unto them, Go ye into all the world and preach the gospel to every creature.... And these signs shall follow them that believe; In my name they shall cast out devils...they shall lay hands on the sick, and they shall recover. So then after the Lord had spoken unto them, he was received up into heaven, and sat on the right hand of God. And they went forth, and preached everywhere, the Lord working with them, and *confirming the word with signs following*" (Mark 16:15; 17-20).

Our Lord said that specific signs would follow belief. His first sign was that devils will be cast out. Could our church be suffering from unbelief? Are we ignoring this sign which is a positive proof of our Lord's victory over Satan? We must take seriously His final words—every one of them.

The scriptural record of the book of Acts gives overwhelming testimony that the ministry of the early church was mightily confirmed by signs. That church moved with visible power. Could it be that our ministry today lacks power because we fear to ask for confirmation? We do not need humanly generated excitement. We desperately need confirmation. If we would claim His promises He would confirm and strengthen our faith.

"The promise is just as strong and trustworthy now as in the day of the apostles... The gospel still possesses the same power, and why should we not today witness the same results?" (DA 823).

The same author indicates that at the identical time the Holy Spirit left the early church the power of healing and deliverance disappeared. The weakness began.

"I saw that if the church had always retained her peculiar, holy character, the power of the Holy Spirit which was imparted to the disciples would still be with her. The sick would be healed, devils would be rebuked and cast out, and she would be mighty and a terror to her enemies" (EW 227).

Every Christian believes in the healing of the sick in harmony with the gospel. In view of the violence of Satan's attack on our world, is it not time for us to renew our authority over devils included in the same gospel? (See Luke 9:1; Mark 3:14-15).

Satan's Power has Increased

In the last 2000 years Satan's purpose to destroy has not changed. Rather, evidence of a vastly increasing activity is everywhere. This needs no proving. The danger is that we become so accustomed to the sin and evil around us that we lose our awareness. It becomes no longer repulsive to us. The need for us to wear the whole armor of God and fight in his power are much more needed now than ever before (Eph 6:11-13).

During these millenniums Satan has gained much experience in manipulating the human mind. His skills have thus vastly increased. He mixes his thoughts with human thoughts. He lead us to believe that these thoughts are our own. He inserts these ideas in subtle and deceptive ways. Those who accept his guidance are not aware that they are being led by his will. He so confuses the minds of men and women that they do not recognize his influence. But his influence is there, and in the end they will do his will rather than God's will (See 2 SM 352,353).

Peter, writing under the inspiration of the Holy Spirit, wrote these words: "Your adversary the devil, as a roaring lion, walketh about seeking whom he may devour" (1 Pet. 5:8). Satan is no less an adversary now, or less aggressive today than when Peter wrote these words. Satan's purpose or nature have not changed. I wish to alert every reader of this book that our only protection is in an unconditional surrender to the Lord.

> "The power of Satan now to tempt and deceive is *tenfold greater* than it was in the days of the apostles. His power has increased, and it will increase until it is taken away. His wrath and hate grow stronger as his time to work draws near its close "(2 SG 277).

Even more —Satan's power is not just ten times greater now than it was in the days of the apostles, but *"it has increased a hundred fold* by exercise and experience" (3T 328).

Satan is even now preparing for his last campaign against the church. But the church is made up of individuals like you and me. So you and I become the target of his temptations, harassments, control, and possession. With the passing of the centuries Satan has been growing more subtle and artful. He is constantly searching for better ways to seduce us (See 1T 342).

Satan is still Christ's mortal enemy. Christ has already won the victory, Satan refuses to acknowledge his defeat although he knows it. It is still his purpose to oppose and destroy God's government. Satan is constantly working through his agents to oppose the authority of God.

As Satan's time gets shorter, we can expect his activity to increase; his desperation becomes greater; his anger gets hotter; his devices and methods, more subtle. We can be sure that he is not going to abandon any device which has proved to be successful in the past. Satan's last exploits will be carried out with more power and cunning than ever before. He has learned from his experience, and his mastermind is full of scientific scheming to accomplish his purposes in these last days.

> "Every ingenious device will be used, every possible method taken advantage of" (TDWG 312).

We Live On The Battlefield

"The fallen world is the battlefield for the greatest conflict the heavenly universe and earthly powers have ever seen. It was appointed as the theater on which would be fought out the grand struggle between good and evil, between heaven and hell. Every human being acts a part in this conflict. No one can stand on neutral ground" (LHU 253).

This world is not only a battlefield. It is a theater for the universe. Every human being on planet Earth is playing a role on one side or the other in this great conflict. Our influence is on one side or the other in this epic struggle. Eternal life is at stake. And the "great controversy going on in the world is waging more sharply today than at any previous period in this world's history" (See UL 20).

Uncompromising Consecration Needed

"Everyone who is not a decided follower of Christ is to some degree a servant of Satan, for he takes control to some extent of every mind that is not decidedly under the control of the Holy Spirit" (TM 79).

To be a nominal follower of Jesus Christ is not enough. We must be followers, not in name only, but "decided" followers. "Every man, woman, and child who is not under the control of God is under the influence of Satan's sorcery" (MYP 278).

This does not mean that all who are not "decided followers of Christ "are demon-possessed as we are using the term in this book. But it does mean that every one of us is "under the influence "of one or the other of the two great powers. It means that "all who are not decided followers of Christ are servants of Satan" (GC 508).

This means that we do not need to choose deliberately to serve Satan in order to come under his influence. *We do not need to enlist in Satan's army in order to march under his banner.* Unless we deliberately and intentionally choose to serve Jesus Christ, we will serve Satan by default. We have only to neglect making that choice. If we do not choose to cooperate with the heavenly agencies, Satan will eventually take possession of the heart and make it his abiding place. (See DA 324).

This is what Jesus meant when He said,

> "He that is not with me is against me; and he that gathereth not with me scattereth abroad" (Matt. 12:30).

When we view the great controversy in this light, realizing that every person on this planet is on one side or the other and that all who are not committed to Jesus Christ are under Satan's influence, it is apparent that there are millions who are yielding their allegiance to the enemy. They may not be demon possessed, but they are carnally minded and to some degree under Satan's power. And the truth is that more of them than we realize are actually possessed by Satan —some of them within the church. Like the Apostles we need to go first to the lost sheep of the house of Israel (Matt. 10:5,6).

The Peril of Ignorance

Ever since Satan disguised himself in the Garden of Eden and spoke through the serpent, he has pawned off on the human race the fictional idea that he does not exist; that there is no deadly foe to battle and to be guarded against. To a dangerous degree he has convinced the world that his existence is pure fable, another Santa Claus myth. And while Satan works with all his cunning and craftiness to defeat God's purpose in our lives, our ignorance and indifference work to his advantage.

It is regrettable at a time when Satan is more active than ever that we have become blinded in regard to his character and power. We remain sleepy and indifferent to the enemy's activity. In our ignorance we do not recognize what he is doing to our youth, our homes, our schools, and our church. We do not appreciate the reality and extent of his warfare (GC 507, 8).

> "It is a lamentable fact that God's servants are not half as much awake to the wiles of Satan as they should be" (3T 196).

> "Day by day the conflict between good and evil is going on. Why is it that those who have had many opportunities and advantages do not realize the intensity of this work? They should be intelligent in regard to this... As a people we do not understand as we should the great conflict going on between invisible agencies, the controversy between loyal and disloyal angels. Evil angels are constantly at

work, planning their line of attack, controlling as commanders, kings and rulers, the disloyal human forces... I call upon the ministers of Christ to press home upon the understanding of all who come within the reach of their voice, the truth of the ministration of angels" (LHU 370, 4ABC 1173).

In view of such statements and appeals from the Lord's servant, I urge that this book be read with much prayer.

"None are in greater danger from the influence of evil spirits than those who, notwithstanding the direct and ample testimony of Scriptures, deny the existence and agency of the devil and his angels. *So long as we are ignorant of their wiles, they have an almost inconceivable advantage...*" (GC 516).

There are multitudes who are *honestly ignorant* of Satan's reality and power. There are many others who are ignorant because they *choose* to overlook or ignore the many evidences of the enemy's activity and success which they see around them. Adventists, who have the Spirit of Prophecy in addition to the Bible to give us guidance, should be more alert than any other people in the world. We should be giving a powerful warning. Has the trumpet been muted?

We know that Satan is constantly on our track, tempting and seducing everyone he can reach, in every walk of life. We have been told that the enemy concerns himself with every aspect and activity of our lives. Our human experience certainly confirms that fact. He intrudes his presence into our homes. Evidence of Satan's presence is in the streets of every city, and even in our churches. The enemy is everywhere, deceiving and seducing. He is everywhere, ruining the bodies and souls of men and women and boys and girls. He is everywhere, breaking up families, causing divorce, strife, confusion and murder (GC 508).

The tragic truth is that even we Adventists have become so accustomed to Satan's activity that we are blind to his wiles. Like the rest of the Christian community, we have come to accept the terrible things happening in our world as though they are part of the natural flow of human events. Seldom do we attribute these things to the out-working of Satan's mind.

My purpose in writing this book is to disclose some of Satan's wiles and thus help to dispel some of the ignorance which he is daily using to his advantage. It is a glorious truth that in the power of the indwelling Christ—even the weakest of us—can be more than a match for Satan and all his angels (5T 293).

God Uses Holy Angels

There are evil angels all around us. Because they are unseen, we seldom recognize their presence. But there is also "an innumerable company," of holy angels who "minister to them who shall be heirs of salvation" (Heb. 12:22, 1:14).

An angel commissioned from heaven attends every soul born on this planet, seeking to draw him or her to the Savior. Ten thousand times ten thousands of angels are at His command. All these heavenly servants have one purpose above all others. They are working to guard and save the human race.

> "None of finite judgment and foresight can conceive of the care God has exercised through His angels over the children of men in their travels, in their houses, in their eating and drinking, Wherever they are, His eye is upon them, They are preserved from a thousand dangers, all of them unseen" (Letter 14, 1883).

These angels work to protect us from Satan's deceptive snares. They bring the word of God to our memory. They influence us to claim His promises. They are tireless as long as there is any hope at all. They are under the direct command of the Holy Spirit. (DA 352).Unless we put ourselves beyond any possibility of help we are guarded by these heavenly beings. (OHC 23).

A very important work of these loyal angels is to fight our battles with the rebel angels who are determined to destroy us in any way they can. The conflict which results is not a mock battle. "It is not mimic battles in which we are engaged"(MH 128). These battles are "as real as those fought by armies of this world" (MB 119). Satan "will not hesitate to engage all his energies, and to call to his aid all his evil host to wrest a single human being from the hand of Christ... They contend and battle with holy angels, and the conflict is severe. And if those who have erred continue to plead and in deep humility confess their wrongs, angels that excel in strength will prevail and wrench them from the power of the evil angels" (MYP 160).

There is an eternal principle that we are prone to forget. "Ask and ye shall receive. (Jn. 16:24) The angels are limited in their work in our behalf by our failure to ask. They need our consent. They will not violate our privacy. We must open the door.

> "I have been shown angels of God all ready to impart grace and power to those who feel their need of divine strength. But these heavenly messengers will not bestow blessings unless solicited. *They have waited for the cry* from souls hungering and thirsting for the blessing of God; *often have they waited in vain.* There were, indeed, casual prayers, but not the earnest supplication from humble, contrite hearts...." OHC 129

We should thank God every day that we are not left to fight the battle in our own power, for God has legions of loyal angels "who excel in strength" and who wage war on our behalf.

Satan Works Through Human Beings

Satan not only uses evil angels as his tools; he uses human beings as well. These human agencies may be individuals, groups or organizations. They may be of a secular or religious nature, depending upon which best serves his purpose. They are often persons from the common walks of life. They may be our own friends, or even members of our families. And, unless we are constantly on our guard and maintain a personal, saving, relationship to Jesus Christ, Satan may use us —that's right!— even you and me to accomplish his purpose.

Satan Used Peter

The Bible furnishes us a classic example of how Satan uses close friends in an effort to destroy . The example is that of Peter—a disciple of Jesus. The full story as recorded in Matt. 16:21-23. Jesus knew that the time had come when He must reveal some of His future to His disciples. He shocked them by saying that He must go to Jerusalem where He would be crucified. This information was so contrary to the expectancy of the disciples that they found it impossible to accept. This was especially true of Peter who began to remonstrate with the Savior. "Be it far from thee, Lord: this shall not be unto thee." Peter thought he was expressing his own ideas. The fact was that he was being directly used by Satan. (2 SM 353; DA 415-6).

In using Peter in this way, Satan hoped to accomplish three things. First, he hoped to keep Peter's heart from being touched by the message of Jesus' anticipated suffering and death. Second, he hoped to turn Peter's attention away from the sacrifice which Christ was about to make for him. Third, Satan hoped through Peter's words—which were really Satan's—to discourage Jesus and turn Him from His mission. Satan was attempting to do through Peter what he had failed to do by his temptation of Christ in the wilderness (See Matt 4: 1-11).

Peter Was Unaware

Peter was totally unaware of Satan's presence and control. Peter had no idea that Satan was speaking through him. Does this happen today? Of course it does! There is no doubt that all of us have many times heard demonic thoughts through human voices. We have heard people remark, "Did I say that? Why—I don't even believe that!" For the moment, another mind was in control. This does happen! We must learn to recognize Satan's presence. There are times when it is appropriate to rebuke the real enemy. "Get thee behind me, Satan" (2 SM 356; 1T 308-9).

There are further lessons for us in Peter's experience. Satan takes advantage of the influence one human mind is capable of exerting over another. This influence is so subtle, so seductive, that the one being molded is often unaware of what is taking place. Satan links the human mind with his own. He hopes to so confuse our thinking that we will hear no voice but his.

The enemy does not control our minds by force. It is when we are spiritually asleep that he most often accomplishes his purpose. If we fail to feed our spiritual nature by Bible study and prayer, and if it is not watered by the Holy Spirit, then Satan can imbue us with his spirit. The enemy spoke through Peter in a moment of weakness. When our guard is down, he can speak through us. It is possible for us to "act the part of the tempter."

Have you ever made what you intended to be a perfectly innocent remark, only to have it grossly misinterpreted? How many family arguments have started over what was intended as an entirely inoffensive comment? Satan distorts the meaning in the mind of the hearer. He will magnify the remark out of proportion. We must brace ourselves against what we consider to be a personal affront, when it is nothing but a satanic ploy.

In such cases, instead of asking God for strength to resist Satan, we often try to defend ourselves and stand up for what we consider to be our "rights." We become defensive. We are blind to the fact that Satan often uses us, or members of our family, to accomplish his purpose. We accept these situations as "human" or "normal. " Little do we realize that Satan is involved in even such seemingly trivial matters (1T 308-9).

Satan and Politics

When it serves his purpose best, Satan uses organizations as well as individuals. These organizations may be secular or religious; or a combination of both. The books of Daniel and Revelation disclose a number of governments and organizations which have served Satan's purpose.

As an example, let us look briefly at the political plot against Daniel which resulted in his being put in the lions' den. This story is known by our Sabbath School children. Daniel was a worshipper of the God of heaven. He occupied a high position in the pagan government of Darius, king of Persia. Satan and his evil angels became frightened when they saw that Daniel's influence was weakening their control over Darius and the other pagan rulers. So Satan put a demon or spirit of envy in the princes. They become jealous of Daniel. It was these satanic agencies who inspired the princes and rulers to plot Daniel's destruction. These jealous government officials did not realize that they were doing Satan's work, and carrying out his plan.

God could have prevented Daniel from being thrown into the lions' den, but He had a greater purpose. He allowed the evil angels and the wicked men under their influence to carry out their plan. Daniel's deliverance from the lions' den resulted in the defeat of Satan and his human instruments and in victory for truth to the glory of Daniel's God (PK 540-543).

The book of Esther gives another example of Satan's using government agencies to carry out his purpose. It also illustrates God's ability to care for His people and to defeat Satan's plans. In these political episodes, God has drawn back the curtain and given us glimpses of the invisible war between Christ and Satan. The same kind of war is being fought today, and each one of us is an active participant in this war. You and I live on the battlefield of this planet we call Earth.

Satanic Harassment

There are degrees of demonic influence in human lives. This fact is so obvious that the statement hardly needs to be made. Satan's most common attacks come in the form of harassment and temptation. We shall discuss harassment here and leave the subject of temptation until another chapter.

Satan's purpose in harassing us is to discourage us; to cause us to lose faith in God and in His Son, Jesus Christ, and eventually to give up the battle. All real Christians will experience some form of harassment to some degree at some time in their lives. "Yea, and all that live godly in Christ Jesus shall suffer persecution"(2 Tim. 3:12). A life of total comfort and ease with no harassment might well raise some questions as to whether we are really Christians.

There are those who become bitter and resentful even against God in times of hardship. This too is part of the enemy's purpose. One other caution—we should be careful not to attribute to either Satan—or to God!—the troubles and problems that are purely the result of our own unwise choices and decisions, a harvest resulting from the seed we ourselves have sown.

Job, a Prototype of the Human Race

The story of the patience of Job is proverbial. However he is not alone. He is only a sample of the human race. True—Job was attacked by Satan in a wider sphere than average, but he is not unique. Let's analyze his whole experience. He was physically harassed . He suffered much pain. He was attacked through his love for his children. Then he suffered great financial loss. His friends turned against him. He was attacked though his marriage. His wife, advised him to "curse God and die." Fortunately he chose not to take her advice. Job's faith and attitude were summed up in his statement, "Though he slay me, yet will I trust him" (Job 13:15).

Job's experience illustrates the fact that harassment may come from many sources. Depression and discouragement are common in our culture today. Physical problems and financial reverses may be the enemy's way of harassing some Christians now just as they were in Job's time. But I must caution again that not every misfortune that comes our way can be blamed on Satan. God is not mocked. If we abuse our body temples or become careless in our managing of God's goods as His stewards, the "harassment" that results must be recognized for what it really is—the consequence of our own bad choices. This principle, of course, may be applied to other areas of our lives in which we may feel that we are being harassed.

The Harassment of Fear

Fear is a common form of harassment today. Unpredictable panic attacks are becoming a matter of national concern. A number of adults with whom I have prayed have said, "I am so scared that I leave my bedroom light on all night." This statement is usually prefaced by some such remark as, "I am embarrassed to tell you this, but—" They do not always know what they fear; they are just afraid.

Mary

Mary is a good example of one who is harassed by fear. She was an attractive teenager, but she was always "on the run." She fled from one city to another, always in great fear. When she came to me she was living in the home of a doctor who, with his wife, had taken her in. I saw Mary only two times; once in the doctor's home very briefly, and again in the church office one evening when she came for help. Although she had come voluntarily, she stayed only a few minutes. She said she was "uncomfortable" and left quite abruptly.

Mary made her exit through the secretary's office. I stayed in my office for a few minutes, talking with the doctor's wife who had brought Mary to the church. After both of them had left I found a note that she had left on the secretary's desk. I have the note before me now. This is what Mary wrote:

Dear Pastor Allen,

I could not agree with you more, that if I don't get help soon my life will be destroyed. *I am afraid.* Please keep praying. May God be with you all. Mary

PS. Please write soon. We are being harassed.

The next day when I phoned the doctor's home I learned that Mary had "sneaked off" about four o'clock that morning. Mary was on the run again. Many young people—and older ones, too—are running in an endeavor to escape the torment of fear. Fear by itself is a terrible thing, but when it is accompanied by doubt and depression its horror is multiplied. These forms of harassment are not new. As great a man as John the Baptist was subjected to Satan's harassment of fear.

"Doubts which otherwise would not have arisen (had they not been expressed by his disciples). were suggested to John. Satan rejoiced to hear the words of these disciples, and to see how they bruised the soul of the Lord's messenger...

"There were hours when the *whisperings of demons tortured his spirit, and the shadow of a terrible fear crept over him*" (DA 314-316).

Satan used fear and doubt to harass John the Baptist. He uses them widely and effectively today. The Psalmist declared, "What time I am afraid, I will trust in thee" (Psa. 56:3).

Jesus Our Only Hope

But there is hope for those who are being harassed. We must always remember that no problem is too big for God. *Not only does God have the answer; He is the answer.* Faith and trust in Him are essential. Like Job, we must say with confidence, "Though He slay me, yet will I trust in Him"

God will give deliverance from harassment when the proper conditions have been met. One of the conditions is that the home be free of everything that Satan might use as an excuse to remain in the house. Demons consider such material as occult literature, pornography, horoscopes, rock music, and similar material as an invitation to make themselves at home. We must clean house. Demons never turn down an invitation.

But, more important than "housecleaning" is "heart-cleaning. " One who expects deliverance either from harassment or possession must make a total commitment to Jesus Christ. When that has been done, the way is opened for the Holy Spirit and the loyal angels to do their work. We are then free to claim God's promises. God never fails to do His part when the conditions have been met and obstructions to the work of the Holy Spirit has been removed.

Shauna

Let me tell you about Shauna. She was a young professional lady who worked in one of our medical institutions. At the time she came for help there were no obvious demonic manifestations. Her speech and conduct appeared to be normal. She came, she said, "because something is wrong." During the interview she suddenly said, "There are no demons in me." There was nothing too unusual about that statement. But when she continued, "In fact, there are no angels; there is no Bible, and no Jesus Christ," it was apparent who was putting those thoughts in her mind and those words in her mouth. Shauna was at that time being controlled by one or more demons.

Before we finished praying with her, the demon admitted to more than twenty different ways in which he had been harassing her. Here are a few examples of her harassment:

I won't let her sleep.	I cause her to doubt.
I make her angry.	I make her forget.
I won't let her eat.	I control her emotions.
I make her jealous. It's fun!	I mess up her finances.

I won't let her have normal social relationships.

This is only half of the list. Other areas of harassment were of a more personal nature. The startling fact is that Shauna had discussed every one of these problem areas with me even before we met to pray. They were what was "wrong."

Paula

Paula, the young woman who told me in the hospital that there was a demon in her, experienced something beyond either harassment or control. During the next few weeks her behavior became abnormal. Her personality deteriorated. She tore her Bible into shreds. She tore the mirror off the wall, leaving large holes where the adhesive took large chunks of the drywall. Three times she attempted to take her life.

Paula was demon-possessed. Before we finished working with her, eight demons were forced to identify themselves and their work and to leave. The full story of Paula's deliverance was told in my book *Delivered from Demon Possession* (Pacific Press-1981). Paula, like Job, is typical of the human family .

The fact is that Satan is still walking about as a roaring lion, seeking whom he may devour. Far from being less active than he was in Christ's time, he is more energetic, for he knows he has only a short time to accomplish his purpose. He still has super-human power and intelligence, and he is still using all his skill and craftiness to accomplish his work of destruction.

The End is Near

The good news is that the war is almost over. There is no doubt that violent battles are yet to be fought. Armageddon is the name of one of them. But we must never forget that the most decisive battle of this war was fought and won at Calvary. I will describe that battle and the victory of our Lord in some detail in chapter sixteen.

Jesus came from heaven to destroy the works of the devil (1 Jn. 3:8). He came to this fallen planet "to expel the demons that controlled the will" of man (DA 38). Jesus met and defeated His enemy on the enemy's own ground, and His glorious victory can be yours and mine through faith in Him and the presence of His Holy Spirit dwelling in our hearts.

One of the best bits of news that mankind has ever heard, or can hear is: "Through divine strength the weakest saint is more than a match for him (Satan) and all his angels" (5T 293). There is no soul in such deep bondage that God's mighty angels cannot come and set the captive free. There is a war going on. The battle is all around us. That is what this book is all about.

CHAPTER
4
War in the Hospital

"My name is Seizure."

The words came from Donna's throat just seconds after I had begun to pray for her in the hospital room. That voice proved later to be only the first of more than sixty such voices who spoke through Donna's vocal chords and who identified themselves during the next few hours as I continued to pray for her healing.

"I won't go! I won't go!"

For a minute or so, the voice continued to protest its having to leave. But soon, after one final loud scream, Donna's body relaxed and the voice became quiet.

Donna was a young woman who had been admitted to an Adventist medical center several days earlier because she was experiencing increasingly frequent and severe seizures. Because of some of the things which transpired later, I must tell you that Donna was an unusually attractive young woman. She was twenty-one years of age.

During her stay in the hospital, a day or two before I met her, several unusual things happened to Donna which were witnessed by some of the nurses and other hospital staff. On one occasion Donna was picked up by unseen hands and thrown against the wall, causing a large "goose egg" to appear on her head. Another time she was literally thrown down a flight of stairs in the hospital. Though uninjured, she became so violent it required six nurses and orderlies to get her back into her bed and put restraints on her. She broke the restraints almost immediately, seemingly with little effort.

The physician in charge of the department told Donna's parents that he could not diagnose Donna's type of seizure and that it was "too deep" for them to treat. It was then that Donna's parents contacted me and asked me to come to the hospital and pray for their daughter.

I met Donna's parents and her older sister around nine o' clock on a Saturday evening in one of the hospital's waiting rooms. I learned that Donna was basically an Adventist Christian, who had recently become careless in her observance of the Sabbath and had developed quite an interest in rock music. She had experienced three recent bouts with pneumonia. And then the seizures had begun. The seizures became so frequent and severe that her parents admitted her to the hospital for examination and treatment. All this I learned as we walked down the corridor to Donna's room.

Other Voices Spoke

A few minutes later, with Donna in her bed and surrounded by her family and friends, I began to pray on Donna's behalf. It was then that "Seizure," the first of more than sixty such voices, spoke from her.

Space does not permit me to discuss each of these voices, nor is it necessary to do so. But I do want to share with you our experience with three or four of the voices in order that you may realize the reality of the situation.

Sabbath-keeping: "My name is Sabbath-keeping," said one voice. "My assignment is to keep Donna from observing the Sabbath." I remembered then that Donna's parents had told me that she had become careless in regard to the Sabbath.

Medication: Two doctors, one of whom was an intern, joined us in several sessions of prayer. During one of those prayer sessions, one of the voices said, "My name is Medication. My work is to see that the doctors give her too much medicine." Some time later as we were walking down the corridor during a break, the doctor said to me, "When you think of it, all we are doing is giving shots and pills and other forms of medication." (For the true effects of many drugs, see 2SM 450-452).

Pride: During the entire experience, while we were praying, Donna was alert and knew what was going on. She prayed with us at times and carried on a conversation at other times; but her prayers and conversation were interrupted by the voices which spoke through her, but over which she had no control. One of the last voices to speak in this way identified himself as "Pride." As soon as the voice said, "My name is pride," Donna began to weep. Tears flowed down her cheeks.

"Oh, yes," she said, "I have been so proud." And then she began to pray. She prayed the same short prayer over and over for the next thirty minutes. I know because I timed it. I prayed silently as Donna's oral prayer was punctuated by the voice shouting, "I won't go! I don't want to go!" I heard Donna's prayer so often during that half hour and it so impressed itself on my mind that I can still repeat it word for word. She prayed:

"Oh, Lord, I have been so proud. Please forgive me. I've spent so much time in front of the mirror admiring my face, my figure, my hair, and my clothing. Please forgive me. From this time on, when I look into the mirror, let me see only the beauty of my Savior."

As we both continued to pray, there was that final loud cry of protest that I had heard so often, and Donna's body relaxed and the voice was silent.

Game-playing: Donna and I, with some members of her family, continued in almost constant prayer from Saturday evening until Monday noon. The last of the voices spoke a little before noon Monday. At about 11:30 Donna suddenly sat up in her bed and looked directly at me. A voice spoke:

"Pastor Allen, I want to apologize to you. You have been so kind. You have spent so many hours with me. I really appreciate it. And it's really all my fault. I am sorry and I apologize again. Please take your Bible and go home. I'm all right, really. Just take your Bible and go home. There aren't any demons here. I did this all myself just to get attention. Now take your Bible and go home."

If this had been my first experience in dealing with demonic forces I might have been deceived, for the persuasive voice sounded very genuine. But this was not my first such experience. There was much evidence indicating that there were demons involved; indeed, it was a demon, who was even then speaking through Donna and urging me to take my Bible and go home.

"You are not Donna speaking," I said, looking straight into Donna's eyes. "You are a demon speaking through Donna. God knows that, you know that, and I know that. Donna has chosen to serve Jesus Christ, and you have no legal right to be in her or to use her vocal chords. In the name of Jesus Christ whom both Donna and I serve, I command that you tell me your name before you leave."

"My name is Game-playing," came the answer. Then, with the usual cry of protest coming from her throat, Donna relaxed and there were no more voices.

Looking back on Donna's experience, I find much Biblical similarity for what transpired. The boy at the foot of the Mount of transfiguration was thrown around violently (Mk. 9:22). The very character of Satan is reflected in pride. His heart was lifted up because of his beauty (Eze.28:13).

Exorcism, Spiritual Battle, and Deliverance

Donna was discharged from the medical center about five o' clock that afternoon. After she left the hospital, Dr. Clarence Carnahan, her Psychiatrist, was interviewed by Editor Steven Mosely, of the *It is Written* magazine, *Channels*. (Fall 1986) The doctor was asked about the seizures. He replied, "They stopped immediately." He commented on the reaction of the hospital personel: "It was quite unsettling. Conferences were sometimes difficult because some wanted to see it entirely as a psychological phenomenon and others chose to see it totally as demon possession." I have no doubt that the latter was the case.

The Doctor called our prayer sessions "an exorcism." I avoid using the term *exorcism* because of its negative connotation in the minds of many people. I prefer to think of such prayer as I engaged in for Donna as a "Spiritual battle" which results in a "Deliverance" involving the ministry of the Holy Spirit and the holy angels. These terms are more in harmony with my understanding of Scripture and the writings of Ellen White.

However, whether we prefer the word *exorcism* or some other word having the same meaning, we must recognize that the doctor is suggesting that demons were present in Donna's body and that it was these superhuman forces who were speaking through her in that hospital room.

Could this possibly have been the case? Is it possible that in this enlightened, sophisticated, scientific age, people—even professing Christians—can be controlled or possessed by demonic powers? Do these beliefs belong back in the superstitions of the dark ages? Do demons speak through human beings now as in Bible times? Were they speaking through Donna?

To find the answers to these and related questions, we must turn to the Scriptures and to the writings of Ellen White, for they are the only authoritative sources of information on this subject.

The Great Controversy

The Bible plainly teaches that the planet on which we live is the scene of the most devastating conflict ever to occur anywhere in God's entire universe. We can understand all other teachings of the Bible only when we view them in the light of this Controversy. We can find satisfactory answers to life's large questions only when we understand the nature, origin, purpose, and outcome of this conflict which is going on between the forces of Satan and the forces of Jesus Christ.

This concept of the Great Controversy—of its origin, its conduct, and its eventual outcome—is central to Seventh-day Adventist theology. More than any other single doctrine, the truth of this Controversy with its many implications forms the backdrop of our beliefs. The great Bible truths which form "the pillars of our faith" (2SM 388-389) the Sabbath truth, the true state of the dead, the sanctuary message, the second advent—are all inseparably associated with the Controversy which is now going on and in which each of us is involved.

Ultimately, when the conflict has ended, only two facts—that each of us is caught up in this war and that Jesus Christ has already won the victory—will be seen to have mattered in this life. Everything else—those things we give so much of our time and attention to now—will then be seen as having been subordinate.

Origin of the conflict: The Bible does not leave us in any doubt as to the origin of the Controversy. It began in the most unlikely of all places——the perfect environment of heaven. This fact alone should tell us something about the subtle nature of sin. Sin is a mystery which cannot be excused, explained, or understood. Lucifer, a perfect being, the highest of all angels, challenged God's government and maligned His character (Eze.28:15). The inspired record states the fact in simple terms: "There was war in heaven" (Rev.12:7-9). Lucifer (later called Satan) and all the angels who sympathized with him fought against Christ and the loyal angels.

Eventually Satan "was cast out into the earth, and his angels were cast out with him." In this way our planet became the battlefield in the greatest war ever waged. It has remained a battlefield ever since. And it will continue to be the scene of conflict until Satan and his followers- both angelic and human- are destroyed, with only a brief interlude during the millennium (Rev.12:1-3, 7-9).

The enemy: Until we understand some things about Satan, who is the instigator and chief proponent of the rebellion, we cannot understand the significance of the Controversy. Many Christians, including some Seventh-day Adventists, are afraid to talk or read about Satan. but his hatred and warfare will not be any less because we ignore him. In fact, nothing makes him happier or pleases him more than for us to pretend that he does not exist, or for us to think of him as having cleft hoofs, horns, a long tail, and pitchfork as he is often portrayed in cartoons. He is pleased when he is regarded as the object of a myth, when he is ignored or made light of. All of this suits his purpose well; it plays right into his plans (1T 342).

On the other hand, "there is nothing that the great deceiver fears so much as that we shall become acquainted with his devices (GC 516). "He (Satan) could not gain advantage if his methods of attack were understood" (1T 308) And so it is my purpose in these pages to help us become acquainted with some of the enemy's devices——to expose some of his methods of attack—and to show how, through Christ, we can gain the victory. In doing this, I shall draw upon the Bible, the writings of Ellen White, and my experience during the past fifteen years in ministering to those who, like Donna, have found themselves severely harassed, controlled, or possessed by the enemy.

Not to extol the enemy: It is true that we have been cautioned against thinking and talking too much about the enemy and his power (DA 493). We must not in any way extol him or overemphasize his influence. But we are also told that one reason we have so little enmity against him—so little ability to resist him—is that we are terribly ignorant concerning his power and hatred. We do not realize the vast extent of his warfare against Christ and the church (GC 507).

Not to remain ignorant: Since we are the church- the objects of the enemy's hatred- it behooves us to know all we can about the enemy, his plans, and his methods. Ellen White tells us that "In the final crisis he (the enemy) will deceive to their own ruin those who do not now seek to understand his methods of working" (RH 7/16/01). She points out that among professed Christians, and even among ministers of the gospel, there is seldom heard any reference to Satan except in an incidental way. We find it very easy to ignore the many signs of his craftiness that are all around us. Of course Satan would be happy for us to remain in this ignorant condition because "his (Satan's) great success lies in keeping men's minds confused, and ignorant of his devices, for then he can lead the unwary as it were, blindfolded " (3SM 423).

Extremes to be avoided: We must never fall into the trap of an excessive and unhealthy interest in demons. We must not automatically ascribe every possible human flaw, struggle, disease or misfortune to direct demonic oppression. On the other hand, to minimize the fact that the devil is very deeply involved in every aspect of individual human life is an equally dangerous distortion of Biblical truth. Either extreme gives him an advantage and must be avoided.

Satan, the enemy: The Bible leaves us no room to doubt or question who the enemy is in this conflict, for it plainly identifies him as "that old serpent, which is the Devil, and Satan" (Rev.20:2) Our enemy today is the same one who caused the downfall of our first parents in the Garden of Eden (Gen.3:1-5,14). But Satan is not our only enemy, for fighting on his side and taking their orders from him are wicked spirits (Eph.6:12). These are fallen angels whom we usually call demons.

The Nature of the War

It is not enough that we recognize the reality and power of the enemy. We must also recognize the reality of the war. The personal, day-to-day battle is every bit as real as the enemy is. "It is not mimic battles in which we are engaged. We are waging a warfare upon which hang eternal results. We have unseen enemies to meet. Evil angels are striving for the dominion of every human being" (MH128).

In recent years most of us have become very aware of the dangers that threaten our property and our lives. Consequently, we resort to locks and alarm systems to protect ourselves. But because we cannot see them, we seldom think of the evil angels who are constantly seeking to harm us, and against whose attacks we have no natural defense. Yet, "if permitted, they (evil angels) can distract our minds, disorder and torment our bodies, destroy our possessions and our lives (GC 517).

The War is More Severe Today

The passing of time since Satan's expulsion from heaven has not diminished his hatred for God or lessened in the least his determination to destroy God's government and the entire human family. In fact, the opposite is true. With the passing of time, Satan, who knows his time is running out, has become more desperate; his anger, hotter; his methods, more subtle; and his attacks, more numerous. We can be sure that at this stage of the war, he is not going to abandon any device or method which he has found to be successful in the past. On the contrary, "every ingenious device will be used, every possible method taken advantage of" (TDWG 312). For good reason does the Bible speak of Satan as "having great wrath, because he knoweth that he hath but a short time" (Rev.12:12).

Satan's power has increased a hundred fold: In the meantime, while the Controversy continues, Satan's power to tempt and deceive is being sharpened and refined by constant practice. Consequently, his power is a hundred times greater today than it was when he rebelled (3T328) and it will continue to increase with use until he is destroyed (2SG 277). Satan's powers of persuasion, too, are almost beyond our human comprehension. Remember that he persuaded one third of the angels of heaven to join him in his rebellion (Rev.12:4).

Never underestimate his powers: The enticing powers he used to trap unfallen angels are more skillful now than ever. Without Christ he can easily deceive and trap us in his snares. It is true that Jesus has "all power in heaven and in earth" at His command (Matt 28:18) yet we must never underestimate Satan's ability to wage war and to charm and persuade. At the very close of the millennium, he will be able to convince his angels and the multitudes of the lost that they can actually capture the New Jerusalem (Rev.20:7-9). And Jesus strongly implied that in the last days the enemy will come close to deceiving "the very elect" (Matt 24:24). Our only protection is abiding in Christ and being constantly on guard.

The battle is worse than at any other time: Because Satan becomes more desperate with each passing year, "the Great Controversy going on in the world is waging more sharply today than at any(other) period of this world's history" (UL 20). We may be tempted to think that the battle is less severe today than it was in the days of the Roman empire when Christian martyrs were thrown to the lions, or in the Middle Ages when many of God's faithful ones were called upon to give their lives at the stake. But that is not the case. It is only that the enemy has temporarily changed his tactics. Instead of persecution as his main tool, he now uses the more subtle tool of compromise to accomplish his purpose.

His methods have multiplied: Through "recreational" drugs, pornography, violent and sexually explicit movies and TV, video tapes, Nintendo games, monster toys for children, various forms of demonic music, Ouija boards, Tarot cards, witchcraft, Satan worship, and in a hundred other ways, Satan is cunningly gaining control of human minds. As a result, we are today witnessing mass murders, suicides, accidents, and other forms of violence on an unprecedented scale. We are amazed at the immorality in the world and the lack of true piety in the church. The divorce rate in the church today is not far behind that of the world. The use of alcohol and drugs is growing in our schools and colleges and among Adventist young people, and some who are not so young. The battle lines are being drawn. The Controversy grows more intense with each passing day.

We are living on a battlefield: Life on a battlefield is never pleasant. It means pain, suffering, destruction, and death. But it also means healing and gains and victories. Life on the battlefield consists of what we see going on around us in the world and in the church. Everywhere we look, we see conclusive evidence that we are living in the war zone.

The War is a Personal One: Adventists have always known that there is a Controversy between Christ and Satan. And we have known that the battle involves "the church". The problem is that we think of "the church" in impersonal terms—

sometimes as a building in our neighborhood. We forget that "the church" is people. The church is *you and me*. It is on this individual level that the war is raging. We are aware that Satan is the cause of strife between nations. We see him working in the moral breakdown of society. But there are few who realize to what extent we are individually under attack by anger, jealousy, lust, and fear. We do not recognize the nature of the battle or how subtle and crafty Satan's devices are. He is exceedingly quick to take advantage of our vast ignorance.

Information is essential: It is no longer optional as to whether we be informed. It is essential to our individual salvation and to the successful mission of the church that we be *fully* aware of Satan's methods and devices. To remain ignorant is to invite spiritual defeat and eternal loss.

We have supernatural Help: Not all the angels involved in the Controversy are fallen. For every angel who joined Satan in his rebellion, there are two who remained loyal. These unfallen angels have an active and important part in the battle. If the curtain could be drawn back so that we could see the battle as it is actually being fought, we would see these loyal angels flying swiftly to help those who are tempted. We would see these angels, commissioned from heaven, actually forcing the evil angels to retreat. We would see that "the battles waging between the two armies are as real as those fought by the armies of this world, and on the issue of the spiritual conflict eternal destinies depend" (MB 119).

Although this world is Christ's battlefield, (4BC 1163), He has not deserted us to fight the enemy alone. Rather than leave even one soul to be overcome by Satan, He would empty heaven of every angel to come to the rescue (GC 516). The angels of God are front-line fighters on this battlefield. They are unseen, but they are all around us—ready to respond to our call for help.

CHAPTER
5
My Name is Legion

"My name is Legion, for we are many." Mark 5:9.

When Christ demanded that the demon in the demoniac of Gadara identify himself, he answered, "My name is Legion; for we are many." The name "Legion" assumed by this particular demon was a military term which denoted a unit of from three thousand to five thousand men in the Roman army. He may well have been the commander of just such a group. Satan's demons are organized into groups in military fashion. This large number indicates the degree of the man's possession. We have prayed with several persons in whom the number of demons who identified themselves, and who were forced to leave, was in the hundreds. It is not unusual today for demons to say their name is Legion.

Names May Indicate Work

Sometimes demons assume ordinary human names, both masculine and feminine, such as Mike or Helen. These can frequently be identified with some person who has had an evil influence in this person's life. Some names seem to be meaningless, however. Or they may identify themselves in terms of the physical problem they are causing, such as Pain, Allergy, Headache, or Seizure.

Cathy

In some cases the behavior will portray the nature of the possession. For example: the telephone rang in the church office one afternoon. It was Cathy asking for help. When I am praying personally with a female I make it a point to have another woman with me. I picked up one of the ladies from the church and drove to Cathy's home. Ringing the doorbell several times brought no response. I tried the door and found it unlocked, so we went in. We found Cathy lying on the kitchen floor. She was in a *fetal position, sucking her thumb* and crying like a baby. This was not my first experience with a demon like this one, so I recognized the problem. Kneeling on the floor beside Cathy, I asked, "Demon, In the name of Jesus Christ, tell me who you are." The answer came, "My name is Immaturity." Her fetal position had spoken volumes.

Millie

And there was also the experience of Millie who during a confrontation laughed steadily for two hours. Understandably the demon identified himself as Laughter. To those of us who were there, it was not a laughing matter, I can assure you.

Dorothy

And then there was Dorothy. She had been admitted to the hospital for several reasons. She was experiencing what her parents thought were epileptic seizures. She also had problems with other types of illness, including three successive attacks of pneumonia. When we prayed with her in the hospital a few days later, the first demon to identify himself and to leave was Seizure. He was only the first of more than sixty, however. Among the others was demon "Sickness." That was ten years ago and Dorothy has experienced good health since that time. In all these cases, and in many others we could cite, the demons' names have corresponded to their work.

Demons do not like to tell their names. Only rarely do they reveal this information voluntarily. I believe that revealing their names weakens their power and influence. In several instances I have heard demonic voices say, "I don't want to tell my name because then I will have to leave." Others besides myself have confirmed this. Jesus stated in Matthew 28:18 that He had all power in heaven and earth. When orders are given in His mighty name they have to leave whether they reveal their names or not. They have no choice.

Some Demonic Names

What names are most commonly encountered? High on the list is demon Pride. Demons working under that name do their best to keep their victims from reaching out for help. They keep their victims from admitting their need. But once the person reaches out to the Saviour for help, the demon's power is weakened. The way is open for the Holy Spirit to continue the work He has already begun. But demon Pride is a powerful enemy, and some of the most severe and prolonged battles I have witnessed have been with him. But this should not surprise us when we remember the basic reason for Satan's rebellion in heaven. "I will be like the Most High" (Isa. 14:14). Pride is still a common but terrible enemy.

Another demon commonly encountered is Hate, or Resentment. In our pre-sessions we ask the oppressed person whether they may be harboring hatred. It is more common than we realize. People hate their spouses, or a close relative whom they feel has treated them unfairly. A surprisingly large number admit hating God at some time. These people must pray *for themselves* for two things: (1) That God will remove all hatred or resentment, and (2) That God will replace the hatred with genuine Christian love. God will answer both requests, if the person sincerely desires it. On these terms God gives freedom.

Also close to the top of the list of names are Depression, Guilt, Fear, Anger, and Suicide. Sex is also quite commonly encountered. Of course he is really perverted sex and he usually has a troop of demons under his control. His troops usually include such demons as Lust, Perversion, Fantasy, Masturbation, and Homosexuality.

It is very important that we realize that these names are not mere figures of speech. They are the names of actual demons whose work, assigned by Satan, is to encourage and foster the sin indicated by their names. The demon is the cause, not the result, of the condition his name indicates. To say it in another way, demon Sex does not exist because our society is sex oriented today. Rather, our society is extremely sex oriented because demon Sex and his troops do exist in many people, and they are carrying on a very active program. This is all part of the war between Christ and Satan. This moral war is real.

Even when we read the names of various demons in the inspired counsel, it is easy to think of the names as being symbolic. *These are not symbols.* We must not fail to grasp the full implication. The expression "demon of selfishness," for example, means more than the carnal tendency to be selfish. The name "demon of selfishness" is one whose current assignment is to manipulate a person into selfish acts and attitudes. An innumerable company of demons work under that name. That is their occupation.

The same principle is true of the "demon of intemperance," "demon of strife," "demon of alcohol," and others previously mentioned. These terms apply to all demons who are doing the work indicated by their names. Every child of God is subject to this kind of intense and studied attack. Without God's armor we have no protection.

The following words from God's servant indicate strongly that Satan has an almost limitless number of demons in his army:

> "The door is left open for him (Satan) to enter as he pleases, with his evil train of impatience, love of self, pride, avarice (covetousness), overreaching (shrewd business deals), and his *whole catalogue of evil spirits*" (4 T 45).

We can assume that it was not the intention or purpose of Ellen White to name all the demons that torment or contaminate the human race. From the ones she does name, and from the ones that have been encountered, it is apparent that demons are assigned to work in every area of human potential weakness.

Whenever we knowingly sin, or do that which we know is contrary to God's revealed will, we can be sure that some demon has succeeded in carrying out his assignment.

Masturbation

One of the most commonly encountered demons is Masturbation. What we call masturbation was called "secret sin," "master passion," or "self abuse" in Ellen White's day. She wrote:

> "Some who make a high profession do not understand the sin of self abuse and its sure results. Long-established habit has blinded their understanding. They do not realize the exceeding sinfulness of this degrading sin... Many professed Christians are so benumbed by this practice that their moral sensibilities cannot be aroused to understand that it is sin and that if continued, its sure results will be utter shipwreck of body and mind" (CG 441).

> "We must do something to stop this terrible tide of moral impurity. Self abuse stands as the most degrading sin, polluting the whole character of man. Unless those who are practicing this vice break off their sin and repent before God, they will find no place in the city of God" (Let. 51, '96)

Most medical and health professionals today do not accept Ellen White's teaching on the results of this practice. In fact, many of them teach that masturbation is beneficial to health in that it releases "inner tensions." Some of our Adventist professionals have been caught up in this teaching. However, recent scientific findings confirm her teaching that *excessive* practice of this habit may result in mental disorders and even in insanity. Notice, for example, the following statements:

"We hate to say it, but in zinc-deficient adolescent, sexual excitement and excessive masturbation might precipitate insanity." (Carl C. Pfeiffer, Ph.D., MD., *Zinc, and Other Micro-Nutrients*, New Canaan, Ct: Keats Publishing, Inc., 1978 p. 45).

"It is even possible, given the importance of zinc for the brain, that 19th century moralists were correct when they said that repeated masturbation could make one mad" (David F. Horrobin, M.D. , PhD. , [Editor] *Zinc* , Vitabooks, Inc. 1981 p. 8).

Notice the expressions "excessive masturbation" and "repeated masturbation" used by these doctors. Their findings agree with Mrs. White's words, "if continued." Sometime in the future medical science may fully "catch up" to the truth regarding the harmful effects of "repeated masturbation." Medical science has confirmed the truth revealed to Sister White regarding the poisonous affects of tobacco, the existence of electric currents in the brain, and the advantages of a flesh-free diet. These truths were revealed to her and to us as a people long before their acceptance by the world at large. In the meantime, it would be wise to accept by faith her statements regarding masturbation.

The demon of masturbation was active in Christ's day. One of his victims is known in the Bible as the demoniac of Capernaum. This man's story is in Luke 4:31-37. It is a tragic story with a happy ending.

Early in life, perhaps while he was a teenager, this man became fascinated with the pleasures of this sexual sin. He did not dream of the experiences that awaited him because of this one choice he made. But, once he started on that downward path, he found himself entangled in a net from which he could not free himself. His evil habit became stronger than he was, and before he was aware of what had happened, Satan had gained entire control over him. He could no longer think his own thoughts or speak his own words. He had no will of his own; he was truly possessed. (DA 255, 256)

In the presence of Jesus the man detected a ray of hope. The demon had brought him there to disrupt the worship service, but the man knew that he was in the presence of Someone who could deliver him from his bondage. He longed for freedom from

Satan's control more than for anything else. The demon in control resisted violently. When the poor man tried to cry out, Satan put *his* words in the man's mouth. The demon cried out in fear, "Let us alone, what have we to do with Thee, thou Jesus of Nazareth? Art thou come to destroy us? I know who thou art, the Holy One of God." (Luke 4:34).

At his time of greatest need and brightest hope the man could not express the greatest desire of his heart. It seemed that his desperate need must go unexpressed. At that moment the conflict between the power of Satan and the man's desire for deliverance was at its peak. Here stood the two arch foes, Christ and Satan, face to face. The demon exerted all his strength to retain control of his victim. The man's face was contorted in agony. Beads of perspiration stood on his forehead. His muscles tensed to the breaking point. It seemed that the tortured man might lose his life. But the Savior spoke with a power and authority which the demon could not resist.

> "And Jesus rebuked him, saying, Hold thy peace and come out of him. And when the unclean spirit had torn him and cried with a loud voice, he came out of him" (Luke 4:35).

I have no wish to belabor this point, but I must tell you that the demons of masturbation are every bit as active and powerful today as they were during the earthly ministry of our Lord. They are more controlling now than they were in Ellen White's time. I have personally witnessed scenes similar to the one in the Synagogue. It is not pleasant. I have seen the contorted face and the tense and tortured body. I have wiped the perspiration from the haggard face and brow. I have heard the "loud voice" cry in protest, "I won't leave." I, too, have seen the demon forced to go in spite of his objections. The record is that:

> "they were all amazed and spake among themselves, saying, What new thing is this! for with authority and power he commandeth the unclean spirits, and they came out" (Luke 4:36).

Jesus Christ still speaks with a power and authority which unclean spirits cannot resist. He still hears and answers the unspoken cry of every soul harassed or possessed by Satan. He turns away none who come to Him for help. Jesus is still the One who sets the captives free. He is Victor in this war.

CHAPTER
6
Satan's Subtle Devices

"Lest Satan should get an advantage of us, for we are not ignorant of his devices" 2 Corinthians 2:11.

Jesus Christ sees each of us as a potential candidate for citizenship in His eternal kingdom. Satan, on the other hand, views every human being as one over whom *he* desires to exercise total control and bring his total destruction

Jesus is motivated by love, for "God is love." Love is God's prime characteristic and the basis of His government. In total contrast, Satan is motivated by undiluted hate. He hates God and His Son, Jesus Christ; he hates every human being made in God's image (FE 299). This hatred has an intensity beyond our comprehension. We see it manifested in every human being over whom he has gained control.

None Of Us Can Be Neutral

There are only two primary forces in the world, Christ and Satan. All influences for good or for evil emanate from one of them. This is the source of the conflict. There are only two banners in the world—the banner of Satan, and the banner of Jesus Christ (MCP 299). Jesus said, "He that is not with me is against me, and he that gathereth not with me scattereth abroad"(Matt. 12:30). We are definitely under the influence either of God or of Satan.

"Every man, woman and child that is not under the control of God is under the influence of Satan's sorcery" (MYP 278). "We must be daily controlled by the Spirit of God or we are controlled by Satan"(5T 102).

"All who are not decided followers of Christ are servants of Satan" (GC 508). "Satan takes control of every mind that is not decidedly under the control of God" (TM 79).

Only those who have a daily personal relationship with Jesus Christ are safe from Satan's influence. This is one of the stark realities of the war in which we are all engaged. We need not enlist in Satan's army to march under his banner.

51

"We must inevitably be under the control of one or the other of the two great powers that are contending for the supremacy of the world. It is not necessary for us deliberately to choose the service of the kingdom of darkness in order to come under its dominion. *We have only to neglect to ally ourselves with the kingdom of light.* If we do not cooperate with the heavenly agencies, Satan will take possession of the heart, and will make it his abiding place" (DA 324).

Satan Works In Subtle Ways

This is not to say that all those who do not serve Christ are possessed by Satan as were the demoniacs of Gadara. But the minds of those who are not committed fully to Christ will gradually be molded and fashioned by Satan as he chooses. And all the rational powers he controls, he will carnalize or pattern after the world. The choices, tastes, preferences, the likes and dislikes will become worldly rather than Christ-like; and in the end, such persons will be found to be servers of Satan rather than servers of God (MCP 328). It is Satan's purpose to influence the minds of men and women until they have no mind or will of their own (MCP 24). In too many cases Satan is succeeding in his purpose. *These individuals can then be delivered only by the power of God in answer to the intercessory prayers of His people* (1T 299).

Even now, Satan and his angels are busy paralyzing the senses so that God's warnings and reproofs and wooing are not heard (AH 401). He diverts our minds to any subject that will create division among God's people and lead them into controversy (MCP 23). We see this being done on an unprecedented scale today.

By his subtle working Satan is now linking human minds with his mind, imbuing them with his thoughts. And he does this in so deceptive a manner that those who accept his guidance do not know they are being led by his will. In this way Satan hopes to confuse the minds of men and women so that they will hear no voice but his. All these plans are part of Satan's devices, of which we cannot afford to be ignorant.

Because Satan has boundless hate for every human being, he has only one goal. He wants to cause as much misery and suffering as he can, and eventually to bring about our ultimate destruction. To accomplish this purpose he will resort to any scheme he can imagine or devise. He is not bound by truth or honesty. He does not operate from any principle except self-interest. He will resort to any deceit and go to any length to gain his purpose. He has no scruples.

Demons Can Inhabit Human Bodies

We have already seen in Chapter Two that when it is in their interest to do so, and when they are permitted, demons torment and can and do inhabit human bodies. This fact is difficult for some people to accept. Since it was true in Christ's day, it is true in our day. Satan's abilities are no less now than then. I am going to give you a few examples:

Paula Green

In Chapter Three we referred to her, the young woman who told me in the hospital that she had a demon in her. Between the time she made that statement to me and the time the first demon revealed himself, certain physical conditions manifested. Paula developed a severe headache which would not go away. She found it increasingly difficult to sleep at night. Then she could hardly stay awake during the day. This was demonic game playing. When she did go to sleep at night, she had terrible nightmares. She would wake up in terror. The same nightmare occurred over and over until she dreaded to go to sleep. She told me, "The nights are terrible."

At times Paula had double vision which came and went at random. One of the strangest physical manifestations was the red splotches which seemed to appear suddenly like bruises on her arms and legs. She told us they were on other parts of her body as well. At first she passed them off casually as something that came "because I bruise easily, I guess." But she had no idea why they came.

Then the most terrifying physical manifestations of all came one night without warning. The movement of her arms and legs became jerky and mechanical. Her speech was so slurred we could hardly understand her. Her physical condition was so bad she had to crawl on her hands and knees to come into the room to ask to be taken to the hospital emergency room. We suspected she had taken some form of drug but she denied it vehemently when we suggested it. Laboratory tests given in the hospital ruled out drugs as the cause of her problem. "There are no drugs in her system at all," the doctor told me later.

Paula stayed in the hospital exactly one week. During that time her physical movements and her speech returned to normal, but the other problems remained. The headache was especially severe. When I talked with Paula's doctor he told me he did not doubt the presence of the headache. "But," he said, "all the tests we have given, including a brain scan and spinal puncture, fail to reveal any reason for the headache. We really don't know why she has the headache." Paula still had the headache when she came home from the hospital.

It was the evening of the day she was discharged that the first demon made his presence known to us. The details have been told in the book *Delivered from Demon Possession.* We will not repeat them here. The point to be made is this: A month later when Paula was delivered from the eight demons that possessed her, all the physical manifestations—the weakness, the headache, the nightmares, the double vision, the insomnia, the drowsiness, the red splotches—all the abnormal physical conditions disappeared. None of them have returned in the years that have elapsed since that time.

We have been told that, "If permitted, they (demonic forces) can distract our minds, disorder and torment our bodies, destroy our possessions and our lives" (GC 517). Many of our experiences in the Deliverance Ministry have involved persons whose physical bodies were being harassed or controlled by demons. Not in all cases have the manifestations of demonic power been as numerous or as severe as they were in Paula's case, however. In many instances the physical body is not involved at all; but Satan works on the emotional, spiritual, intellectual, or sexual aspect of the person. This ability is another one of Satan's many devices.

Shelly

In Chapter Four I related Donna's experience in the hospital with the demon "Seizure." We had an interesting and unusual experience while we were praying for Shelly, too. We had several encounters in the early part of the day. Later, in the afternoon, Shelly telephoned me and said, "Something strange has happened. I have a burn on my lower arm about the size of a silver dollar. But I don't know how it got there. I have not used my stove at all today. How do you suppose I burned my arm?" Of course I had no explanation of the burn either.

Early that evening at Shelly's request we returned to her home where there was another encounter. During the encounter I read Revelation 20:7-10, which contains these words:

"...and fire came down from God out of heaven, and devoured them. And the devil that deceived them was cast into the lake of fire and brimstone, where the beast and the false prophet are, and shall be tormented day and night forever and ever" (Verses 9,10). I had hardly finished reading these words when the demon said, "That's why I burned her." It was the last thing he said before he was forced to leave.

That Satan can harass and torment the human body and, in some cases, even cause disease is indicated in these words:

"The fact that men have been possessed with demons is clearly stated in the New Testament. The persons thus afflicted were not merely suffering with disease from natural cause. Christ had perfect understanding of that with which He was dealing and He recognized the direct presence and agency of evil spirits" (GC 514).

"Satan again counseled with his angels, and with bitter hatred against God's government told them that while he retained his power and authority upon earth their efforts must be ten-fold stronger against the followers of Jesus....He related to his angels that Jesus had given His disciples power to rebuke them and cast them out, and *to heal those whom they should afflict*. Then Satan's angels went forth like roaring lions, seeking to destroy the followers of Jesus" (EW 191, 192).

Velda

Velda Thorne's experience illustrates the extent to which satanic forces are carrying out their orders to afflict the human body. Velda's healing shows the continuation of the same power that Jesus gave His disciples to rebuke them and cast them out, and also to heal those that they should afflict.

Velda made an appointment with me by telephone. When she came to the church office the next day she described her case of extreme allergy. Her diet was limited to five items. She could eat corn, collard and mustard greens, almonds, and alfalfa sprouts. Any variation from this regimen caused a variety of reactions, not just a rash or sneezing. Her mental and emotional well-being were affected. Eating other foods caused a breakdown of her physical system. Her ability to concentrate was diminished to a great degree. She lost control of her emotions. She would cry easily and became upset at the slightest provocation.

She enjoyed normal health so long as she limited herself to the five items which experience told her she could tolerate. Those five foods plus a small amount of corn oil supplied all the nutrients essential to her life and health over a period of ten years. But the monotony of such a limited and unusual diet become intolerable. Of course it was very inconvenient to her and her family. Eating out or being a guest in another home was, of course, very awkward and embarrassing.

Twice she had undergone a series of tests in one of our large medical centers to discover the cause and possible solution to her problem. These efforts had been futile. She had been told that nothing could be done. She would just have to learn to live with the her illness. All of this I learned in our first conference. We prayed and I suggested that she make her problem the subject of special prayer during the next week and return at the end of that time. Others would be praying for her as well.

When she came back a week later, she reported that her condition had not changed. She had experimented with her diet and found out the hard way that her allergies were still very much with her.

During Velda's second visit, we prayed again, but we did more than that. In the name of Jesus we rebuked the demon Allergy and commanded that he leave. We then anointed her in harmony with God's instruction in James 5:14-16.

I did not hear from Velda again until I met her in the local market three weeks later. She said, "I am so thankful for God's goodness. I am eating a normal diet. Everything changed the day I was anointed." I talked with Velda again some months later. She was still praising God for what He had done for her. And of course I join her in that praise. Some of the most remarkable healings that it has been my privilege to witness have involved allergy. I do not believe that all allergies are demon-related. However, in a search for relief from severe allergic conditions that possibility ought not to be disregarded.

It is important that we accept as fact that demons can and do to afflict the human body. Job's experience confirms this. "So went Satan forth from the presence of the Lord, and smote Job with sore boils from the sole of his foot unto his crown" (Job 2:7). If Satan could afflict Job with boils, why should he not be able to afflict human bodies in other ways today? The truth is that he can. I can truly testify that the ability of the enemy to afflict human bodies is very real—just as real as God's word and the Spirit of Prophecy say it Is. The enemy imposes physical afflication more often than we realize.

Another device Satan uses is to observe our individual frailties and weaknesses. He takes note of the sins we are most inclined to commit. Then he makes sure we are tempted in those weak areas (GC 555). In light of this it is well for us to recognize where we are weak. We must ask God for special strength and protection in the ways we are prone to fall. Of course we have a responsibility not to place ourselves in any situation that invites the temptations of the enemy and leaves us vulnerable.

Satan assigns a work, a part to act, to each of his angels. And he admonishes them all to be sly and cunning in carrying out their particular responsibilities (EW 90). We might say that they are all "professionals" in their specialty. They are extremely well organized (GC 513, MCP 24).

Demons Can Speak

The idea that demons always speak in loud or coarse voices is not based on fact. Basically they use the voice of their human victim. Because they use the same vocal chords of the one they possess—the resonance of the voice is rarely different. However, at times we do hear a great difference in personality. When a voice says, "He belongs to me."—the switch of pronouns tells everything. Also many times his words will betray him.

For example, when Shauna, at the beginning of an encounter, said in her usual soft voice, "There are no demons here," we might have believed her. But when she went on to say, "There is no devil and no God and no Bible," we knew at once who was speaking. Imitating the voice of their victim is another demonic device.

Incidentally, language is no barrier to demons. They can speak any language they choose. We have known of a number of encounters in which an English-speaking person spoke perfectly in a foreign language—a tongue of which the victim had no personal knowledge.

And Hear

Not only can Satan and his demons imitate or use the human voice; they can also hear and understand every word we speak (See 1 SM 122, 123). The pastor who said he never told anyone what he was going to preach about had a point. He did not want Satan to know his subject.

"The adversary of souls is not permitted to read the thoughts of men; but he is a keen observer, and *he marks the words...*"(1 SM 122). An experience we had a few years ago with a young man whom we shall call Kenneth demonstrated the truthfulness of that fact.

Kenneth

Kenneth had gone through a time in his life when he had prayed to Satan. Because of this, he had come under the enemy's control, but now he wanted to be free. He called to ask if I would pray with him for his freedom. We agreed to meet at a church office at six o'clock the next *Monday* evening.

My telephone rang late *Sunday* evening. The voice on the other end of the line came immediately to the point—"So, you are going to pray for Kenneth tomorrow evening. What if I kill him before then?" The timbre of the voice was Kenneth's; the mind behind that voice was not Kenneth's.

You can be sure that we did much praying for Kenneth during the next day. To the glory of God, Kenneth met the appointment. The battle was severe, but Kenneth was freed from his bondage.

Incidentally, this demonic voice is only one of several such voices that have called me on the telephone during the fifteen years I have been involved in Spiritual Warfare. The spiritual war is real!

It is well for us to remember that the heavenly angels also are acquainted with our words. Even our thoughts and the intents of the heart are open to them (MYP 27). Demons cannot read our minds, as loyal angels can, but they watch our faces. Nothing escapes them. They study us and then formulate their attack.

Another ability or "device" that demons have is that of doing more than one work at a time. One demon may carry out several different assignments in the same person simultaneously. He may cause headaches and nightmares in the same individual, for example. The same demon that tempted Christ in the wilderness also possessed the demoniac of Capernaum. And he was this same demon who controlled the unbelieving Jews. This demon was none other than Satan himself (Matt. 4:1,5,8).

It is also true that more than one demon may be assigned to the same general work in one person. For example, there may be several demons whose work is to promote a variety of pressures, reasons and situations to make an individual want to smoke.

Satan has reserved some of his devices for use in these last days, perhaps in desperation because of the shortness of time. It is his special aim to take possession of the minds of young people, to corrupt their thoughts and inflame their passions (MCP 22). We can see his purpose being accomplished all too successfully today through drugs, rock music, television, video games, pornography, witchcraft, and other media. Never have our youth been attacked in so many ways as they are today.

Our Ignorance Is Satan's Advantage

None of these facts should surprise us. We were told years ago that Satan's last exploits will be carried out with more power than ever before through "scientific scheming." He will use "every ingenious device" and take advantage of "every possible method" (TDWG 312). Today Satan is preparing for his last campaign against God's people. Before the battle ends he will bring into use every scheme and trick that his immense intelligence can devise.

"So long as we are ignorant of their (evil spirits') wiles, they have almost inconceivable advantage..."(GC 516). Why should you and I continue to give the enemy the advantage of our ignorance, in view of the light God has given us in the Bible and in the Spirit of Prophecy? How can we willingly remain ignorant and at the same time profess to be on the side of Jesus Christ in this greatest of all battles?

"There is nothing that the great deceiver fears so much as that we shall become acquainted with his devices" (GC 516). The purpose of this book—and especially of this chapter—is to help us to be more alert to Satan's devices. If we understand his subtle tricks, we are better able to defend ourselves against his attacks. Shielded by the truth that God has given us, he has less advantage over us than he has had in the past.

CHAPTER
7
The Christian and Demonic Oppression

"Cast not away therefore your confidence,
which hath great recompense of reward" Hebrews 10:35.

Can a Christian be harassed, controlled, or possessed by Satan? The question can hardly be answered satisfactorily by a simple "yes" or "no" without the risk of being misunderstood. The answer deserves some careful thought and discussion.

We must recognize that there are degrees of Satanic influence. Harassment, control, and possession indicate progressively stronger demonic influences in human life. None of these terms come from the Bible. The Greek text does not contain the word "possessed." The Bible supports the idea of being "demonized" or "oppressed," which we by usage apply to the extreme degree of demonic influence or "possession."

Demonic harassment exists when demons are permitted to cause circumstances which annoy or harass an individual. The purpose of harassment is to discourage the individual, to cause him to lose faith in God, and eventually to reject God's influence in his life.

The Experience of Job

The Scriptures contain a number of examples of demonic harassment. Job's experience comes to our minds. Job was "perfect and upright, and one that feared God, and eschewed (hated or avoided) evil" (Job 1:1). He was a worshipper of the true God, the Old Testament equivalent of a Christian. But, in spite of that—actually, because of that!—he was terribly harassed by Satan himself. He lost most of his family and his property. He suffered severe physical pain over much of his body. His friends blamed him for his misfortune, and even his wife suggested that he curse God—just what Satan wanted him to do—and die.

This is not the place for an in-depth study of the book of Job, but God had a special reason for allowing the record of his experience to be preserved. The message is that every human being has a part in the great conflict between Christ and Satan. We must remind ourselves that we, too, are personally involved. Like Job, we are constantly choosing sides. Job could well be a prototype (sample) of every human being.

Take note of the many ways that Job was attacked—financially in the loss of his property; by grief through the death of his children; by the false theology of his friends; by physical pain; and by his wife's lack of confidence in God. Yet through it all Job's faith in God did not waiver. He remained steadfast in spite of all of these severe tests. "Though he (God) slay me," Job said, "yet will I trust in him" (Job 13:15). Job did not cast away his confidence. Faith and trust in God are the most important antidotes for any and all forms of demonic harassment.

Job 42:10 is significant. It says, "And the Lord turned (or ended) the captivity of Job when he prayed for his friends." In spite of his own misery, Job came to the place in his experience where he was more concerned about his friends and their needs than he was about his own condition. When Job took his eyes off himself and turned to God on behalf of others, he placed himself in a position where God's channel of blessing could reach him. It was then that his period of trial ended.

Satan knows that when our minds are turned inward toward self, we are turned away from Christ who is the Source of our strength. So he will do anything he can to cause us to divert our attention from our Savior and in this way prevent our communion with Him. This is one of Satan's purposes in any form of harassment.

Job 42:10 says, "Also the Lord gave Job twice as much as he had before." But not everyone's experience involving demonic harassment ends that happily, as the apostle Paul testifies.

The Experience of Paul

Paul was harassed all his life after he was converted on the road to Damascus. He wrote, "There was given me a thorn in the flesh, a messenger of Satan to buffet me" (2 Cor.12:7). The word "messenger" comes from the Greek *angelos*, which in most cases is translated as "angels" who are, of course, messengers. We may substitute "harass" for "buffet" without doing violence to Paul's meaning. So, Paul is really telling us that one of Satan's angels—a demon, if you please—was harassing him. Paul recognized, however, that God permitted the harassment for a reason. In this way God was keeping Paul humble, "lest I should be exalted above measure. "

Three times Paul prayed that the harassment might end. God's answer was, "My grace is sufficient for thee" (2 Cor.12:8,9). When Paul wrote, "God is faithful, who will not suffer (allow) you to be tempted (or harassed) above that ye are able," he was writing from experience. Paul had learned that God "will with the temptation (harassment) make a way of escape, that ye may be able to bear it" (1 Cor.10:13). God knows exactly how much "pressure" each of us can stand. If we depend upon Him we will not fall. If we depend upon our own strength we easily become captive to temptation.

Elijah Was Harassed

The prophet Elijah experienced the harassment of a deep depression. He wanted to die. "It is enough," he said, "Now, O Lord, take away my life" (1Kings19:4). Depression is epidemic today, but it is not new, as Elijah's experience testifies. We are not suggesting that all depression is of demonic origin. There may well be "human" causes, too. But we quite commonly encounter demons whose assignment is to cause depression, and they usually operate under that name. In many cases, demon "Depression" is accompanied by demon "Suicide."

But there was hope for Elijah, and there is hope for those who suffer from depression today. Notice what happened in Elijah's case. "An angel touched him" (I Kings 19:5). Thank God for the ministry of good angels! They are still there to do battle with the demons that harass today. We should thank God that "Holy angels are on the track of every one of us" (LHU 209).

John The Baptist

Even John the Baptist, of whom Jesus said there is no one greater, was not free from harassment. There were times when the whisperings of demons harassed his soul, and the shadow of a terrible *fear* crept over him (DA 216).

Fear is a terrible, but common, form of harassment. And when it is combined with doubt it can cause deep discouragement. John suffered from doubt as well as from fear. His inquiry of Jesus, "Art thou he that should come, or do we look for another?" is very significant when we see it in this light (Matt. 11:3).

Ellen White writes of a night when her baby, Edson, could not sleep but kept lashing out with his hands at something invisible to her. The child cried out in fear, "No! No!" She recognized this as Satan's effort to harass the family. For two hours she and her husband prayed before relief came. (See LS 138). Physical discomfort and fear as forms of harassment are not relics of the past. They are still very real today

Annoyance

Sometimes the harassment takes the form of pure pestering. Some time ago I was called to a home where annoying things were going on. Doors were opening and closing with no visible cause. Dresser drawers were pulled out when no one was in the room. A knickknack shelf came off the wall. It was hurled across the room, just missing the mother's head as she put the baby into its crib. The most terrifying manifestation came when the ten-year-old boy's pajama bottoms literally danced around the bathroom while the boy was taking his shower. It was a frightening experience for the boy. It happened more than once.

In one home where we were doing spiritual battle there were audible footsteps all evening. The young woman had heard them over a period of several months. This can be a very terrifying experience when one is alone in the middle of the night, especially when it goes on night after night. We encountered the demons who harassed the young lady. One of the demons identified himself as Tormentor. He confessed he had made the footsteps. The sounds have disappeared since her deliverance. We asked God to cleanse the home, banish all demonic forces, and fill the home with loyal angels.

Donna

Donna suffered a brief, but very severe harassment. She ran a low-grade fever. Periodically she suffered from a sore throat. She felt weak. Her situation became so bad that her doctor ordered her to stay home from work and rest. During that time she was subjected to two series of tests and examinations. None of these tests revealed any natural cause.

Donna lived a few miles from my home and she knew something about my involvement in the Deliverance Ministry. She called me periodically to keep me informed of her physical problem. We had discussed in a casual way the possibility of the problem's being caused by demonic activity. Then at one-thirty in the morning, she called me on the telephone. "Pastor Allen, I've been harassed for the past hour or so, and I don't know how much more I can take," she said. "It's terrible! Maybe I should go to a friend's house for the rest of the night."

"No," I advised her, "I understand what you are saying. But don't run away. God will protect you. You don't need to be afraid. Claim God's promise of protection in James 4:7."

She explained how she had been awakened by the feeling of a hand pressing on her shoulder. She prayed and the pressure was released, but then her bed began to shake. When she rebuked the demon, her bed became quiet, but she began to feel pain in one of her legs. The pain increased until it became very severe. Again she rebuked the demon and the pain subsided.

Donna's Variety of Harassment

But when one form of harassment ended, another began. When she called me, she was experiencing pain in her chest. In the name of Jesus I rebuked the demon causing the pain in her chest and the pain stopped.

By this time Donna was able not only to rebuke the demon but to say to it, "Demon, I am not afraid of you. I have Jesus in my heart and you cannot hurt me. I claim His promise that you cannot hurt me."

Suddenly her lower jaw began to hurt. As I was rebuking the demon who was causing that pain, Donna cried into the phone, "Are you there? I can't hear a thing. He has made me deaf. Are you there? I can't hear you."

I rebuked the demon of deafness. (Mk. 9:25) Donna's deafness seemed to last a long time but it was probably not more than a couple of minutes. As suddenly as it began, the deafness left.

Then I heard a bang and a clatter which sounded as though Donna had dropped her telephone receiver. Everything became quiet. My first thought was that Donna had fainted. "Donna, are you all right? What happened? I can't hear you now. Are you all right? Can you answer me?"

For about thirty seconds there was no voice, only a strange sound I could not identify. Then Donna spoke again: "Are you still there?" "Yes, I'm still here." "It sounded to me as though you dropped the phone. What happened?"

"No, I didn't drop it. The receiver was yanked out of my hand and thrown as far as the cord would allow it to go. I didn't want to get out of bed, so I pulled the receiver back by the cord. He's still here. He's making my face tingle. "

I continued to rebuke demons as they manifested themselves in various ways in different parts of her body. There was a short period of time when her heart beat abnormally fast. Donna kept up a running commentary, at times rebuking the demon and at other times telling him that she was not afraid. And she also kept me informed of what was happening.

Her heart began to beat very fast. Then she said, "I just picked up my Bible and I have placed it over my heart." In a few seconds she told me that her heart was beating normally again.

"I don't feel pain any more, and I think he's getting weaker," she said at one point. "But he is making a pounding noise. I can't tell exactly where it is coming from. It's just a kind of thump that seems to fill the whole room."

All the physical manifestations in Donna's body gradually weakened and disappeared, and only the thumping sound remained. It went on for some time. Of course we continually rebuked the demon who was causing it. Suddenly the sound stopped and everything was quiet.

"The thumping just stopped," Donna reported. "I think he's gone. I believe it's over. " And it was. I looked at the clock on the night stand. It was four o'clock in the morning. We had battled for two and one-half hours. We both prayed and thanked God for His mercy.

Donna called the next afternoon. "I feel fine," she said. "I have my strength back. It's like I'm a new person. "

And, in a way, she was a new person. We were told years ago that when they are permitted to do so, evil angels can weaken and torment our bodies and distract our minds. Demons can work the nerves and the organs of human beings (DA 36 341). Donna's experience, and others like it which we have witnessed, verifies the truthfulness of what we have been told. Sometimes demons control the organs of those they possess, but in Donna's case they only harassed. It was a brief experience, but quite terrifying while it lasted.

Can Christians be harassed by demons? The answer seems obvious. Job "was perfect and upright. He feared God and eschewed evil" (Job 1:1). John the Baptist was chosen by God. Paul was both preacher and prophet. Ellen White was God's messenger. All these people experienced harassment. So the answer must be, Yes, Christians can and do experience demonic harassment. Even Christians of long experience are often attacked by awful doubts and insecurity (OHC 76).

And why should this not be true? Satan hates every human being with a deadly hatred, and he has a special hatred toward Christians. But above and beyond this, he reserves a particular animosity against members of the remnant church (EW 191). "Never is one received into the family of God without exciting the determined resistance of the enemy" (PK 585). Therefore, we should not be surprised when we are harassed by the enemy. But God forbid that any of us should invite harassment, control or possession by our unsanctified homes or lives.

Demon Control

Demon control exists when Satan's agents influence one's words and thoughts and actions temporarily and externally. That is, the control is exercised only for brief periods of time and without the demon's inhabiting the body. Satan's speaking through Peter, "Making him act the part of the tempter," is a good example of demonic control (see DA 416).

It is possible and even probable that you and I have been the object of demonic control at some time. Have you ever resorted to sarcasm? Have you ever made a hasty retort that you later regretted? Have you ever engaged in gossip or unjust criticism? When we allow ourselves to become involved in such activities we are being controlled to some extent by Satan. He uses us at times just as he used Peter. After all, sarcasm, criticism, and gossip do not originate with God. There is only one other source (1T 308, 9).

Demon Possession

When, in the power of God, we successfully resist Satan in one area of our lives—in the matter of appetite, for example—it becomes easier to resist him again, either in that same area or in another area. We pointed out that the opposite is also true. That is, when we surrender to the enemy and give in to the temptation, it is easier to give in again—either in that area or another area of our lives. Every time we capitulate to the enemy, we turn a little of our wills over to his control. If this process is repeated often enough, Satan will eventually control that area at his will. Our wills may be so weakened that we may lose even the power to *choose* or even know what is right.

Satan's influence can be exerted in one or more areas of a person's life. To the extent that the person has lost control of that area, that person is said to be "possessed." There are, of course, degrees of demon-possession. The Spirit of Prophecy speaks of Judas as being "possessed" although only two demonic forces, selfishness and greed, are named in that connection (5ABC 1102). In contrast to this is the case of the demoniac of Gadara who was possessed by thousands of demons (Mark 5:9).

When we prayed with Paula Green, whose experience initiated us into the Deliverance Ministry, there were eight demons who identified themselves and who were forced to leave her. Since then, we have prayed with those who have been possessed by demons ranging in number from one demon to several hundred.

It is commonly believed that a universal sign of possession is rolling on the ground, or frothing at the mouth. To the contrary, most of those with whom I have prayed in the Deliverance Ministry and who were possessed, have walked into the office under their own power. They were living apparently normal lives. They have discussed their problems rationally, talked about their need, and have been able to pray about their lack of control. A few, however, have not been able to pray.

The Tragedy of Judas Iscariot

There is much to learn from the experience of Judas Iscariot. Although he was "demon-possessed" (Jn. 6:70), outwardly he lived what we would call a normal life. His problem was known only to himself and the Savior. Judas Iscariot gave no obvious evidence of his possession. The other Apostles were completely unaware of his condition. At the last supper when Jesus said, "One of you shall betray me" (Jn. 13:21) *every man at the table asked, "Lord, is it I"* (Matt. 26:22). Judas had left no trail of evidence. Such can be the deceptiveness of a hidden possession. Like Judas' case, much possession goes unrecognized.

For example, when Mary Magdalene broke her costly alabaster box of ointment to anoint the Lord's feet, Judas spoke of this as a waste. He said the money should have been given to the poor. (Jn. 12:5, 6). An evil spirit can hide behind pious language.

"Judas had naturally a strong love for money;...The love of mammon overbalanced his love for Christ. Through becoming the slave of *one vice* he gave himself to Satan, to be driven to any lengths in sin" (DA 716).

From the experience of Judas, I have many times warned that one vice indulged—one cherished and unforsaken sin—can lead to terrible consequences.

Bizarre Behavior

In most cases, it is only after we have begun to pray a warfare prayer for their deliverance that the behavior and/or language of Satan's victim has become bizarre. It is when Satan realizes he is actually about to lose a victim that the real battle begins, although many of these people have told me that the demonic activity became worse as soon as they made the appointment for prayer.

It is when we begin to intercede on behalf of Satan's captives that they sometimes, not always, manifest bizarre behavior. In some cases their bodies convulse. In rare instances they froth at the mouth, and I have seen them crawl with snake-like gyrations on the floor and with protruding tongue, "hiss" like a snake. In a few exceptional cases I have seen the victim's face change in shape and appearance to such an extent that the person was not recognizable.

It is at these times, when the battle is raging at its peak, that demonic voices may speak through their victims in a vile, vulgar and blasphemous manner, to manifest an extremely violent temper, and threaten the lives of their victims and of those who are praying. But, in spite of numerous threats, I have never been attacked or seen anyone else attacked.

On several occasions I have heard demonic voices say, "I would like to kill you; but I can't because there are angels around you." Such experiences make us very humble and help us to realize how real the battle is, and how dependent we are upon God for protection. These experiences also help us to be sure that everything is as it should be between us and our Savior.

In contrast to those who become active and vociferous during the spiritual battles will go into an apparent sleep or stupor, moving only their lips through which the demons may speak. The voice coming from the victim's mouth generally sounds like the person. This makes sense inasmuch as they are using the victims voice box. The differences are frequently seen in the personality more than the sound. Occasionally there may be a strange voice, harsh and coarse. The idea that demons always speak in discordant voices is just not true. They can speak with a soft feminine voice when that suits their purpose.

In connection with "bizarre behavior" I want to make one emphatic statement. This type of behavior is happening much less frequently in the last few years than it did when I first became involved in Spiritual Warfare in the 1970's. I feel that God permitted these dramatic responses early in our experience in order to impress us with the reality of the conflict (DA 428).

In most cases during the last few years we have been able to sit or kneel around a table in the church office, or sit in the comfort of a home during the entire prayer session, and the only unusual activity will be the victim's coughing, blowing, yawning, burping, and frequent gagging which usually accompanies deliverance—the reason for which I cannot attempt to explain. I can only tell you that it happens. On a few occasions I have seen frothing at the mouth. Many deliverances I have witnessed which involved alcoholism have been accompanied by vomiting.

Demonized Christians?

At this point I would like to remind my readers that most of those for whom I have interceded in Spiritual Warfare, and whose experiences I have related, are members of the remnant church. They are your spiritual brothers and sisters who sit next to you in church from Sabbath to Sabbath, but who, unfortunately, have been caught in Satan's net. Some of them are leaders and officers in their local churches. Others are musicians whose talents some of you who read these pages have enjoyed. In a few cases they are professional people employed in our institutions. And, in a few rare cases, these people who have become victims of Satan's devices are pastors who are preaching the Word from Sabbath to Sabbath.

These examples should alert us that every one of us is at war. The more intelligent, talented and gifted people are the ones Satan will work harder to entrap; for them he lays his most subtle plans. We must always remember that, were it not for the power of God, each one of us would become Satan's victim.

And that brings us to an important question: Can a Christian become possessed? The answer is not as simple as it may appear. It depends, first of all, upon our definition of a Christian. If we equate being a Christian with being a member of a church, the answer must be, "Yes." Most of the several hundred people with whom I have prayed in the Deliverance Ministry have been members of the Seventh-day Adventist church. I am quite sure that, had you asked, every one of them would have replied that he or she was indeed a Christian.

But regardless of what the spiritual condition may have been when each of these persons came for help, deliverance—in every case—always follows a desire to reform. Sins have been confessed and made right; changes have been made in the life style. Everything must be brought into harmony with God's expressed will. In some cases complete deliverance has been delayed until such reformation and commitment was made.

Some have discovered they could not fool God. He knows when the heart-change is genuine and complete. Paul admonishes us, "Examine yourselves, whether ye be in the faith" (2 Cor. 13:5).

And Jesus warns us, "Not every one that saith unto me, Lord, Lord, shall enter into the kingdom of heaven; but he that doeth the will of my Father which is in heaven" (Matt. 7:21).

There are many whose experience consists only of a profession. Many whose names are on the church roster are not truly Christian. Only those who are allowing the power of God to daily transform their lives will be saved; they alone are safe from Satan's delusions, and from the possibility of demon possession.

"Satan takes control of every mind that is not decidedly under the control of the Spirit of God" (TM 79). "When the mind is not under the direct influence of the Spirit of God, Satan can mold it as he chooses" (MCP 22).

Can a genuinely committed Christian become demon-possessed? The answer is No! Harrassed?—Yes. Buffeted?—Yes. Possessed?—No!

"What fellowship hath righteousness with unrighteousness? And what communion hath light with darkness? And what concord hath Christ with Belial?" (2 Cor. 6:14,15; MCP 22; 2 Cor.12:7)).

Jesus is not in partnership with Satan. He will not share our minds and our affections with the enemy. The Savior said, "Thou shalt love the Lord thy God with *all* thy heart, and with *all* thy soul, and with *all* thy mind" (Matt. 22:37). *Every genuinely committed Christian is already possessed—by the Holy Spirit.* When Jesus returns, every living human being will be possessed by one of the two great powers—Christ or Satan.

Day by day the polarizing of the human family goes on. Daily we are deciding—by the exercise of our wills—which of these two powers will possess us this day. Each day—and at times in the hottest battles, each minute—we make that decision.

The point that should catch and hold our attention in all this is not the fact that some unfortunate professing Christians have been temporarily trapped in Satan's snare. The precious truth is that Jesus Christ is still victorious on the Battlefield. He is still Commander in Chief of the armies of heaven.

CHAPTER
8
Inviting Satan In

"Neither give place to the devil" Ephesians 4:27.

Police departments and other law-enforcing agencies spend much time and effort studying the *modus operandi* of wanted criminals. The more the authorities know about a criminal—his habits, his thought patterns, his motives, his method of operation—the easier it is to apprehend him.

Satan is the arch criminal of the universe. Each of us is his potential victim. The more we know about him and his methods the easier it will be for us to recognize his presence and activities, and to avoid his traps. There is nothing Satan fears more than that we shall become acquainted with his devices and methods (GC 516).

We must realize that Satan has an almost unlimited number of ways to accomplish his purpose, but He cannot touch our minds or intellects unless we yield them to him (MS. 17, 1893). So he studies our individual weaknesses to learn how he can best gain access to us, and then he tempts us in our weakest points. Your weakness may not be my weakness, therefore Satan may not tempt you in the same area that he tempts me. None of us knows the area or degree of temptation which others are experiencing. We have no way of measuring the heat of the battle being waged in another's heart. Because of this we should be sympathetic rather than critical when someone becomes a victim of temptation. It would be well for each of us to remember that "There except for the grace of God go I."

Our Weak Spots

We all have our particular weaknesses. Something that may tempt you, may be repulsive to me—and vice versa. However, there are traps in which any of us may fall. One thing is sure—at no time can any of us let our guard down. Keep in mind that every word we say, every tone of voice, every facial expression, every gesture—are all under demonic surveillance. Satan is always looking for a weakness. If he sees one, he will make his move. I want to point out some common vulnerabilities.

73

"Satan studies every inclination of the frailty of human nature, he marks the sins which each individual is inclined to commit, and then he takes care that opportunities shall not be wanting to gratify the tendency of evil" (GC 555)

The Senses

God does not allow Satan to have unlimited access to our minds. He and his angels can reach us only through our senses. These are sight, hearing, taste, touch, and smell. God has given to each of us the ability to control the use of these senses. They are the avenues to our souls, and each of us chooses what travels over these avenues. This power of choice is one of the God-like abilities we have because we are created to some degree in God's image.

We must maintain a faithful guard over all the senses if we expect to control our minds and prevent vain and corrupting thoughts from contaminating our souls. If we would avoid falling prey to Satan's temptations, we must avoid reading, seeing, or hearing anything which suggests impure or unholy thoughts (MYP 76).

If God's word is faithfully observed, it will serve as a protection. "Finally, brethren, whatsoever things are honest, whatsoever things are just, whatsoever things are pure, whatsoever things are lovely, whatsoever things are of good report: if there be any virtue, and if there be any praise, think on these things" (Phil. 4:8).

If with God's help—and we cannot do it without His help—we would honestly and consistently practice this advice, what a difference it would make in our personal lives in our homes! And it would be a very frustrating experience for Satan, for it would go a long way toward curtailing his present success in enticing us into sin.

"Those who would not fall a prey to Satan's devices must guard well the avenues of the soul; they must avoid reading, seeing, or hearing that which will suggest impure thoughts. The mind must not be left to dwell at random on every subject that the enemy of souls may suggest... or evils without, will awaken evils within, and the soul will wander in darkness" (AA 518).

Television

We all know that very little of what appears on the television screen is lovely, pure, or of good report. Little of it is either true or honest. And almost none of it has any virtue. And that raises an important question: How can a Christian, one who is "decidedly under the control of the Spirit of God," sincerely ask God to keep him from temptation when he intentionally exposes his eyes and ears—two of his most important senses—to so much evil, and in doing so deliberately invite Satan's enticements? It's something to think about, to pray about. There is a time to say, No ! Perhaps that time is now.

Music

These same principles apply to two other tools which Satan is using very successfully today to gain access to the mind. One of these tools is music. I need not prove that rock music is a tool of Satan. It is public knowledge that many of the rock groups and stars are Satan worshipers. Some have thought that there are subliminal evil suggestions mixed with the "Music." MTV is a burgeoning addiction. Yet, these video tapes and records are in the homes of some who consider themselves Christians.

It is not too unusual to encounter demons working under the name of Music, who say they entered their victims through rock, heavy metal, and other forms of Satanic music. Satan considers such records and tapes as an open door to that person's house.

Pornography

Another tool Satan uses to appeal to our carnal natures is pornography. It comes in many forms and unexpected places. Pornography is not limited to Playboy and similar magazines; it is found in many so-called "Family journals." Advertisements of everything from automobiles to tooth paste and motor oil feature subtle—and sometimes not so subtle—pornography as attention grabbers. As for television, "soap operas" have the reputation of being almost synonymous with pornography.

From my experience, I have found that many more Adventists than we dare think have been entangled in a web of pornographic material. Frequently their personal tragedy is compounded when these same victims, reacting to this sexual stimulation, become involved in masturbation, incest, and child abuse.

We have confronted demons of pornography, in both male and female victims. Their assignment is to create a perverted appetite for this sort of material. To protect ourselves we must learn to turn our eyes away instantly from such material. To stop to look is extremely dangerous. We must pray earnestly that God will protect us from these subtle, or not so subtle, enticements by which Satan molds many minds.

Thoughts and Feelings

Closely related to our senses are our thoughts and feelings. Just as we must guard our senses, so we must control our thoughts, feelings, and imaginations. Before the flood "God saw that the wickedness of men was great on the earth, and that every imagination of the *thoughts* of his heart was only evil continually" (Gen. 6:5). The thoughts and feelings of many people closely parallels those of Noah's day.

But God does not intend that our minds should fantasize on every subject which Satan may suggest. Our imaginations must not be allowed to run riot without any effort or restraint on our part. If our thoughts are wrong, our feelings and emotions will be wrong; and the combination of our thoughts, feelings, and imagination determines what we are, and what we do. They must constantly be under the control of the Holy Spirit, or Satan and his evil angels will move in and usurp that power. Satan will gradually take control of our behavior (PP 460).

Use of Leisure Time

Time is a talent which God gives to each of us, and it is the only talent He gives to all of us in an equal amount. To everyone He gives twenty-four hours each day as long as He gives life. During each of those twenty-four hours we are either serving Christ, doing His will and promoting His kingdom, or we are being influenced by Satan to enhance his cause. Each of us makes our own choice.

Necessity does not require us to work from twelve to sixteen hours a day as was the custom a few generations ago. For this we should be grateful. But what are we doing with the extra time we have gained? Since God holds us responsible for our use of the time He gives us, we should be concerned with the answer to this question. Sociologists and other students of social trends are concerned about the answer to this question. They point out that with the increase of leisure time that has come during the last century there has come a terrible increase in crime and violence. It seems apparent that the large amount of leisure time now available to so many people has created a situation which Satan is using to his advantage.

The Curse of Idleness

Idleness is one of the greatest curses that mankind can experience, for vice and crime invariably result. Satan lies in ambush, ready to surprise those whose leisure gives him an opportunity to become active in their lives.

It is not enough that we avoid doing wrong with our time. We must use it for good. That is one of the lessons Jesus taught in the parable of the talents. Read the parable in Matthew 25:14-30. The man who was given one talent did not waste or destroy it. He did not abuse or misuse the talent. But he did not use his talent, either. He just buried the talent until his master returned. *He just let time slip by.* But Jesus called him an unprofitable servant.

It's so easy for us to make the same mistake the unprofitable servant made. We just let time slip by. It's not so much that we deliberately use our time for sinful purposes as it is that we fail to put forth the necessary effort that is required to use it for right purposes.

Our time is not really ours, but God's. We must give as strict an account of our use of time as of any other talent God has given us (COL 342). There is a cliché which says that an idle mind is the devil's workshop. This is also true of idle hands, and when both mind and hands are idle, we place ourselves in double jeopardy. If we are genuinely concerned with gaining the victory in this great controversy, we will use every hour to the best advantage. Otherwise we may be sure Satan will use them to his advantage. That's his business! "He is never more successful than when he comes to men in their idle hours" (TDWG 133).

The Devil In Our Homes

Harsh words: There is no place where we show our true natures more than we do in our homes. It is there that we relax the reserve and front we often put on in public, and we become our "natural" selves. And too often that is literally true; that is, the "natural" man—the carnal man—becomes evident. This pleases Satan. We do not have to be shrewd observers to realize that our homes are often the object of his attacks. If he can cast his influence over the parents in the home, he will reach the children through them. Satan sees real progress.

Parental Behavior: Few factors determine the atmosphere of the home for good or for evil more than the attitude and words of the parents. If the parents are cross and speak harsh words, the children will be influenced to act and speak the same way. Because it is "natural" for us to yield to the carnal nature and speak sharply, we must constantly be on guard against it and ask God to place a seal upon our lips, for God' angels will not stay in the home where harsh words are spoken, where there is bickering and quarreling (MCP 179). And when the loyal angels leave the home, evil angels come in to reinforce the work they have already begun. In this way we open the door for Satan to enter our hearts as well as our homes.

I suspect that we do not yet fully realize the significance of our conduct in our homes as it pertains to the great controversy in which we are all engaged. Notice these two short quotations:

> "It is from your conduct at your home that we shall be able to judge in a large measure whether or not you are a real Christian" (RH July 2, 1889).

> "Much will be gained by self-discipline in the home... Let each make life as pleasant as possible for the other. Cultivate respect in the speech. Preserve unity and love. *Satan will have no power over those who fully control themselves in the home*" (MLT 84).

Lack of discipline: We must remember that the battle between Christ and Satan is really a battle over the control of human minds. Good angels and the Holy Spirit are exerting a heavenly influence upon us, wooing us heavenward while Satan and his rebellious angels are continually seeking to cause our spiritual destruction (AH 405).

This battle over our minds begins with the tiny baby in the mother's arms. Have you ever seen a baby kick and scream and throw itself in anger? The enemy even then is attempting to control the mind of the little one. That is the time to rebuke the evil spirits. To wait until the child is older before we meet the enemy is to give him an advantage we cannot afford to give, and an advantage he does not deserve.

In more cases than not, the persons we have worked with who have been demonized have felt that their enslavement began when they were children or teenagers. Most of these persons grew up in very permissive homes, according to their own testimony. Discipline in the homes was lax. Consequently, the children did not learn self-control. The truth is, however, that no child ever goes undisciplined.

> "Someone disciplines them. If the mother or the father does not do it, the devil does. That is how it is. He has the control..." (3 SM 218).

Permissiveness in the home, so common in today's society, opens up the door for Satan's control, and he comes right on in.

There must be a balance in our homes, as well as in all other matters. Order and discipline must be maintained, but it must be done always in kindness and love. The atmosphere of quarreling and bickering found in too many families today creates tension, lays the groundwork for future hatreds, and opens up our homes to Satan.

The fifth commandment requires children to honor their parents. But this also implies that parents must earn and deserve that honor and respect by the way they treat their children. In their zeal to maintain discipline, too many parents become harsh and dictatorial. Firmness must always be balanced by love, compassion, sympathy and the application of the golden rule.

Too many adults who have grown up in Adventist homes find it very difficult to see God as the loving Father He is, because their human father—the only role model of God they knew—was harsh, critical, dictatorial, overbearing, and emotionally abusive.

In light of the warning Jesus gave in Matthew 18:6 about offending "one of these little ones," conscientious parents should make the matter of child discipline the subject of prayer and reformation. Both laxness and severity in the home open up the door to Satan.

Exposure to Satanic Influences

Parents sometimes expose themselves and their children to Satanic forces through ignorance. Satan worship and witchcraft are more common in our so-called Christian culture than is generally realized. Often Satan's influence is exerted in disguise. Many who would be repulsed by the idea of openly consulting spiritualistic mediums are attracted to the teachings of Oriental religions, Science of Mind, or Christian Science. Parents take their children to so-called faith-healers, or to others who depend upon the latent forces of the human mind, rather than to trust in the healing power of God and the God-given skills of well-qualified physicians. In doing this parents place themselves, and especially their children, in the hand of Satan as truly as if he were standing by their side. As a result, in many cases the future of the child is controlled by a satanic power which is seemingly impossible to break (PK 210-11).

Edna's experience is an example of how this principle works. In our pre-session she commented that when she was a child her mother took her to a Christian Science practitioner rather than to a physician. A day or two later during an encounter with a demon, he volunteered this information: "I've been in her since she was a child. I got in through Christian Science." Demons do not always tell the truth unless they are forced to do so by the Holy Spirit, but in this case the demon's statement harmonized with the information I had been given, and with truth that has been given us.

This attempt on Satan's part to exert his influence over the minds of children may seem unfair. Sin and everything about it is unfair. That's one of the realities of the war in which we are all engaged. Satan is not bound by any rules of fairness. He is governed only by self-interest.

Unconverted Children

With a determination that most of us do not dream of, Satan is seeking to gain control of children's minds, and thus to bring about their eventual destruction. He takes advantage of every possible opening.

> "Children who have not experienced the cleansing power of Jesus" —who have not been converted, in other words—"are the lawful prey of the enemy, and evil angels have easy access to them" (CT 118).

Many children today come from homes where the name of Jesus is unspoken except in profanity, where the Bible is never opened, where television is the prime influence and where permissiveness is the accepted style of life. Given these conditions, and knowing Satan's ambitions and methods of operation, why should we be surprised at what is happening in our culture today? We are only reaping the crop we have sown.

But children are not left defenseless. God has made provision for them. The power of evil angels may be broken by the faithful and untiring efforts of their God-fearing parents, and by the blessing and grace bestowed upon the children in answer to the prayers of these same parents. Through these intercessory prayers a sanctifying influence is shed upon the children, and the powers of darkness are driven back (CT 118). God's promise is, "I will contend with him that contendeth with thee, and I will save thy children" (Isa. 49:25).

The promise is for those who contend with Satan by cooperating in every possible way with God. There is no such promise for parents who cooperate with Satan by allowing their children to watch violence and sex on television, allowing them to play satanic games, buying them toy guns and other implements of war and destruction, allowing the careless practices of the pagan culture that surrounds us to creep into our homes, and neglecting family worship. How can parents who do these things sincerely feel that they have Christian homes? Isn't it presumptuous of us to ask God's blessing on such homes?

Wake up, parents! If you are not disciplining and educating your children properly in harmony with God's will and the light that has been given to us, you can be sure that Satan is disciplining and educating your children for you.

"The enemy will work right through these children (in permissive homes) unless they are disciplined. Someone disciplines them. *If the father or mother does not do it, the devil will. That is how it is. He has the control*" (3 SM 218).

"Unless parents plant the seeds of truth in the hearts of their children, the enemy will sow tares" (MCP 15).

When parents neglect their God-given responsibility to educate and discipline their children, they are opening up the door and inviting Satan to take control of their children.

Playing with Satan's Toys

Many of those who have come for help have, at some time, in some way, played with Satan's toys. Pornographic material, books and magazines dealing with the occult, horoscopes, Tarot cards, the Ouija board, and rock music are all used by Satan to ensnare human minds. Nintendo games and the popular *Dungeons and Dragons* are in many instances nothing but a form of witchcraft. These are only a few of the means he uses to entice his intended victims. Too many are eager to play with these dangerous toys.

A full-page book advertisement in a tabloid newspaper reads as follows: "The Magic Power of Witchcraft." In the body of the article the reader is assured that, if he follows the advice given in the book, he will "enjoy a life of unbelievable riches, lasting love, and constant protection." Thousands will tragically turn to this type of material rather than to the Bible for the "unbelievable riches" of God's grace, the "lasting love" of our Saviour, and the "constant protection" of loyal angels. Hidden in the smaller print the reader is assured that he will learn from the book how to cast spells that really work, how to dominate others, and how to keep evil forces away.

This book—and the magazine which features the ad—are typical of the material that thousands are feeding their minds on today. Satan considers the presence of this type of material in the home, along with his other toys, as a standing invitation to join the family circle. And Satan never turns down such an invitation!

By these many means Satan gradually molds their minds after his fashion and exercises his power over them. When they wish to control their minds, they find they cannot do so. They yielded their minds to Satan, and he does not easily release his claims (1T 299).

"Tell The Enemy"

Kenneth was one of those who had walked on Satan's ground. Although he had grown up in an Adventist home, he had wandered so far from his Savior that he had prayed to Satan on several occasions. I was not totally surprised when, during a prayer session, a demonic voice said, "I don't have to leave. He has prayed to me, and he is mine."

Under such circumstances, what should we do? We are told that we must "tell the enemy." Notice the following example:

"When Satan comes to tell you that you are a great sinner, look up to your Redeemer, and talk of His merits. That which will help you is to look at His light. Acknowledge your sin, but *tell the enemy* that Christ Jesus came into the world to save sinners" (SC 41).

"*Look the tempter firmly in the face and say.* 'No, I will not imperil my soul for any worldly attraction. I love and fear God. I will not venture to dishonor or disobey Him for the riches of the world or the love or favor of a host of worldly relatives. I love Jesus who died for me. He has bought me. I am the purchase of His blood. I will be true to his claims, and my example shall never be an excuse for any turn from the straight path of duty. I will not be the servant of Satan and of sin. My life shall be such as to leave a bright track heavenward.'" (UL 32).

We have this valuable counsel:

"When Satan points to your filthy garments, repeat the promise of the savior, 'Him that cometh to me I will in no wise cast out.' *Tell the enemy* that the blood of Jesus Christ cleanses from all sin. Make the prayer of David your own: 'Purge me with hyssop, and I shall be clean: wash me and I shall be whiter than snow' " (PK 320).

Yes, there are times when we must *"Tell Satan* that you do not trust your own righteousness, but in the righteousness of Christ" (LHU 273). Tell him of the firmness of your commitment to Christ. We are told that "When Satan tells you that your sins are such that you need not expect any great victories in God," we are to *"tell him* the Bible teaches that those who love most are those who have been forgiven most" (LHU 333).

Ordinarily I do not communicate with the enemy, but I felt that in this case I should "tell the enemy," since Kenneth, at that time, was so possessed by the enemy that he could not speak.

In response to the demon's statement that he did not have to leave Kenneth, I said, "Yes, Kenneth has prayed to you. That was a sin, but that sin has been confessed and forgiven. It is covered with the blood of Jesus Christ. Therefore, you can not hold that sin against him. You have no ground to stand on. In the name and power of Jesus Christ I demand that you leave." Before that prayer session ended the demon was forced to leave. But the battle that took place was a severe one.

This battle was proof that Satan "will not hesitate to engage all his energies and call to his aid all his evil host to wrest a single human being from the hand of Christ ... Satan and his angels are unwilling to lose their prey; they contend and battle with holy angels and the conflict is severe" (MYP 60).

Cherishing Known Sins

People sometimes ask what the unforgivable sin is. Our answer is that it is any sin which we refuse to give up. Such a sin is unforgivable simply because we do not ask for the forgiveness which God offers. We cherish the sin more than we cherish forgiveness. Sins not repented of are sins not forgiven. If we think ourselves forgiven of sins, of which we have never felt the sinfulness and over which we have never felt contrition of soul, we deceive only ourselves.

Everyone who willfully cherishes a known sin is inviting Satan to tempt him. separates himself from God and from the protection of His angels. Everyone who willfully departs from the keeping of God's commandments and deliberately chooses to live contrary to God's known will places himself under the control of Satan. As Satan presents his deceptions, the deceived one will be left without defense and will fall an easy prey.

Such a person will be lured on and on until he finds himself controlled by a will stronger than his own. Unless he allows the Holy Spirit to change the direction of his life, he will eventually find himself serving Satan rather than serving God.

Most of us have some cherished sins in our lives. Not big ones, perhaps, but little habits that we intend to get rid of *some* day, such as a bad temper; a gossipy tongue; indulgence of appetite; carelessness regarding the edges of the Sabbath; a spirit of criticism; lack of a devotional life; and intemperate habits. These are the doors we open to Satan. Some day we plan to let God take care of them, but Satan will do his best to see that the day of reformation never comes. None of us can risk delay. "Behold, now is the accepted time; behold, now is the day of Salvation" (2 Cor. 6:2). Why not ask God to take care of your problem right now?

Appetite

I have given no priority to the order in which I have considered these weak spots in which the enemy most often attacks us. Possibly I have saved the most delicate one until the last.

Appetite is a very sensitive subject. As we are using the word here, "appetite" means anything that we take into our bodies. Satan knows that "if he can control the appetite, he can control the whole man" (Te 276). Therefore, he attacks us in this area as often and as severely as he can, and in as many ways as he can. Satan concerns himself with what we eat, when we eat, and how much we eat.

> "Satan is constantly on the alert to bring the (human) race fully under his control. His strongest hold on man is through appetite, and this he seeks to stimulate in every possible way" (CD 150).

Working closely with demon Appetite is demon Intemperance, "who is of giant strength, and not easily conquered" (Te 176). I have heard both of these demons speaking through their victims, as well as the demons of alcohol and tobacco. (Te 32, 63). And working in close cooperation with appetite and intemperance is the demon of sugar. Some of you will be tempted to smile at that suggestion, and that is exactly what Satan wants us to do. *Demon Sugar does exist.* Sugar is a compulsive destroyer. I have heard him speak and identify himself through his victims many times.

Bonnie's Experience

Let me tell you about Bonnie's experience. She called one evening and made an appointment to meet me at the church the next day. At the church she told me, "I can no longer control my appetite for sugar. That's why I called you. I need help." Then she told me how the day before she had eaten a half-gallon of ice cream, six brownies, six doughnuts, six candy bars, and still her craving for sugar was overwhelming. "That's when I knew I needed help," she concluded. Bonnie was right. She did need help. Satan had taken control of that aspect of her life.

God has told us that "The free use of sugar in any form tends to clog the system, and is not infrequently a cause of disease" (CD 197). In view of this fact, why should we find it hard to believe that Satan would use some of his demons to encourage us to use this poison? After all, it was Satan himself who invented alcohol (Te 12). Why should he hesitate to use sugar to his advantage?

Appetite was involved in the first battle of this war fought in the Garden of Eden. It was successful then. It is successful now! This is the reason why God in His mercy has given us so much light on this subject. We should be thankful to Him for this! The seemingly trivial matter of our eating and drinking has a more important bearing on the outcome of our spiritual battle than most of us have realized. We need constantly to remember that Satan's "strongest hold on man is through appetite" (CD 150). But through the divine strength that comes from the indwelling of Christ, He is able to set us free of the appetite demon.

In this chapter we have considered some of the methods which Satan most often and most successfully uses to exert his influence over us. There are many other ways in which Satan attacks us. But, in every encounter with him, God through His Son, has made it possible for us to be free, no matter how deep has been our bondage. "Thanks be to God who giveth us the victory" (1 Cor. 15:57).

CHAPTER
9
Omnipotent Wills and Impregnable Hearts

"For it is God which worketh in you both to will and to do of his good pleasure" Philippians 2:13.

When God planned to populate this planet with human beings, He decided to do something He had never done before. "And God said, let us make man in our image, after our likeness" (Gen. 1:27). An entirely new race of people was about to be brought into existence. For the first time God was about to create a people patterned after Himself. All heaven must have tingled with excitement, for "Human beings were a new and distinct order. They were made in the image of God" (1 ABC 1081).

The Will

Adam and Eve were to some degree fashioned like their Creator physically. They were also patterned after Him mentally and spiritually. Every faculty of mind and soul and body reflected the Creator's glory (Ed. 20). He also gave to Adam and Eve the capacity to develop characters patterned after His character. God has given to each of us the ability to form God-like characters, just as He gave it to Adam and Eve. He had given this same capability to the angels when He created them. The development of character, which distinguishes us from other forms of animal life, is made possible by the power of choice. We sometimes refer to this as the will.

What is the Will?

The human will is the God-given power to make a free choice. We are to use it to make a heart-felt, intelligent decision to forsake any and every practice, act, thought, behavior and attitude that is not in harmony with the character of the Lord Jesus Christ.

The will is not inclination or taste. To will is more than to want. It is more than hoping or desiring. Many who hope or desire to be saved will be lost because they did not *will* to be saved (MH 176). In the Garden of Eden the human race gave its will into the control of Satan. Ever since Eden Satan has molded the human will like clay to the doing of *his* pleasure. On the other hand the reason Christ came to this world was, "to expel the demons that had controlled the will" (DA 38).

More Than a Wish

The power to change involves a positive determination to *carry out* the choices that we make. The use of the will involves a Christ-centered decision to change. So the use of the will involves more than a wish. It is easy to wish for a Christ-like character. Many people make proper choices mentally, but knowing what to do and doing it are two different things. Many people are *hoping* for salvation, but will be lost.

Conversion is a cross-roads where we choose to make His will our own. Yet this is only the beginning. Every day, moment by moment, the will is making choices. Every decision must be made in the light of that *one great choice.* The will must continue to operate and to give force to every decision.

We are in real danger until we understand the correct use of the will. Everything, happiness in this life and the goal of eternal life, depends upon it. The will is not passive, but forceful. It is the God-given governing power we must use to control all our other faculties. It motivates and empowers all our actions (5T 515).

But there is an equally vital matter to remember—while the choice is ours, the power to carry out that decision comes from God. "It is God which worketh in you both *to will* and *to do* of His good pleasure" (Phil. 2:13). "None but Christ can fashion anew the character that has been ruined by sin" (DA 38).

It is vital that we understand that a major issue of the Great Controversy concerns the control of the will of man. Man has a choice. For us to turn the will over to the sanctifying influence of the Spirit of God is the way to eternal life. To make such unconditional commitment is not easy. Such a decision often goes against every fibre of our nature. There are times when our prayer must be, "Lord, make me willing to be made willing."

Omnipotent Wills, Impregnable Hearts

By constantly keeping our wills on the Lord's side, every impulse and desire will be brought into captivity to Him. At times this will take every ounce of will power that we possess, and sometimes more. But God knows this, and He has made provision to supply what we lack. Notice this assurance:

"As the will of man cooperates with the will of God, it becomes omnipotent" (MYP 101).

Consider for a moment what this means. When we totally surrender our wills to the divine will of God, our weak, wavering, powerless wills take on the God-like quality of omnipotence. We then have access to that divine strength which makes even the weakest of us more than a match for Satan and all his angels. Then we have supernatural strength with which to battle supernatural powers, for "Greater is he that is in you than he that is in the world" (1 Jn.4:4). "A soul thus kept in possession by the heavenly agencies is impregnable to the assaults of Satan" (DA 324).

When we submit ourselves to Christ, our hearts and wills are merged with His, and our minds become one with His mind. A new power then takes possession of our hearts. A change takes place which we cannot make for ourselves. It is a supernatural work which brings a supernatural element into our human natures. The indwelling of Christ in our hearts through faith in His righteousness is our only defense against the evil one.

The Freedom of the Will

One thing God has forever renounced—the use of force against our wills. He will not transform our characters against our choice. For God to do so would mean that we are no longer made in the image of God. It would also confirm Satan's accusation that God is a dictator who ignores man's wishes.

"It is not the work of the good angels to control minds against the will of the individual" (MYP 53).

God *will* not control us against our wills, and Satan *cannot*. But in Christ's day many had yielded themselves to Satan. They had allowed themselves to come under the influence of one whose will was stronger than theirs.

"They brought unto him many that were possessed with devils; and he cast them out with the power of His word and healed all that were sick" (Matt. 8:16).

As in Christ's time, Satan is putting forth every possible effort to control, harass, and possess all whom he can. He knows that Jesus will soon return to take His people out of this sin-polluted planet. He is determined to destroy as many people as he can before that day. He will influence your mind and mine in one way or another if we permit him to do so.

Agencies that we cannot see, both good and evil, are at work to control the mind and the will. Good angels are exerting a heavenly influence upon our hearts and minds. At the same time Satan and his angels are continually working to bring about our destruction through control of our minds (AH 405).

You and I, as we go about our daily routine, are being influenced by one group of angels or another. Our minds are given to the control of God or to the control of Satan.

Tragically, more people listen to Satan than to God. Whenever men and women reject the Saviour's invitation to accept Him, they are yielding to the devil. Millions in every aspect of life, in the home, in business and even in the church, are doing this today. As a result, violence and crime and moral darkness cover the earth like a cloud (DA 341).

The Need for Intercessory Prayer

When they are permitted to do so, evil angels will control the minds of men and women. Many have no mind or will of their own. Many of those with whom we have worked have at first been unable to exercise their own wills. Karen is a good example. Many times we found it necessary to encourage her to pray the most simple prayer on her own behalf. Her response most often when we suggested that she pray was, "I can't pray. I want to, but I can't." It took as long as forty-five minutes of our praying with her before she was able to pray the most simple request, "Jesus, help me." This is typical of those whose minds and wills are controlled by Satan.

Karen's experience illustrates the need of intercessory prayer for those who are under Satan's control. *Because they are possessed, they cannot seek God's help on their own behalf.*

Karen's experience is comparable to that of the demoniac of Capernaum who in place of prayer could utter only the words supplied by Satan (MH 93). Because Satan controlled all his faculties, he was unable to utter the most simple request for help. Can you imagine the agonizing frustration in such a situation? To realize one's desperate need of help, to know that help is available, and yet not to be able to express that need must be a terrifying experience indeed. But God is always aware of every unexpressed cry for help.

Mark 2:1-12 tells the story of four men who brought their friend, "one sick of the palsy," to Jesus to be healed. Verse five is significant. "When Jesus saw *their* faith, he said unto the sick of the palsy, Son, thy sins be forgiven thee." Jesus healed the sick man and forgave his sins *because of the faith of his friends who interceded for him.*

There is power in intercessory prayer. Jesus honored the faith of the paralytic's four friends, and He will honor our faith today when we come to Him on behalf of those in need. I believe that the prayers and presence of committed Christians with their accompanying loyal angels weakens and frustrates the influence of demonic forces. That is one reason I often take several others with me when we minister to the needs of one who is possessed. "No power can deliver the ensnared soul but the power of God *in answer to the prayers of His followers*" (1T 299).

Intercessory prayer—prayer for the sick among us, for unconverted relatives and friends, and for those who cannot pray for themselves—should grow as a vital ministry among God's people. This should be especially true "as we approach the close of time, when Satan is to work with the greatest power to deceive and destroy" (GC 516).

The Enemy's Power Multiplied

Satan was created with a mastermind and noble capabilities; and although He has prostituted these gifts, He is still a being of great power and ability. For thousands of years he has experimented with the properties of the human mind. In subtle ways he implants his thoughts into our minds. He does this in such a manner that those who come under his influence may not know that they are being led by his will, rather than their own. Satan's aim is to so confuse the minds of men and women that they will hear no voice but his (MCP 18). He endeavors to accomplish his purpose by paralyzing our senses, by diverting our minds to any subject that will cause division and dissension. (AH 401; MCP 22, 23).

Satan's power to tempt and deceive us is now *ten times greater* than it was when Jesus and the apostles walked on earth. (2 SG 277). By his experience in dealing with human minds for thousands of years, and by his continual practice during that time, the enemy's power and control is a *hundred times greater* than it was when he rebelled in heaven. (See 3T 328).

His anger and hate will continue to increase until Jesus returns and puts an end to his work. It behooves us who are living in these testing times to ask ourselves, Who is influencing my mind and will today? For when our minds are not directly influenced by the Holy Spirit, Satan can mold them as he chooses. (See MCP 22).

God Restores the Will

But we are not left to Satan's mercy. Just when Satan thought that he had succeeded in debasing the image of God in humanity beyond any possibility of help, Jesus Christ left heaven and came down to this planet to restore in man the image of his Maker. He came to lift man up from the dirt and mire into which he had fallen, to reshape the marred character and to make it beautiful again with His own glory.

To conclude this chapter, I wish to underscore one more time that in order to save the lost race, it was mandatory that the *human will* be set free. Man's will had been in bondage ever since the Garden of Eden. God in His love gave man a second chance—a chance to make the right choice. Jesus came here in order to expel the demons which for ages had controlled man's will. (See DA 38). He made an infinite sacrifice to make this choice possible. To neglect or fail to use this opportunity is a sin against the blood of the Cross. Let us use our wills to His glory! No victory is won on this Battlefield without a sanctified will.

CHAPTER
10
Victory Through Submission

"Submit yourselves to God. Resist the devil and he will flee from you." James 4:7.

God has promised that when we submit to Him and resist the devil, he will flee from us. But why is it that many people, even professed Christians, are harassed, controlled or possessed by Satan? Has God lost His power to fulfill His promise? Has Satan at last grown more powerful than God? Is Satan so strong that he does not have to flee? Of course not!

It is well for us to remember that Satan's fleeing is conditional upon our submitting to God and our resistance to Satan. The fact that Satan lingers around more than we like is an indication that we need to consider seriously our part in the fulfillment of God's promise. If the promise is not fulfilled, the fault lies not with God, but with us. In this chapter we shall look at the matter of submitting to God.

Our Filthy Rags

As Satan's captives we are naturally inclined to do his bidding. To submit to God is contrary to our carnal natures. We cannot take even the first step back to Christ without His help. Jesus said, "Without me, Ye can do nothing" (Jn. 15:5). Nothing is *zero*. Without the divine strength that comes when Jesus is in the heart, through faith in His righteousness, we can do nothing good; only evil.

It is easy to think, "But I'm really not that bad. I've never robbed a bank or killed anyone. I don't smoke or drink. I don't lie or cheat on my income tax. I'm true to my spouse. And besides, I keep the Sabbath. I pay tithe, and I....," and we compile quite a list of the bad things we don't do, and the good things we do. It's quite an impressive list! Not really. It's so easy for us to forget that basically we are sinners, not so much because of what we *do* as because of what we *are*.

When Paul wrote in 1 Timothy 1:15 that he was the chief of sinners, he did not mean that he was intentionally doing any wrong. He was not an immoral man. Paul is saying that every thing he did —the very best life he could live—apart from Christ and His righteousness, is still sin. Paul was agreeing with Isaiah that "all our righteousnesses"—the best things we do and think are as filthy rags," if they are done apart from Christ (Isa. 64:6). In God's eyes, there is absolutely nothing good about us except that which comes as a result of our personal relationship with Christ.

"There is none righteous, no not one. " "All unrighteousness is sin." "And this is his name whereby he shall be called, The Lord our Righteousness" (Isaiah 64:6; Rom. 3:10; Jer. 23:6). The Lord is the only righteousness we will ever have.

"Without Christ we cannot subdue a single sin or overcome the smallest temptation" (4T 353).

The first two words, "without Christ," are the key. They make the difference between defeat and victory. God has given us assurance of victory over Satan and his temptation, but the victory comes only from the indwelling of Christ, never from ourselves.

That is why James 4:7 says, "Submit yourselves therefore to God. Resist the devil and he will flee from you." We must submit or surrender our wills to God's divine will before we can resist effectively. We can resist only as we submit. Unfortunately, most people have reversed this counsel. Many people—most people, in fact—have submitted to the devil, and they spend most of their lives resisting God. Is it any wonder that our society is sick?

The Bible defines sin as the transgression of the law (1 Jn. 3:4). But in a broader sense sin involves more than the outward breaking of the Ten Commandments. Sin is the result of a severed relationship with God.

"Behold the Lord's hand is not shortened that it cannot save; neither is his ear heavy that it cannot hear. But your iniquities have separated between you and your God, and your sins have hid his face from you, that he will not hear (Isa. 59:1, 2).

A Love Relationship

Sin did not and does not change God. But sin did and does change us. It changes our natures and interferes with our ability to relate to God. The purpose of the plan of salvation and all that it involves is to restore that lost relationship. God's goal for us is perfection of character. Character is a result of the restoration of that perfect relationship with God which sin destroyed. That relationship is restored only when Christ comes into the heart and abides there. Obedience to God—the keeping of the law—will be the natural result of this relationship. The Saviour who kept His Father's commandments when He was on earth will also keep them when He lives in our hearts. (John 15:10).

It is important that we recognize that we are saved by our faith relationship with Christ, not by the obedience that results from the relationship. But, if the relationship truly exists, the obedience will inevitably result. We are saved by faith alone, but faith is never alone. Faith, love, and obedience are always together.

The Bible is very plain in teaching us that our salvation depends upon a relationship, not upon obedience. "And this is life eternal, that they might know thee, the only true God, and Jesus Christ, whom thou hast sent" (Jn. 17:3). "He that hath the Son hath life; and he that hath not the Son of God hath not life" (1 Jn. 5:12). Obedience—the keeping of the law—will be the fruit of that love relationship. "If ye love me," Jesus said, "keep my commandments" (Jn. 14:15). "He that hath my commandments, and keepeth them, he it is that loveth me" (Jn. 14:21). Commandment keeping and love are united. One cannot exist without the other. Our submission to God and our love for Christ empower our resistance to Satan.

Submission

But Jesus cannot abide in our hearts as long as they are full of self. As long as we insist on doing the fighting against Satan, depending upon our own strength to gain the victory, we are bound to be defeated. There won't be any real and lasting victories. God can help us only when we are willing to admit to ourselves and to Him that in our own strength we cannot cope with Satan. When we admit our helplessness, our lack of strength, He will supply what we lack. That is the only circumstance under which we can expect to resist Satan. God has promised victory only as we meet that condition.

The Indwelling Christ

In his letter to the Ephesians, Paul writes about the indwelling Christ in these words, "That He (Jesus Christ) would grant you, according to the riches of His glory, to be strengthened with might by his spirit in the inner man; that Christ may dwell in your hearts by faith; that ye being rooted and grounded in love" (Eph. 3:16,17). These two verses contain the formula for coping with Satan successfully—*"That Christ may dwell in your hearts by faith."* That is the only solution to the problem of Satan and sin. Without this personal acquaintance with Him, and a continual communion with Him, we are at Satan's mercy and eventually we will do his bidding (DA 324).

Our Helplessness

God knows better than we do how weak and helpless we are. He knows that we are battling supernatural forces that are beyond our strength. And so, when we surrender our wills to Him, He performs a miracle for us, and in us, that makes up for our weakness. When we accept by faith the righteousness of Jesus Christ, He makes us partakers of His divine attributes. He makes up for our human deficiency with His own divine merit (1 SM 382). God does for us what we cannot do for ourselves.

God promises this in His word. He tells us about it in Paul's letter to the Thessalonians. "And the very God of peace sanctify you wholly; and I pray God your whole spirit and soul and body be preserved blameless unto the coming of our Lord Jesus Christ" (1 Thess. 5:23). This is a higher standard than any of us can reach by ourselves, and God knows that. And so He immediately gives us this assurance, "Faithful is he that calleth you, who also will do it" (1 Thess. 5:24). This is God's promise to do for every submissive and believing soul what he cannot do for himself (DA 98). The same God who calls us to the impossibly high standard will "do it." That is, He will enable us to reach that standard if we trust in Him and cooperate with Him.

By Invitation Only

When we submit ourselves to Christ, a new power takes control of our hearts and lives. A change is brought about which we can never accomplish for ourselves. It is a supernatural work, which brings a supernatural element into our human natures (DA 324).

But Christ will not come into our hearts and bring about this change for us without definite invitation. His presence in our lives is always the result of our personal choice. He responds to the invitation we extend. God will not control anyone against his will. Satan, on the other hand, will use force to enter any part of our lives not already occupied by Christ. We cannot keep Satan out in our own strength; only Christ has the power to keep him out. The victory comes from Christ, but only at our invitation.

Let me say it another way: The Bible emphasizes the source of our strength— "be strong in the Lord." We stand against the enemy in "the power of His might" (Eph. 6:10). It is certain that we have no natural power of our own against this vicious and persistent enemy; however, it is absolutely essential that we understand that God has left something for us to do. We have a part to play in this victory. God provides the armor, but we must "put on." It is His righteousness, but in order to wear it we must submit completely to His revealed will. Only then can we win. God provides the sword—His word—but we must take it in our hands. (Study it). Then, and only then, can we have victory in this battle.This is a positive prerequisite to being released from Satan's captivity.

> "Christ may entreat, His angels may minister; but all will be in vain unless they themselves are roused to fight the battle on their own behalf" (Te 111).

One more thing: We must wear the breast-plate of His righteousness. There is no "back-plate." Those who turn their backs have no protection. We cannot run from this conflict. On this battlefield there is no place for cowards. To try to avoid the fight is to lose. When the Apostle Paul came to end of his life, he said, " I have fought a good fight" (2 Tim. 4:7). Freedom is certain, but it is never cheap. The Cross of our Lord is the proof of that.

Praise God! He has promised never to leave us or forsake us. He will make our hearts impregnable to Satan's attacks (DA 324). Through His divine strength Christ will make even the weakest of us more than a match for Satan and all his angels. With Christ at our side, our captivity is broken. Jesus is victor on the Battlefield.

CHAPTER
11
Non-practicing Sinners

"Resist the devil and he will flee from you" James 4:7.

Submission or surrender to Christ is essential to a victorious life for anyone. But it is especially important to those who seek freedom from demonic oppression in any form. God is not in partnership with the devil. He will not free from Satan's influence anyone who is going to continue to use his efforts and time to advance the enemy's cause.

But when, by surrendering our wills entirely to Jesus Christ, we show our allegiance to Him, He will make us more than a match for Satan and all his demons. He makes us partakers of His divine nature (7ABC 929). Christ's presence in our hearts enables us to resist Satan's temptations which we cannot do even in the smallest degree without His help. In this chapter we shall consider two basic reasons as to why we may not resist Satan as strongly as we should.

Our Dangerous Ignorance

One of the reasons we do not resist Satan as we should is that we do not really see sin in its true light. We do not see its horror and repulsiveness. We have become so accustomed to sin that in some ways it has become attractive. (See Heb. 11:25) As a result, we do not meet it with the determined and decisive resistance with which our Savior met it.

Parallel to this is the fact that we are also blinded to the character and power of Satan. Because we are so ignorant of his power, malice and extent of his warfare against the church collectively and each of us individually, we manifest little enmity against him or his work. "He (Satan) could not gain advantage if his method of attack were understood" (1T 308).

There are relatively few, even among the remnant church, who recognize the enemy for the mighty general that he is. Few appreciate his power to control their minds—and thus their actions. Each of us are being carefully studied by evil angels who seek to devise and carry out their skillful plans to destroy us (See GC 507, 508). There is fatal danger in ignorance.

An Appeal to Ministers

I hesitate to say it—but even among Adventist ministers there is often a fearful and tragic hesitancy—and in some cases, outright refusal—to engage in intercessory prayer for those who are bound by Satan and who are seeking help. I usually ask those who come to me, "Have you talked with your pastor about this problem?" In too many instances the answers are something like this: "Yes, I went to my pastor for help, but he did not know what to do." Others tell me that the pastor offered a perfunctory prayer that did not help. Some tell me the pastor only suggested that they "see a psychiatrist."

Many of these people have been severely disappointed in their pastor's inability to help them. In most cases the pastor's hesitancy or inability to meet the needs of these people who are crying for help, is due to a fear of becoming involved so directly with the enemy, or to an ignorance of what is involved in real Spiritual Warfare.

I write this in all kindness, for I was once in that same ignorant situation. It was because of my ignorance that I told Paula Green she was wrong when she told me. "There is a demon in me." Only when demonic voices spoke through her in my presence did I realize how right she was, and how wrong I was.

Ellen White made an indirect appeal to the ministry to warn their flocks about the sly, destructive work of the enemy.

> "Among professed Christians, and even among ministers of the gospel, there is heard scarcely a reference to Satan, except perhaps an incidental mention in the pulpit. They overlook the evidence of his continued activity and success; they neglect the many warnings of his subtlety; they seem to ignore his very existence" (GC 508).

In kindness I appeal to my fellow pastors to study again the Gospel commission and all its implication. As a starter in this direction, I suggest that you read—or read again—chapter two of this book. Check out the quotations for yourself. Discover for yourself what the Bible and the Spirit of Prophecy really teach about the Deliverance Ministry, which is nothing more or less than intercessory prayer with the specific purpose of freeing our fellow human beings from Satan's bondage through the power of Jesus Christ, given according to His promise.

The Malignancy of Sin

I must stress a vital truth: we do not resist temptation as we should! We have little perception of the danger and disastrous nature of sin. We must pray that God will help us to grasp its lethal nature; pray that He will give us a genuine hatred for it. Nothing gives greater resistance to Satan than this.

But hating sin and Satan is not enough. If we are to resist Satan with effective power, we must first be convinced that we *can* resist his temptations. We will never be victorious over temptation as long as we allow the devil to deceive us into believing that there is an acceptable reason for our sinning. We will never be able to cope with Satan if we allow him to convince us that our case is different, that it's really not our fault, or that God really is not that strict. These are all pieces of human reasoning. They are part of Satan's deceptive devices.

Partakers Of His Nature

When Jesus comes into our hearts, He makes us partakers of His divine nature. He gives us victory *now*, in this *present* life. He makes it possible for us to overcome temptation.

> "Satan declared that it was impossible for the sons and daughters of Adam to keep the law of God. . . . Men who are under the control of Satan repeat these accusations against God, in asserting that men cannot keep the law of God." 3ST 264

> "Satan is jubilant when he hears the professed followers of Christ making excuses for their deformity of character. It is these excuses that lead to sin. There is no excuse for sinning. A holy temper, a Christlike life, is accessible to every repenting, believing child of God." DA 311

Many look forward to His second coming to change their characters. I must tell you earnestly that the change must be made *now!* To believe otherwise is dangerous.

> "When He (Jesus) comes, He is *not to cleanse us from our sins*, to remove from us the defects of our characters, or to cure us from the infirmities of our tempers and dispositions. If wrought for us at all, this work will be accomplished before that time. When the Lord comes, those who are holy will be holy still" (2T 355).

The belief that it is impossible to overcome sin in this life is "a fatal sophistry of Satan" (GC 489). God has promised "to keep you from falling and to present you faultless before the presence of His glory with exceeding joy." To deny this is to contradict God's word and limit His power to change our lives (Jude 24).

God admonishes us to "be diligent that ye may be found of Him in peace, without spot, and blameless" (2 Pet. 3:14). Paul says that Christ gave Himself to the church "that He might sanctify and cleanse it with the washing of water by the word, that He might present to Himself a glorious church, not having spot or wrinkle, or any such thing; but that it should be holy and without blemish" (Eph. 5: 26, 27).

Consider this: the church is composed of individuals. God saves us as individuals. How can His church collectively be without blemish if the individuals who make up the church are spotted and wrinkled and blemished with sin?

John wrote it this way: "Whosoever abideth in Him sinneth not: whosoever sinneth hath not seen Him, neither known Him. Little children, let no man deceive you: he that doeth righteous is righteous. He that committeth sin is of the devil; for the devil sinneth from the beginning. For this purpose the Son of God was manifested, that He might destroy the works of the devil. Whosoever is born of God doth not commit sin; for His seed remaineth in him; and he cannot sin, because he is born of God" (1 Jn. 3:6-10).

Victory is Essential

If we find it difficult to accept as truth the idea that we must gain the victory over sin in this life before Jesus returns, it is probably because we have tried and failed so many times. We have come to believe Satan's fatal sophistry that it is impossible to overcome. This, of course, pleases Satan. But God does not require us to do what for us is impossible. That is why He supplies the divine strength that makes us more than a match for Satan. Christ overcame and obeyed as a human being. If we attribute to His human nature a power that is not available to us, we destroy the completeness of His humanity.

Jesus did not come to this planet as a lesser God, to give obedience to a greater God; but He came as a *man* to obey God's holy law. He is our example. He came to our world, not to show what a God could do, but to reveal what a human being can do through faith in God's power to keep him from sinning. In the same way, man through faith is to be a partaker of the divine nature and to overcome every temptation that besets him. The law now demands that you and I, through faith in Jesus Christ, obey Him in the human natures we have. Jesus, by bridging the gulf sin has created, made it possible for us to do just that. (See OHC 78; 7 ABC 929).

Non-practicing Sinners

There is a vital difference between being sinners by nature and practicing sin. If Christ is in our hearts, Satan cannot force us to sin against our wills. Satan cannot control our minds unless we yield the control to him. He cannot control our wills or force us to sin without our consent. He can distract us, but he cannot contaminate us; he can cause us agony, but he cannot defile us. He can tempt us; he can make sin appear pleasant and enticing; but it is up to each person's choice to decide as to whether or not he will yield to the temptation. (See AH 402; 1T 301; GC 510).

Wearing His Yoke

Jesus spoke of our taking His yoke (Matt.1:29). A yoke is a joining together to bear a common burden—a joint enterprise—if you will. Just as God will not save us against our wills, so He will not force us to stop sinning against our wills. By linking our wills with His, His will becomes ours. "Thy will be done becomes our daily prayer" (Matt 6:10). So long as we *want* to sin, so long as we cherish sin more than we cherish God's approval, we will continue to sin. But when we learn to hate sin because it is sin, and because of what it did and what it does to the Savior, when we have Christ in our hearts and when we *will* to stop sinning, God will enable us to overcome every temptation.

We are not to think or to say that we cannot overcome every temptation or remedy our defects of character. If we come to this conclusion, we will never experience the everlasting life God has made available to us (COL 331).

God has made provision that the Holy Spirit shall be imparted to every repentant soul, *to keep him from sinning* (DA 311). Satan is jubilant when he hears professed followers of Christ making excuses for their sins. It is these excuses that lead to sin. There is no acceptable excuse for sinning.

To believe that we can live above sin in this life requires faith. But faith is the thread from which the fabric of the Christian life is woven. "Without faith it is impossible to please him: for he that cometh to God must believe (have faith) that he is, and that he is a rewarder of them that diligently seek him" (Heb. 11:6).

Both the Old and New Testaments teach that the just must live by faith. "The just shall live by his faith"(Hab. 2:4). Paul attached enough importance to this statement under the inspiration of the Holy Spirit to quote it in Romans 1:17 and again in Galatians 3:11. This statement is quoted a third time in Hebrews 10:38. We do not yet fully appreciate how great an element faith must be in our lives if we are to be overcomers.

Christ has sufficient grace and strength to make us more than conquerors in our warfare against Satan. He came to this world and lived a sinless life so that in His power His people might also live sinless lives. But we must reach out by faith and claim that grace and strength which Christ has made available. Otherwise Christ's ministry and sacrifice will avail us nothing. Now notice this significant statement:

> "He who has not sufficient faith in Christ to believe that he can keep from sinning, has not the faith that will give him an entrance into the kingdom of God" (RH, March 10, 1904).

We never appear more helpless, yet really are more invincible than when we realize our nothingness and depend entirely on the merits of Jesus Christ. At that time God will send every angel in heaven to come to our aid rather than to allow us to be overcome by Satan. (7T17). Only when we have the divine strength which Christ's presence supplies can we exercise any really determined resistance to sin.

Bumper Sticker Religion

During the last few years bumper stickers have become quite popular. Recently I saw a sticker which read, "It's O.K. not to drink." The message does state a truth, but it is a pretty weak protest against the use of alcohol. More recently I noted a slight change in word order. It now reads, "It's not O.K. to drink." What a difference! It is not a recommendation. It is a warning!

Satan, too, plays word-games. His bumper sticker reads, "It's O.K. not to sin." Satan implies that sin is not a big issue, It's O.K. not to sin, but don't worry about it if you do. This is deception.

God's sticker has never changed. His always reads, "It's not O.K. to sin" This is not a recommendation. It is a clear and certain warning. Satan's bumper sticker is weak and enticing. God's is true and faithful: "It's not O.K. to sin"

In His love, God has been fair to us. He has clearly warned: "Ye shall not eat of it, neither shall ye touch it lest ye die"(Gen. 3:3). "The soul that sinneth, it shall die" (Eze. 18 : 4). Death is not an arbitrary decree on the part of God. Sin is deadly; It kills! Death is the wages that sin earns. (Rom. 6:23).

Can We Live Above Sin?

This book is written in the faith that Christ came to set us free of sin—not partially free—all-the-way-free. The victory over Satan is total. The victory over sin is total. If this is not true then the plan of salvation falls short of being adequate. If it is inadequate in the slightest degree—then it becomes *totally* inadequate. The death of Christ in our place, and His presence in our hearts through the Holy Spirit make it possible for us to gain complete victory over sin. Notice this significant sentence:

> "To everyone who surrenders fully to God is given the privilege of living without sin in obedience to the law of heaven" (RH 9/27/06).

All that has been written by Bible writers and God's messenger to the remnant church about the possibility and necessity of living sinless lives is true. But there is a corollary to all this which is also true. The corollary is this: Never, until these corruptible bodies become incorruptible, can we have any claim to perfection. The clearer perception we have of Christ's spotlessness and purity, the more conscious we will be of our own imperfections in contrast. Those who catch even a fleeting glimpse of the loveliness and exalted character of Christ will never say, "I am sinless." By grace, God may write that word in His books, but we should never speak it about ourselves.

Think of Moses and Daniel, Joseph and Elijah. No sin is recorded against these men, but none of them claimed to be sinless. Daniel's prayer was, "We have sinned, and have committed iniquity, and have rebelled, even departing from thy precepts and from thy judgments" (Dan. 9:5). This is not the prayer of one who considered himself sinless. The soul in closest relation to Jesus, beholding His purity and excellency, will fall before Him in humility as did Daniel.

Looking to Jesus and meditating upon His goodness, mercy, and love will create in our souls an utter abhorrence of sin. The more distinctly we see Jesus, the more clearly will we also see our own defects of character. As we confess these faults to Jesus, and with genuine humility cooperate with the divine power, the Holy Spirit will enable us to put those things out of our lives.

For it is the Holy Spirit who changes our characters into the image of Christ, and when this has been done we shall reflect His character. The character of the one who thus beholds Christ will become so like Him that those looking at him will see Christ's own character reflected as in a mirror. Imperceptibly to ourselves we will be changed day by day from our ways to the ways and will of Christ. Thus we shall grow up into Christ and unconsciously we will reflect His image.

Only when the battle with Satan is over, when the armor is laid at the feet of Jesus and we have been translated from the kingdom of grace to the kingdom of glory, can we claim to be saved and sinless (3 SM 353-356).

In the meantime—while we retain our sinful natures, *we have stopped practicing sin.* We must *never* confuse these two concepts. At His second coming, it is our *natures* that will change—not our characters. Before our Lord's return we must become *non-practicing sinners,* if you please. He has made this possible for us. If this is not true then the salvation of the Cross falls one step short of being fully adequate. But here is the good news! By His grace, we can have complete victory over Satan and all his angels. Total victory is possible on this Battlefield by the grace of our triumphant Lord. To Him be the glory!

CHAPTER
12
The Weapons of our Warfare

"For the weapons of our warfare are not carnal, but mighty through God to the pulling down of strongholds" 2 Cor. 10:4.

A genuine hatred for sin and a conviction that sin must be overcome in this life are essential to victory over Satan and his temptations. How can we ever expect to rid our lives of sin if we enjoy it and believe that it is unavoidable?

When we really hate sin for sin's sake and see its horror in the light of the Cross; when we are genuinely convinced that there is no excuse for sin and ask God for divine strength to resist Satan, He will answer our prayers and come to our aid. He will make us more than a match for Satan. He will fight the battle for us and give us the victory. He has already won!

Although victory is dependent upon the presence of Christ in the heart, there is a work we must do. We must continue to resist temptation in Christ's strength. In this chapter we shall consider some practical ways of resisting the devil so that we can claim the promise of James 4:7, that Satan will flee from us.

Bible Study

No one has resisted Satan perfectly as did our Savior. So we can do no better than to learn how He coped with Satan, and then follow His example. We can be sure that Satan was on Christ's track every moment of His life, seducing Him in every possible way. So much was at stake in that one Person's life! He "was in all points tempted like as we are, yet without sin" (Heb. 4:15). The Scriptures give a detailed account of three specific temptations and Christ's response to each one. Read the record in Matthew 4:1-11. One important fact stands out: Jesus met each of the temptations by an appropriate answer from the Bible. His response to temptation was, "It is written." Jesus was a student of the Scriptures. If He, the divine Son of God, felt the need of knowing the Word, how much greater must our need be?

In the sixth chapter of Ephesians, Paul admonishes us to "Put on the whole armor of God," that we may be able to resist Satan's temptations. A very important weapon is "the sword of the Spirit, which is the Word of God" (Eph. 6:17). No Roman soldier would engage in battle without his sword. It could be used both offensively and defensively. In the same way, no Christian is prepared to engage in battle with the enemy without fortifying his mind with the Scriptures.

"Thy word have I hid in my heart," wrote the psalmist, "that I might not sin against thee" (Psa. 119:11). When the Bible is prayerfully studied, the Holy Spirit takes the scriptures and fortifies the mind against the temptations of the enemy.

The study of the Bible is a vital channel through which God communicates His ideas to us. Think of it! In place of our own narrow, mean ideas and plans, the great God of Heaven, the Creator of the universe, implants His noble thoughts in our minds. In this way God leads us away from self and sin toward heaven and eternal life.

There never has been a time when study of the Bible was more important than it is now. We are surrounded by deceptive influences. Everything that can be shaken will be shaken, and only those whose minds have been fortified by the study of the Word will be able to stand.

Satan Hates the Bible

Satan knows very well the strength and resistance that comes from the Bible. And so he takes action against it. Many with whom I have prayed have told me they were unable to study the Bible. In some few cases the individual was physically unable to pick up or open the Book. In other cases their vision would blur or become obscure so that they could not read the Bible. Other material, yes, but not the Bible. Others have been unable to understand or comprehend even the most simple biblical concepts during the time of their bondage.

These conditions disappear when freedom from Satan's bondage is attained. In these and other ways Satan manifests his hatred of God's Word. Sometimes the demons express their disdain for the Bible verbally. "I hate the Bible" is a common statement. Others have said, "The Bible is trash" or "It's rubbish." Several we have worked with have thrown the Bible across the room. One young woman tore the Bible into shreds. She realized what she was doing but was unable to control her actions. In spite of their hatred of the Bible, demons know its message and they can quote parts of it from memory.

Although no other book can take the place of the Bible, there is a wealth of excellent devotional material which can help to supply the inner spiritual strength that is necessary to resist Satan. At the top of the list of such material is a classic little book, *Steps to Christ*. I recommend it to all who want to maintain a close relation to their Savior.

Prayer

Bible study has a partner, which is prayer. Prayer provides us the opportunity to talk with the Creator of the universe in a personal relationship. "Our Savior spent entire nights in prayer. If He felt such need of prayer, how much more should we feeble sinful mortals realize its necessity?" (SC 98).

It is almost impossible to over-emphasize the importance of prayer as a defense against temptation and sin. The darkness of the evil one surrounds those who neglect to pray. Through his whispered temptations, Satan entices them to sin and his work is made easier because they do not use the privilege God has given them in prayer. If they do not open their hearts and communicate with Christ, Satan will communicate with them.

Satan and his demons hate Jesus, and they detest His very name. They know that Christ's has given His ministers power to rebuke them, to cast them out, and to heal those whom they afflict (EW 191,192). They know they are already a conquered foe and when we earnestly appeal to Jesus for help they become alarmed. We should not wonder that the devil and his angels do all they can to keep us from praying, for this serves their purpose well (MCP 26; 1T 296).

Just as Satan hinders them from studying the Word, so he tries to prevent them from praying. "I know I should pray, but I can't" is a common statement of those who come for deliverance. It has taken as long as an hour of rebuking Satan and of intercessory prayer before the possessed one could pray the most simple prayer, "Jesus, help me."

To neglect the privilege of prayer is to give Satan a major advantage. On the other hand, it is impossible for Satan to overcome one whose heart is in continual communion with Him (SC 103). So important is prayer that Paul recommends "praying always with all prayer and supplication in the Spirit" (Eph. 6:18).

Since Satan is always on our track, why should we not always be in an attitude of prayer? Satan is busy every moment, going to and fro, walking up and down in the earth, seeking whom he may devour. The earnest prayer of faith will baffle his efforts.

Of all the practical things we can do to assure victory over sin and Satan, nothing is more important than Bible study and prayer. Neither can be neglected except at great risk of spiritual defeat. But when these two weapons are used together, they go a long way in assuring victory.

The importance of Bible study and prayer in maintaining victory over the enemy is emphasized in these words from the Lord's messenger:

> "Beware how you neglect secret prayer and a study of God's Word. They are your weapons against him who is striving to hinder your progress heavenward. The first neglect of prayer and Bible study makes easier the second neglect. The first resistance to the Spirit's pleading prepares the way for the second resistance. Thus the heart is hardened and the conscience seared" (LP⁻ ⁻99).

Faith

There is another weapon without which all other weapons are useless. That weapon is faith—faith in the indwelling Christ in His righteousness and power to save.

> "But without faith it is impossible to please Him for he that cometh to God must believe that He is, and that He is the rewarder of them that diligently seek Him" (Heb. 11:6).

Just now, as you read these words, you do have some faith. It may not be as much as you want, or feel you need; but you do have some, for "God hath dealt to every man the measure of faith" (Rom. 12:3).

"Prayer is the key in the hand of faith to unlock heaven's storehouse" (SC 99). Unless prayer is accompanied by genuine faith, even our prayers have little value in supplying spiritual strength. In the Bible the Lord has made some incredible promises. We must take them seriously. "If ye abide in me, and my words abide in you, ye shall ask what ye will and it shall be done unto you" (Jn. 15:7). This is not a prayer over a catalog want-list. It applies in the realm of our spiritual needs. We must learn to hold up these promises to our Lord. Press these promises to his throne. He will prove faithful.

Do you sometimes feel the need of more faith? If you do, don't despair. You are in good company. Jesus' disciples felt the same need. "Lord, increase our faith" (Luke 17:5). This is a perfectly proper prayer for anyone who sincerely wants more faith. It is good to realize our needs. Take note that Jesus answered the disciples' request by referring to a grain of mustard seed.

"If ye have faith as a grain of mustard seed," Jesus said, "ye shall say unto this mountain, Remove hence to yonder place, and it shall remove, and nothing shall be impossible unto you" (Matt. 17:20). The mustard seed is one of the smallest of seeds, yet it has a mysterious power to produce one of the largest trees. In this ministry it has always amazed me how God will take our mustard seed of faith and explode it to His glory (Matt 17:20). Obstacles that appear insurmountable will disappear on the demand of faith. With that faith "Nothing is impossible unto you" (Matt. 17:20).

And as you exercise the faith you have—which may not seem any larger than a grain of mustard seed—it will increase. Study of the Bible with the proper purpose to learn God's will and to know Jesus more personally will increase your faith, for "faith cometh by hearing, and hearing by the Word of God" (Rom. 10:17).

Testing the Promises

Faith grows only when it is exercised and tested. One of the reasons why we do not have greater spiritual strength is that we do not give God opportunity to reveal His power on our behalf. He will help us in every time of need if we will place our entire faith in Him. But we must give God that opportunity.

Let me tell you a little story that illustrates this point. There once was a philosopher attached to the court of Alexander the Great. With the passing of years the old philosopher came upon hard times. In desperate need of help he appealed to Alexander. In reply to the old man's request Alexander replied, "Go to the royal treasurer and draw out what you need." So the philosopher followed the emperor's instructions. He asked the royal treasurer for the equivalent of one million dollars.

"A million dollars!" exclaimed the treasurer when he heard the request. "I can't possibly let you have that amount of money. I will have to talk to his majesty about this." And so the treasurer asked the emperor about the matter.

"Pay the man at once!" Alexander ordered. "He has done me a great honor. By the largeness of his request he has shown great faith in me, in my wealth and in my generosity. "

Too often we fail to honor God by our requests. We have so little because we ask for too little! We may even insult Him, His love and His ability to fill our need by the smallness of our petitions. Too often the reason why His professed people have no greater strength is that they do not give the Lord opportunity to reveal His power on their behalf. (See PP 493).

We often become concerned about what we feel is a lack of faith when all God really expects of us is that we exercise a mustard seed of faith. He is not only powerful—God is eager to answer our prayers. Satan causes us to be overly anxious about our seeming lack of faith. He causes us to look inward to ourselves instead of upward to Him who is the source of our strength.

"You know you don't have much faith." Satan whispers this in our ears. He says that our prayer and petitions mean nothing. By such insinuations he opens our minds to doubt. "You know your God can't answer your prayers." And sure enough, there are times that our prayers aren't answered just as and when we feel they should be, and our faith becomes still weaker.

God hears and answers every prayer that comes from a humble and sincere heart. When the answer does not come in just the way we have asked, and at the time we expected, we must still believe that He has heard and that He will answer in the way and at the time that God in His wisdom sees is best. By faith we must claim the promise and know that the answer will come and that we shall receive the blessing we most need (SC 100).

Satan knows that faith is a mighty weapon in the heart of the Christian. One of the demons we most commonly encounter is demon Doubt. His work is indicated by his name. His target may be God, Jesus Christ, the Bible, all three, or any combination of them. Like all demons, Doubt may be rebuked and expelled in the name and power of Jesus Christ. There are practical steps we can take that will prevent his returning.

Doers Of The Word

As we have already stated, study of the Bible is a powerful antidote for doubt. But to make this study really effective we must live up to all the light that is revealed. We must be doers as well as hearers of the Word. When we begin to reject the light of truth, we open the door to Satan again.

We must accept the loving Jesus who is revealed in the Bible. We must continually ask Him to abide in our hearts. To fail to do this opens up the door to Satan. But as we accept Jesus Christ daily in our hearts, doubt and darkness will disappear. They cannot exist in His presence. (SC 117).

Daily learning God's will from the Bible, talking with God in prayer, and the exercise of a simple faith—these are the most effective weapons we have in our battle with sin and Satan. But there are other weapons, too. God has given a full suit of armor to each one who is willing to face the enemy.

> "Wherefore take unto you the whole armor of God, that ye may be able to withstand in the evil day, and having done all to stand. Stand therefore, having your loins girt about with truth, and having on the breastplate of righteousness, and your feet shod with the preparation of the gospel of peace; above all taking the shield of faith wherewith ye shall be able to quench all the fiery darts of the wicked. And take the helmet of salvation and the sword of the Spirit, which is the word of God" (Eph. 6:13-17).

God has supplied us with both defensive and offensive weapons. But all these weapons must be kept in good repair, sharp and bright, which is best accomplished by using them daily. When they are left unused, or are laid aside even for a day, they become dull and ineffective. But their constant daily use will accomplish much in causing Satan and his demons to flee from us in fulfillment of God's promise in James 4:7.

Protective Angels in Personal Ministry

When Christ is in our hearts we have means of defense which are not otherwise available. Angels that excel in strength are sent from heaven to protect us. The wicked one cannot break through the angel guard which God stations about us (GC 517). In our work with those who have been demonized, we have had experiences which demonstrate that this is not an idle promise.

We had worked for several hours with Dorothy, and the series of prayer sessions ended late in the evening. Because Dorothy lived some distance away, we decided to let her stay in our home that night. Pastor Paddock, who was working with us, also stayed in our home, and the night passed uneventfully.

The next morning we returned to the church for another prayer session. As we were praying the demon said, "Why did you take her to your home last night? I tried to get in, but there were angels around your home and I could not get through. Even when I sent for reinforcements I could not get in. The wall was too tight. But let me warn you. If there is ever a crack, I'll get through." Since that experience, I have heard almost the same words several times. Such experiences have a very humbling effect. And they make us keenly aware of the reality of the battle being waged between the evil and loyal angels. My family is determined that by God's grace there shall be no "cracks" in the wall of protection around our home.

We thank God for the ministry of loyal angels, which is manifested in many ways. When those who have erred confess their faults and plead for help with deep humility, angels who excel in strength will wrench them from the power of the evil angels. God would send every angel in heaven to rescue just one soul who wants to overcome. (See 7T 17).

During a prayer session with Dorothy, the demon in power suddenly spoke. "Why are there so many of you?" he asked. Apparently he was referring to angelic beings who were visible to him but invisible to us. Then he continued, "Don't send any more! Get them away from me! There are so many I can't count them. I'm confused." Then, speaking to those of us who were engaged in Christian warfare for Dorothy, he said, "Why don't you guys get them away from me?" There was a pause. "I'll go! I'll go!" the voice shouted. And the demon left.

When we were praying with one young lady, she opened her eyes and looked up toward the ceiling. Her eyes moved in a pattern as if she were watching something the rest of us could not see. Then the demon spoke. " They have swords of fire! They have swords of fire!" This was repeated several times as the eyes continued to follow an invisible (to us) moving object. Then the young lady closed her eyes and frowned. Moments later the battle was in full force. I am happy to be able to tell you that the young woman has been delivered and is now rejoicing in her new freedom.

While we were praying with a young man several years ago, a demonic voice said, "You don't know how weak I really am." I would not minimize the power of the enemy, but Satan and his angels know they are already defeated. They know that, compared to Christ and the loyal angels, they are weak. They know that the weakest saint, with Jesus in the heart, is more than a match for all of them. This is positive proof that any captive may be free. By the grace of Christ none need lose any skirmish on this Battlefield.

The Cup He Drank

"The mission of Christ to the world was to break
the chain of Satan from the soul, and to set at
liberty those that are bound. It cost an infinite
price to deliver the captives of Satan from the
captivity of sin...Jesus, the Prince of life, took
the battle field to meet and to contend with
the prince of darkness, and to dispute his
claims. From the time of his birth until
he hung on Calvary's cross he warred
with the evil one in our behalf. His
purity of character was a rebuke to
the world, and men hated him
because of his divine and
holy character. He did
not come to our world
as an angel
of glory, but as
a man. He was
made in the
likeness
of sinful flesh, and condemned sin in the flesh.
With his human arm he encircled the race, and
with his divine arm he grasped the throne of
the infinite, linked man with God, and earth
with heaven. Oh, who are there who are
colaborers with Christ, who are feeding
the starving flock of God?" 3 ST 109

CHAPTER
13
With Power and Authority

"Then He called His twelve disciples together, and gave them power and authority over all devils, and to cure diseases. Luke 9:1.

One of the last acts of the Lord before His ascension was to define again the nature and scope of the Gospel commission. The importance of the timing cannot be overstated. In His mind this was a matter of the highest priority. "Go ye into all the world, and preach the Gospel to every creature," Jesus said. And then He told His disciples that certain signs would accompany the preaching of the Gospel. "And these signs shall follow them that believe; In my name shall they cast out devils ..." (Mk. 16:15, 16).

By His Word

Nowhere in the Bible are we told exactly how demons were to be cast out, but we do know that Jesus "cast out the spirits with his word"(Matt. 8:16; GW 250). By His word He stilled the sea and raised the dead (GW 250). It was with this same word of power that He expelled demons from human minds and bodies (Ps. 33:6,9). This is verified by the examples in the Bible.

In English *"word"* in our minds means a *single* word. In Biblical Greek and other languages it carries a much larger meaning. It means a *speech, or discourse.* This definition gives a more accurate picture of His deliverances. Obviously, the man (or men) of Gadara was not freed by a *single* word—the scripture is clear that many words were exchanged (Mark 5:2-15). The idea that Jesus cast out devils with a *single* word is not supported in the scripture.

Jesus Ordered Them

When the demon-possessed boy was brought to Jesus at the foot of the Mount of Transfiguration, "Jesus *rebuked* the foul spirit, *saying* unto him, Thou dumb and deaf spirit, *I charge thee*, come out of him, and enter him no more" (Mk. 9:25). And to the demon who possessed the man in the synagogue at Capernaum, Jesus spoke, "Hold thy peace and *come out of him*" (Mk. 1:25). It

117

is apparent that the specific examples cited in the Bible are only a few of the many cases that took place during the ministry of Christ. The record says that Jesus healed "many that were possessed with devils" (Matt 8:16). In nearly every case Christ addressed the demon as an intelligent entity, *commanding him to come out* of his victim and to torment him no more (GC 516).

After the ascension of Jesus the disciples continued to cast out demons in fulfillment of His commission. "Unclean spirits, crying with loud voice, came out of many that were possessed with them" (Acts 8:7). Paul cast out demons in the name of Jesus. There is the account of a girl "with a spirit of divination." Paul said to the spirit, "I *command* thee in the name of Jesus Christ to come out of her. And he came out the same hour" (Acts 16:16,18). In the early church "A multitude... were vexed with unclean spirits; and they were healed every one" (Acts 5:16).

Jesus recognized the casting out of demons as a miracle (Mk. 9:38, 39). And miracles are performed only when God wills it. Even the disciples were not always able to perform miracles at their will. The Lord grants His servants that special power only as the progress of His work and the honor of His name require it (6 ABC 1064).

No Fixed Formulas

The Bible does not give a "method" or "formula" or "procedure" to be followed in casting out demons other than to say that Jesus "cast out the spirits with his word" (Matt. 8:16). The most logical reason for the Bible's lack of a "fixed method" is that there is none. The Bible records at least three blind men whose sight was restored by Jesus. In each case Jesus employed a different approach. In Spiritual Warfare the methods are equally varied. In fifteen years of experience no two persons have presented the identical set of problems. There is no identical set of answers. At the same time there are always similarities. Others engaged in the Deliverance Ministry have told me that their experience is comparable. One thing is certain— no captive can be set free except in the name and authority of Jesus Christ. It is a serious matter that the authority God gave His church to free the captives has been forgotten. "God's word was robbed of its power, and evil spirits worked their will" (DA 257-258).

One of the most common criticisms of the Deliverance Ministry is that "you are not doing it right." The critics have not yet demonstrated "the simple method." One thing we know—the Lord said, *"Cast them out!"* This fact is clear and plain. This we do. We sincerely welcome the help of experienced leaders.

The purpose of this chapter is to present some suggestions for the benefit of anyone who may find himself in an emergency. We believe such needs will grow as the coming of the Lord draws near, and Satan becomes even more active (GC 516).

No Accusations

We would like to emphasize the fact that all those persons we have dealt with have *come to us* for help. We have never approached anyone with the suggestion that he or she is possessed or needs help. We believe this approach is the one Christ took in His ministry. Judas was possessed by a demon of selfishness. Jesus was aware of this, but although He cast demons out of many others, He never delivered Judas. The reason was simply that Judas never asked for help. Perhaps Judas' pride kept him from acknowledging his need. Jesus never forced Himself on anyone. Jesus never frees a captive against his will. Judas might have become a citizen in God's kingdom had he reached out to Jesus for help (DA 294).

With very few exceptions, those who experienced deliverance during the ministry of the early Christian church also came voluntarily for help. One exception to this is the "damsel" who was possessed by a spirit of divination. Her work was to distract people from listening to the Gospel. Paul discerned the true situation, and said to the spirit, "I command thee in the name of Jesus Christ to come out of her. And he came out the same hour" (Acts 16:16-18). Like Jesus, Paul cast out the demon by verbal command.

Not In Control

People often ask, How do the people who come for help know they need help? Every individual's case is different from all others, but basically each person has realized that his life is "out of management." This is seen in the form of *compulsions* over which the individual has no control. Each one has come to realize a destructive and evil power is governing his conduct in one or many aspects of his life.

"I'm not in control" and "Another power is controlling me" are statements they quite often make when they ask for help. I do not know exactly *how* they *know* that a demonic power is working in their lives. One thing I do know for sure, they are very much aware.

Paula Green, the first person who came to me for help, insisted "There is a demon in me," even when I argued that this could not be true because she was a baptized church member. It was six weeks later, when demonic voices began to speak out of her, that I learned how right she was and how mistaken I was.

Indicators of Demonic Presence

I an going to list some of the more common "problems" that are characteristic. It is important to remember that these "symptoms"—if we may use that term—are manifested in varying degrees in different individuals. It is important to know that no one person is going to experience all of these problems. Many of the "symptoms" are exact opposites of each other. One person is depressed and will not talk; another is a compulsive talker. Some suffer from insomnia and have trouble sleeping; others have to fight off sleep. Some are compulsive eaters (bulimic), and others refuse to eat (anorexic). Incidentally, I am not saying that all cases of eating disorders are demon-related; but from experience I know that some of them are.

We must keep in mind, too, that those of us who consider ourselves "normal" may have some of these abnormalities to a limited degree. We consider these as personality "quirks" and in no way demonic. *When these abnormalities are numerous and unusually pronounced, they should be eyed with suspicion.* These problems frequently interfere with, or prevent their living a normal life. People come for deliverance when they are no longer in control of their own lives.

Let me give you one example. Several years ago a young man, probably in his early thirties, called on the telephone and made an appointment with me. He would say only that he was desperate and needed help. When we met in the church office he was very brief in what he said. I can still quote him almost word for word.

"I am a married man. I love my wife and I would not hurt her for anything. But these last few weeks there wells up in me a rage which I cannot control. If I don't get help, there is going to be a tragedy in our family. I am either going to injure my wife, or I am going to kill her. Please help me."

That's all he said, but it was enough. We prayed together and in the name and power of Jesus Christ I rebuked the demons of rage, temper, anger, and murder. That man was right; he was not in control and he realized it. For a while there was a severe battle. But he was a different man when he walked out of that office an hour or so later. I had never seen that man before, and I have not seen or heard from him since. Jesus is still Lord and Savior. The demons are still subject to us through His name, and I thank Him for that.

One by One

As in the case of this young man, it is not unusual that demons will surface one at a time, identify their work-assignment, resist departure, and go. This takes time. This time factor has been highly criticized in academic circles. With all due respect for those who maintain that all demons should leave instantly upon one simple command, this concept does not concur with practice. We could wish they would all leave instantly, but they don't! There are at least two reasons.

The first reason is simply that the Lord Jesus Christ is the Bondage Breaker. He is the one who sets captives free. We are his co-workers and nothing more. The decisions are His, not ours. It is not for us to tell Him how to do His work.

The second reason is the *human will*. Many captives are not aware of the sources of their bondage. It may be a TV addiction, an irrational fear, jealousy, or an indulged vice. The Lord reveals to the captives the points of their bondage—*One by One*. In this way, He allows them to see, one by one, where surrender is needed. The choice is theirs whether they want to be free. Jesus could put them all out in an instant; we know that; but there are times that He won't! He leaves the choice with us—whether the demons go or stay. Adam and Eve had a free choice—it is so with us today. Choices often have to be made *One by One*. Demons frequently leave that way. This fact should not be a major problem.

One more caution must be given in regard to the following list of "symptoms." We must always avoid seeing demons in anyone just because he may be a bit eccentric or different from what we consider the norm. For that reason I never suggest to anyone that he has "a demon problem." On the other hand, persons under demonic attack will, in all probability, manifest some of these "symptoms." *The more numerous and severe the problems are, the greater is the probability of demonic oppression.*

Frequently parents recognize the presence of demonic oppression in one or more of their children, and to seek help for them. It happened in Christ's day, and it happens today. A father, you remember, brought his demon-possessed son—first to the disciples, and then to Christ—for deliverance. The event is recorded in Matthew 17:14-18, Mark 9:17-29, and Luke 9:37-42.

In my experience with such cases involving very young children—toddlers, as we call them—a rather unusual thing happens. Any "manifestations" that occur, such as yawning, coughing, or burping, involve the mother—she becomes surrogate for the under-age child. I do not remember any exceptions to this. However, this is not true with older children who have reached the age of accountability. I believe that this fact and its implications are worth noting.

I am here listing some groups of symptoms. These groups were not discovered by reasoned study, but rather they have been discovered as tormented people have come seeking help.

A LIST OF POSSIBLE SYMPTOMS

A. **Social abnormalities**

1. Tends to isolate self from others.
2. Has fear of crowds.
3. Has relatively few friends.
4. Experiences loneliness.
5. Is unable to function to capacity in daily life and work.

B. **Physical Manifestations**

1. Has abnormal or "superhuman" strength.
2. May be violent at times; may require restraint.
3. Is abnormally destructive.
4. Suffers from physical weakness.

C. **Personality problems**
   1. Has dual personality; sudden changes.
   2. Is hard to get along with—rebellious
   3. Lacks initiative.
   4. Has periods of silence.
   5. Becomes angry without cause.
   6. Is compulsive talker.
   7. Is sullen, withdrawn.
   8. Has extremely weak will.
   9. Physically, or verbally abuses others.
   10. Uses vulgar or blasphemous language.

D. **Restlessness and insomnia**
   1. Constantly "on the go," unable to "settle down."
   2. Suffers from insomnia.
   3. Is drowsy during the day.
   4. Has frequent nightmares, often same ones repeated.

E. **Inner turmoil**
   1. Suffers from deep depression and despair.
   2. Has great and abnormal fears.
   3. Has hatred toward God, Jesus, Bible, Sabbath.
   4. Uncomfortable in religious meetings.
   5. Is not able to read Bible, pray.

F. **Physical and mental injury**
   1. Has suicidal tendency.
   2. Has feelings of self-depreciation and self-reproach.
   3. Experiences feeling of worthlessness.
   4. Experiences feelings of failure.

G. **Functional disorders**
   1. Suffers from pains and aches for which no organic cause can be determined.
   2. Suffers from migratory pain (Moves around the body).
   3. Has unexplained allergies, seizures.
   4. Is compulsive eater.
   5. Starves self.
   6. Has excessive minor sicknesses.
   7. Has physical problems which routinely prevent attendance at religious activities.

H. **Excessive use of prescriptive drugs**

    1.   Uses tranquilizers.
    2.   Uses sleeping pills.
    3.   Uses pep pills.

I. **Sex life**

    1.   Practices masturbation.
    2.   Practices homosexuality.
    3.   Has excessive heterosexual drive.
    4.   Experiences extreme sexual fantasies.

The Counseling Session

I do considerable counseling before beginning an actual prayer session. I am careful to investigate the possibility of any underlying medical or emotional problem. I do not rush to judgment. I must have rather conclusive evidence that the problem is indeed of a demonic character. There are fanatics who blame everything on demons.

I do have a caution. Persons who are demonically oppressed often manifest the same characteristics as those who are mentally or emotionally disturbed. The Bible teaches that many mental and emotional problems are caused by demonic oppression. This was true in Christ's day, and it is true today.

> "The fact that men have been possessed with demons is clearly stated in the New Testament. The persons thus afflicted were not suffering with disease from natural causes. Christ had perfect understanding of that with which He was dealing, and He recognized the direct presence and agency of evil spirits" (GC 514).

One fact I would like to emphasize is that the counseling session is not a "confessional," as some critics have thought. But I have found that, in many cases, discussing the problem insofar as the person is comfortable in doing so, is in itself healing.

Some have felt a need for years to talk about their problem with someone who would sympathetically listen. I still remember the woman who sobbingly told me that her husband said that if she ever mentioned her problem to him again he would have her committed to a mental institution.

Some Guidelines

I try to have at least one other person with me, a fellow prayer warrior, during these times of spiritual battle. If it is a female I am praying with and for, I try to have at least one other woman present for obvious reasons. I say "try" because I have found myself in a few situations where that was not possible.

We always begin our counseling session with prayer, committing ourselves anew to Jesus Christ. We ask Him for wisdom and claim His promise that it will be given (James 1:5). We ask for protection from any demonic deception or lies. We also ask for God's continued protection, and claim His promise that "Nothing shall by any means hurt you" (Luke 10:19). God has always kept His promise. Although threats of injury and death are sometimes uttered by demonic voices, we have never been the subject of physical attack.

We never seek out an individual and tell him that he is possessed, or that he has a demonic problem of any kind. By coming for help he is admitting that he may have a problem.

In the second place, it is not always easy to determine at that stage that the person actually has a demonic problem. Most of the people walk into the room or office as normally as you or I would. It is usually only later, as we begin to pray a warfare prayer that the one for whom we are praying sometimes begins to display bizarre behavior.

It is at that time that demonic voices may speak through their victim, stating that they are not going to leave, or object to going. I have seen these people froth at the mouth, crawl on the floor, hiss like a snake, assume a fetal position, and do other strange things. Often the captive has no recollection of his behavior after he has been freed from Satan's power.

I must emphasize that the demonic voices and the bizarre behavior are the exception and not the rule. In most cases we can kneel in prayer, or sit around a table during the entire prayer session, and the only unusual happening will be yawning, coughing, and sneezing on the part of the one for whom we are praying. I have observed that these odd behaviors occur much less frequently during recent years. However, I have noted a marked increase in the number of entire families coming under Satan's attack, and asking for deliverance.

Total Surrender Essential

In the pre-counsels we discuss the importance of making a full surrender to Jesus Christ. Total surrender to do the will of God is a prerequisite to deliverance from Satan's domination. God is not in partnership with the enemy. God cannot give deliverance to one who continues to choose to serve Satan. Of the several hundred persons who have come to me for help, I remember only three who refused to make such a surrender.

Making a commitment to Jesus Christ is not easy for one who has been, and is, under the domination of the enemy. Paula Green's deliverance was delayed six weeks until she was able to put her will on the Lord's side, and decide to make the necessary changes in her life-style to bring it into harmony with God's will. Others have required days or hours to make that decision.

This surrender of the will is often accompanied by evidence of reformation even before we begin our prayer session. I remember one young lady who reached into her purse, took out a pack of cigarettes and handed them to me with the remark, "Here, I won't be needing these any more." Then she reached into her purse again and handed me a copy of that month's horoscope. A short time later we were engaged in a real spiritual battle with the enemy who hated to lose his captive. But to the glory of God, that young lady was delivered; and to my knowledge she is free of both the cigarettes and astrology.

At the conclusion of what I call the "pre-session," we pray again and ask God to cover all of us with the blood of Jesus, to forgive our sins, and to give each of us a full suit of armor as we engage in Spiritual Warfare.

The Right to Command

Those who are praying such a warfare prayer must not hesitate to command that the demons leave, in the name and authority of Jesus Christ. Christians must believe that the "power and authority over all devils," which Jesus originally gave to His church, is still in effect (Luke 9:1; Matt.10:1). *This is absolutely essential in Spiritual Warfare.*

Those who engage in such spiritual battles must believe, not only that this commission applies in general, but that it applies to them personally as a servant of the Lord Jesus Christ. They must take command over all demons in the name, power and authority of the Savior and Lord whom they have chosen to serve without reservation.

Those who do not have this kind of faith, and who are not prepared to assume this authority, should not be present at such prayer sessions, for the sake of themselves and of others.

I recall an experience that illustrates this point. I had invited a member of my congregation, whom I thought was qualified to serve as a "prayer warrior" to intercede for a young man who had called for help. When seated in the church office I noticed that this man had taken a seat in the far corner of the room—as far away as possible from the young man and myself.

I did not think anything of this at the time. But soon, after we had begun our warfare prayer a demonic voice spoke out of the young man. It said, "What is that man doing here? He should not be here. He does not have faith. "

My partner looked surprised, as though he wanted to leave. But I was hesitant to allow him to go on the advice of a demon; so urged him to stay, which he did. However, he later said that it was true that he did not have faith. He said he did not wish to take part in such a prayer session again; and so far as I know, he hasn't. He has grown spiritually since that time, and I would like to believe that he would serve again as a prayer warrior if the opportunity were presented.

I pray that God will bind all demons involved in the forthcoming battle (Matt 18:18-21); that God will protect all of us from any harm or violence that the demons may wish to do (Luke 10:19); that there be no sharing of strength between demons; that they not be allowed to accept any new assignments; that all previous commands and assignments given to them by Satan be canceled and counteracted by the blood and power of Jesus Christ; and that all Satanic pacts, spells, curses and occult holds be broken and smashed by the Savior's blood. Some people scoff at the idea of curses and spells and occult holds, but I have learned that these things are very real to those who have come under the power of Satan.

Spiritual Battle

After claiming the promise of God's presence and protection, I invite everyone present to pray, including the one for whom we are praying. In some instances that person has been unable to pray because of Satan's bondage. I have at times given that individual a printed prayer to read, and in some cases the captive has been unable even to read the printed prayer. In a few cases the person has torn up the paper , or attempted to do so. Such actions are often accompanied by demonic voices. I want to say again, though, that such behavior is the exception rather than the rule. It was true in Bible times. No one should criticize if, on occasion, it is true today.

It is important that we trust in God to take care of any situation that may arise. When I first became involved in the Deliverance Ministry some years ago, there were times when we physically restrained the "victim" (Satan's victim). Since then I have learned to trust God and to ask Him to have His angels do whatever restraining is necessary. The team work between God's earthly servants and His angel troops is a joy to behold. Physical violence is seldom seen.

Deliverance from Satan's domination requires real Spiritual Warfare, a warfare in which the battles are "as real as those fought by the armies of the world" (MB 119). In these battles our primary weapons are faith and prayer. But the actual power that gives victory is not in the prayer itself, but in our God who hears and answers prayer (Matt.28:20; Heb.13:5); the One with whom all things are possible (Matt.19:26); the One who came to give "deliverance to the captives, and... to set at liberty them that are bruised" (Luke 4:18).

"It is part of God's plan to grant us, in answer to the prayer of faith, that which He would not bestow did we not thus ask" (GC 525). Spiritual Warfare involves more than a perfunctory "God bless you" type of prayer. Warfare prayer is as specific and direct as knowledge of the need will permit. We ask God through the ministry of the Holy Spirit and loyal angels to do battle against specific demons—fear, depression, alcohol, pain, pride, lust, witchcraft, suicide, or whatever the need may be. In most cases the one for whom we are praying knows what we should pray against.

Power in the Promises

To pray for deliverance from the enemy and to claim that victory in the name of Jesus Christ is not presumptuous, for such prayer is based on the promises of God's Word. Such texts as Matt. 10:1, 8; Mark 16:15-17; Luke 9:1 and Luke 10:17-19 give divine authorization for such spiritual battles. These verses all state a truth which Satan and all his demons already know—that Jesus has won the victory, and that He has given His disciples power and authority over them, to cast them out. The demons may hesitate and resist; but provided their captive has fully surrendered to Jesus (so far as is possible under those conditions), and all known sins have been confessed and forgiven, they must leave. Under those conditions, they have no choice, and they know that.

Power in Hymns of Praise

With experience and prayer, those who engage in such Spiritual Warfare will discover additional Bible texts and promises which are powerful weapons in battle. Verses which speak of forgiveness are effective. Psalm 51 and 1 John 1:9 are examples. The singing of hymns which speak of Christ's sacrifice and His blood are also effective weapons. "There is Power in the Blood" and "The Old Rugged Cross" are good examples of this type of hymn. Some of the strongest protests I have heard expressed by demonic voices have been uttered while we were singing such hymns. "Don't sing that song!" "Stop singing that song! I can't stand it!" are typical responses. We have been asked why the singing is so effective against them. We feel that it calls to their memory the singing they once did in heaven. It is painful to them to remember how much they have lost. They suffer with these memories. Needless to say, we sing more enthusiastically when they complain.

What I have suggested in the last few paragraphs outlines the procedure which I follow under normal circumstances. However, every person's situation is different; and in the Deliverance Ministry we must deal with every circumstance as it arises and trust God to give wisdom and ability to deal with the needs of the occasion.

I remember a man who called on the telephone and arranged to bring his wife to the church office for intercessory prayer. But his wife "passed out" in the car before he reached the church. He and their two daughters who came with them had to carry her into the office.

And there was the young woman who came to the church office with her brother-in-law. As the young woman opened the office door a voice said, "There are five of us, and we are not going to leave." Her brother-in-law feared that I would not recognize what was happening. In a stage whisper he said, "That's not her speaking. That's a demon." Obviously, in such situations, we can't follow the procedure I have been describing in the last few paragraphs. Instead, we go immediately into Spiritual Warfare. Incidentally, the young woman whose experience I just related in this paragraph is the same young woman who gave me her cigarettes and horoscope from her purse, as I related a few paragraphs earlier. In spite of their statement to the contrary, the five demons did leave, to the glory of God. We have had some interesting experiences, but God has never failed us; and He never will.

Why Does It Take So Long?

People frequently ask why it takes so long for some individuals to be set free. Why does it require more than one confrontation in many cases? I do not know a simple answer to these questions. But an understanding of several facts will supply some insights which, when taken together, may answer the question.

Understanding Scriptural Brevity: This is a general perspective that we must bear in mind. The extreme brevity of most Bible records can easily lead to false conclusions. For example, the late night interview between Jesus and Nicodemus as recorded in John's Gospel can be read in one minute and forty five seconds. No one in his right mind would contend that this was the length of their conversation. They probably talked for an hour or more.

This same principle as we have seen in the example of Nicodemus must be applied to all the Bible records of Jesus' deliverances. The Gospels gives us only an outline of these events. To say that the casting out of demons, even by the Lord, was always instantaneous is an unjustified conclusion.

Consider Jesus' healing of the demoniac of Gadara. Mark's record of this event reads that "He (Jesus) asked him, What is thy name? And he answered, saying, My name is legion" (Mk. 5:9). On the surface of the text one might gain the impression that Jesus addressed the demon one time and immediately the legion of demons was gone. But in the Greek, the verb *asked* (eperotoa) is the imperfect active, indicating a continuous action, or an action that is repeated. More accurately translated the sentence would read, "And he kept on asking him, what is thy name?" This indicates a series of demands rather than instantaneous obedience to one command. Several Bible versions say, "He continued to ask, what is thy name?"

Clues from the Greek Text: In addition the Greek text of Mark 5:10 indicates that the demons begged Jesus repeatedly not to send them to the (Pit) Abussos (Luke 8:31). I believe that the scriptural record of the deliverance of the men of Gadara indicates a prolonged confrontation—the exact length of which is not known. Internal evidence does not support the position that the deliverance was instantaneous.

Other Factors to Consider

Increased Demonic Skills and Avenues: "Satan has the same power and the same control over minds now, only it has increased a hundred fold by exercise and experience. Men and women today are deceived, blinded by his insinuations and devices, and know it not" (3T328). Why is this true? Two thousand years ago there was no television with lurid sex and violence. There were no "porno shops" and racy novels and magazines in every store. The world enjoys being entertained by sin. Ellen White said it this way: "The power of Satan now to tempt and to deceive is tenfold greater than it was in the days of the apostles. His power has increased, and it will increase, until it is taken away. His wrath and hate grow stronger as his time to work draws near its close" (2 SG 277). Satan has told his demons to "Battle every inch of ground" (EW 267). Be assured, they do just that.

Weakening of the Will: An essential factor in deliverance is the human will. It is not always easy for one who has been under Satan's domination to surrender the will to Jesus Christ. We can be sure that Satan will do all he can to keep that from happening. There are people who enjoy their demons such as lust and fantasy. Sin is more seductive today. It is "packaged" more attractively via all the media. I recall a young woman who frankly said she would "have to think about it." She wrestled three days before she decided for Christ ; then the battle was easily won, and she was freed.

The Battle is more Fierce: Daniel 10:12,13 tells us about a battle that went on in the mind of Cyrus for twenty-one days. Even then, Jesus Himself had to enter the conflict before the Satanic powers could be overcome and the victory could be won. "For three weeks Gabriel wrestled with the powers of darkness, seeking to counteract the influences on the mind of Cyrus; and before the contest closed Christ Himself came to Gabriel's aid" (PK 572). In view of this three week conflict why should we question the validity of a spiritual battle that goes on for three hours?

The Need of the Prayer of Faith: James and Ellen White were harassed by demonic powers on several occasions. She wrote of a time of depression that was so intense that she began to doubt her Christian experience. She tells of her intense mental anguish until her husband began to pray for her. In telling her experience, she wrote, "He (Satan) would not yield until my voice was united with his for deliverance" (LS 136).

On another occasion of satanic harassment, Ellen White's head became so swollen that "both eyes were closed, and her face was so disfigured that it no longer looked like that of a human being." She was not freed from this harassment until both her husband and Elder John Loughborough interceded for her. (See Appendix B, p. 196).

Regardless of what the harassment may be, or the source of the bondage, the fact is that the battle is seldom easy. Often more than one confrontation is necessary before complete deliverance comes. But most important is the fact that people who have been captives of Satan for years are being set free to the glory of Jesus Christ. There is Victory for both Christ and the human soul on the Battlefield.

CHAPTER
14
Jesus Answers His Critics

"But if I cast out devils by the Spirit of God, then the kingdom of God is come unto you... whosoever speaketh against the Holy Ghost, it shall not be forgiven him, neither in this world, neither in the world to come" Matthew 12: 28, 32.

One would think that the perfect ministry of the sinless Son of God would escape all criticism, but the opposite is true. Nothing that He did or said pleased His critics. They were always looking for flaws. His critics despised Him. They could not wait to see Him dead. The Cross is the ultimate proof that even a perfect ministry cannot escape criticism.

Nothing that He did pleased His critics. He opened the eyes of a man born blind, and they did not like that (John 9:34). He healed a man crippled for 38 years and they did not like that (Jn. 5:9,10, 16). He set possessed people free. They did not like that. He was considered to be an agent of Satan (Matt. 12:24).

In keeping with the message of this book, perhaps we should examine more closely the complaints of His critics when Jesus cast out devils. In our ministry we can never claim His perfection. Yet in my efforts to help oppressed people I hear again and again the same objections that He met two thousand years ago. I will point out this fact from time to time throughout this chapter.

The Critics and Backsliding

One of the most solemn warnings that Jesus ever gave was in connection with backsliding. This is what He said:

"When the unclean spirit is gone out of a man, he walketh through dry places, seeking rest: and finding none, he saith, I will return unto my house whence I came out. And when he cometh, he findeth it swept and garnished. Then goeth he and taketh to him seven other spirits more wicked than himself; and they enter in, and dwell there; and the last state of that man is worse than the first" (Matt. 12:43-45).

Why would the Lord make such a grim warning? No question about it—He said that people who had once been free could get worse—even seven times worse than before! But there is more behind His warning than meets the eye. *He was replying to a criticism directed at His own ministry.* The possibility is that not a few— perhaps many—of the people He set free went back into bondage. The Lord gave no idle warning. Backsliding existed then; backsliding exists now. His critics lost no opportunity to point this out in an effort to discredit Him.

His Candid Admission

How did He handle their complaint? He made an open admission that it was true. He fully recognized the possibility of re-enslavement. We too make every effort to prevent regression. We are not always successful. The problem existed in His time. It exists in ours. This is sad, but true.

Take notice that while Jesus fully recognized the possibility of reinfestation, this did not prevent Him from "ordaining "twelve...to cast out devils" (Mk. 3:14,15). Jesus never took the position that nothing should ever be done. The danger in the modern church is that if it knows or hears of a "failure" it draws a false conclusion—deciding that nothing should ever be done. The experience and leadership of our Lord would not endorse such a policy. The many victories on this battlefield are worth the "failures."

Today's Critics

On a few occasions, I have come under the criticism of a fellow minister. Someone of his acquaintance who was having severe problems had come to me for intercessory prayer. The pastor observed that for awhile this person seemed better; but more recently she had became worse. She had even stopped coming to church. The Pastor was convinced that my ministry was faulty. It hurts when we learn that someone for whom we have prayed and cared about deeply has fallen back into sin and despair. It hurts when a fellow minister harshly condemns what I feel is a much needed part of the Gospel commission (Mk. 3:14-15). Instead of condemning this ministry, that time and energy could better be used praying for the persons who had received their freedom and then lost it.

Jesus' Critics Demanded Lifetime Warranties

Jesus gave no such warranties! Consider the healing of the man at the pool of Bethesda (Jn. 5:1-14). This man had not walked in *thirty eight years*. Now he was walking! However, this is not the end of the story. Later Jesus *found* the man in the temple (vs. 14). The implication of the word *found* is that Jesus deliberately sought him out. Jesus told him, *"Sin no more lest a worse thing come upon thee."*

Check this out: if this man *had* become worse after his spectacular healing *would this have proved Jesus to be a false healer?* Jesus put the responsibility of keeping his wellness directly on the man himself. Jesus gave this man indispensable counsel—"Sin no more!" It is always true that Deliverance or healing of any kind can be lost. Freedom can be kept—but only by the daily choice of the one set free.

Jesus gave no lifetime warranties for His physical healings. The same holds true for spiritual healings—both then and now.

Ellen White gave the following illustration to indicate the disappointment that comes at times to those who minister the Gospel:

> "Some of the work that has been done is represented as being like men rolling large stones up a hill with great effort. *When nearly at the top of the hill, the stones rolled again to the bottom.* The men succeeded in taking a *few* to the top. In the work done for the degraded—what effort it has taken to reach them, what expense, and then to lead them to stand against appetite and base passions!" (3 SM 42).

I have had some disappointing "stone-rolling" experiences. They are heartbreaking. But those who stay on "top of the hill" are worth it all. I include Mrs. White's illustration for one reason. I wish to repeat that there are well-meaning people who demand absolute perfection—a quality that neither the Gospel or the Spirit of Prophecy teaches. Those who have never met the forces of hell in direct combat do not understand their strength. Let me assure you, the joy of seeing a captive truly set free is a rewarding experience.

They Criticized His Methods

At the heart of their criticism of Jesus was their vigorous opposition to His methods. The scriptures indicate that the way He dealt with demons was new and different.

> "And there was in their synagogue *a man with an unclean spirit*; and he cried out, saying, Let us alone; what have we to do with thee, thou Jesus of Nazareth? art thou come to destroy us? I know who thou art, the Holy One of God. And Jesus rebuked him, saying, Hold thy peace, and *come out of him. And they were all amazed, insomuch that they questioned among themselves, saying, What is this? what new doctrine is this? for with authority commandeth he even the unclean spirits, and they do obey him"* (Mk. 1:23-27; Lk. 4:33-36).

The thing that astonished the witnesses to this Deliverance was Jesus' use of authority and command. Jesus rebuked the demon. *The use of authority and command was the new thing.*

Whatever method the leaders of Israel were using at that time, rebuke and command was clearly not one of them. What Jesus did was "new." Because of King Saul's experience (1 Sam. 28), Jesus' critics might well have had a rule forbidding anyone under any circumstance to speak to a demon. *Jesus broke their rule.* Immediately His critics shouted, "Witchcraft." Their censure was false then; it is false now!

Let me amplify on the fact that Jesus spoke to the demon. There is no question that He spoke to the demons who possessed these unfortunate souls; and that the demons spoke to Him. However, we need to compare two different experiences:

> Case One: Jesus "rebuking them suffered them *not to speak:* for they knew that He was Christ" (Luke 4:41).

> Case Two: "And He asked him, What is thy name? And he answered, saying, My name is Legion: for we are many" (Mark 5:9).

The circumstances in these two instances were different. While Jesus would not permit them to identify *Him,* He *commanded* them to speak and to identify *themselves.* To say that Jesus *always forbade* them to speak does not stand up in scripture.

The Man of Gadara

There was another confrontation between Jesus and a hierarchy of demons. It generated a great deal of opposition. On the shore of the sea of Galilee Jesus met the man (men) of Gadara. This man was possessed of a legion of demons (Mark 5:1-20; Luke 8:26-39). After the Deliverance of this man, the people wanted Jesus out of the country. Take note: If *He* could not prevent opposition, *we* can't prevent it. Any challenge to the powers of evil will always meet with resistance.

"When the Lord is about to do a work, Satan moves
upon someone to object" (DA 535).

Securing Names

It is impossible for me to believe that the Lord ever set us a bad example. In the Gadara encounter He asked the demon his name. His name was Legion (Luke 8:30). Certainly the Lord was not engaging in playful conversation. He had a vital reason for everything He did. Asking the demon his name must have been imperative to the man's freedom. As in the Gadara case, I have found that there are times when securing names is indispensable. This is far from *always* needed, but is sometimes required. Many modern critics say that securing names is not essential. If we say that it is *never* needed we are criticizing what Jesus did. Take care! He made no mistakes! He set a perfect example. He must have felt that names were needed.

Every criticism leveled against Jesus is still in vogue. To speak directly to a demon; to rebuke him; to ask his name; to challenge his control; to command him—is still considered to be witchcraft. Ministers engaged in Deliverance Ministry are accused of being Spiritualists. These echoes are 2000 years old.

Jesus' Critics Demanded Perfection

At no time did Jesus teach that the Gospel would have perfect results. To the contrary, He spoke of a sower who scattered good seed everywhere (Matt. 13:1-9). Some seed fell on a hard pathway and was soon devoured by birds. Some fell on shallow ground. It sprang up, but because the soil had no depth, it was scorched by the sun and withered away. Some fell among thorns and was choked out. Some fell on hard ground and yielded nothing. Only a portion of the scattered seed was productive. There was no perfection then; there is no perfection now.

In harmony with His teaching, we freely admit there are some people for whom we have prayed and the result was temporary. There are times when there is no harvest at all. Many of our efforts are wasted. Equally true—when the seed falls on a fully surrendered heart, the harvest is abundant and frequently quick. Take special note of how Ellen White applied this parable specifically to Deliverance.

> "There were many in Christ's day, *as there are today*, over whom *the control of Satan for the time seemed broken;* through the grace of God *they were set free from the evil spirits* that had held dominion over the soul. They rejoiced in the love of God; but *like the stony-ground hearers of the parable,* they did not abide in His love. They did not surrender themselves to God daily, that Christ might dwell in the heart; and *when the evil spirit returned, with 'seven other spirits more wicked that himself,' they were wholly dominated by the power of evil"* (DA 323, 324).

True to the above quotation, there will never be a guarantee for the permanence of any Deliverance. We scatter the seed. The Gospel seed is perfect. Its results are not always perfect. Yet, there is nothing wrong with our efforts to help the oppressed. We pray for a perfect harvest. When it comes, we thank our God!

Testing by the Cross

The cross is the ultimate test of every truth. Jesus openly discussed the dismal results of His atoning sacrifice. He was fully aware that the majority would reject His salvation. He said that most would travel the "broad way." Only a "few" would find the way to life (Matt. 7:14). Yet He died for those He knew would only be a "few." His death on the cross was a perfect sacrifice. Not one soul need ever be lost, but *most are lost.* Not even the Cross of Christ produces perfect results.

The principle of the Cross applies to Deliverance. We plead the shed blood of Calvary over the enemy. We plead His grace and power to free the captive. We do what He ordained his church to do in the Gospel commission (Mk. 3:14-15). It is our responsibility to make every effort to set the captives free (Luke 4:18). More than a "few" keep their freedom. Praise God!

The Testimony of the Apostles

"Stand fast therefore in the liberty wherewith Christ hath made us free, and be not entangled again with the yoke of bondage" (Gal. 5:1).

"For if, after they have escaped the pollutions of the world through the knowledge of the Lord and Savior Jesus Christ, they are again entangled therein, and overcome, the latter end is worse with them than the beginning" (2 Pet. 2:20).

Can a person escape the world's pollutions and then become entangled again? The testimony of the Apostles agrees with Jesus. Their initial "escape" was not defective. The person himself became re-entangled. *Every Deliverance must consider these apostolic counsels.*

Jesus' Critics Underestimated Satan

We human beings almost always under-estimate the terribly subtle and destructive nature of Satan's control over human minds. He exerts an influence that is almost impossible to break. Only Christ can do it in response to prayer. Without Him we are helpless against this foe. We need the prayer support and understanding of all of God's people.

"When men and women fall under the corrupting power of Satan, *it is almost impossible to recover them* out of the horrible snare so that they will ever again have pure thoughts and clear conceptions of God's requirements. Sin...is never again regarded in the loathsome light that God looks upon it. After the moral standard has been lowered in the minds of men, *their judgment is perverted,* and they look upon sin as righteousness, and righteousness as sin" (5T 143).

These words tell us that our best and only safe course is to walk in obedience to Christ to avoid the initial entrapment. Not one of us can afford to play with Satan's toys, walk on his ground, tempt him to tempt us in any way, or to yield even to the "smallest" of his temptations. Many of Satan's victims have sacrificed their ability to tell right from wrong. They feel no need to reach out for help. Many people enjoy their sins and reject freedom. If we miss the delivering power of the Savior now, it is a sad thought that we may miss the eternal fellowship with Him in His glorious kingdom.

The Ultimate Criticism — Beelzebub!

Jesus had the ultimate confrontation with His critics over the Deliverance of a man who was blind and dumb. Here is the record:

> "Then was brought unto him one possessed with a devil , blind, and dumb: and he healed him, insomuch that the blind and dumb both spake and saw...But when the Pharisees heard it they said, *This fellow doth not cast out devils but by Beelzebub the prince of devils*. And Jesus knew their thoughts and said unto them, Every kingdom divided against itself is brought to desolation; and every city or house divided against itself shall not stand. And if Satan cast out Satan, he is divided against himself; how shall then his kingdom stand? And if I by Beelzebub cast out devils, by whom do your children cast them out? therefore they shall be your judges" (Matthew 12:22, 24-27).

Review the scene of this conflict. First, His critics could not deny that a miracle had occurred. The man was there; he could *see*; he could *speak!* How could they respond to this miracle? They had to invent some evasion tactic. If they admitted that the man was healed by God's power, they would have to accept Jesus as a man of God; and even more—the Messiah of Israel.

Only one other option was open. They took it. It was the worst mistake God's people ever made. They cried, "Beelzebub." In their ultimate effort to discredit His ministry they accused Him of being possessed. (Mark 3:22-30; Luke 11:15-18; John 7:20; 8:48, 52; 10:20) Then He told His disciples to prepare for the worst: "If they have called the master of the house Beelzebub, how much more shall they call them of his household? (Matt. 10:25). If Christ himself could not convince His critics *then*—we should not be astonished if it becomes almost impossible to convince the critics *now*.

Jesus Replies

Take notice that by three different illustrations—a kingdom, a city, and a family—Jesus categorically denied that Satan ever casts out Satan. He was unequivocal that this *never* happens. He could not have been more firm in His denial. Then he followed this denial with the most awesome warning that ever escaped his lips. *Jesus said that to credit Satan with the work of the Holy Spirit is to commit the unpardonable sin* (Matt. 12:32). They committed this sin. We must not repeat the same mistake. This is a very serious matter. It was then. It is now!

Two thousand years ago the religious leaders interpreted this man's Deliverance as satanic. In modern language they were saying that Jesus was a spiritualist. To them Jesus was himself deceived and a deceiver. (Matt. 28:63). But it was they who were deceived. They had resisted the Holy Spirit and declared Him to be an agent of Satan. This fatal decision determined the final fate of ancient Israel. They had gone too far. The suffering in Jerusalem a few years hence was the terrible consequence.

The reaction of His critics that day has a modern counterpart. Frequently when a person is set free, his "friends" converge upon him. "Are you sure it was God who healed you? How do you know it wasn't Satan who freed you?" These words plant seeds of doubt which can easily mature and ripen into the fruit of re-enslavement. "Friends" assume an awesome responsibility when they question God's work. To put unbelief into the mind of someone newly set free is indeed a solemn thing to do.

The Caring Church Could Help

I want to assure you, dear reader, that when Satan loses a prisoner, he makes an all-out effort to re-enslave his victim. That is the time when the prayers and understanding of fellow Christians are most needed. Unfortunately, it is in this crucial period that many fellow church members fail. They do not understand or appreciate the intense struggle a person goes through to keep his freedom. Instead, some church members withdraw their support and even their friendship. They do not realize that in this way they are cooperating with the enemy. By becoming critical they destroy a struggling soul. How tragic! Satan's former captives need the sympathy, under-standing and prayers of fellow believers. Lord, let it be so!

Being rejected by one's brethren for whatever reason can be a very discouraging experience. We rightfully expect better treatment from our fellow Christians. Such shunning as I have described can quickly push a person into re-enslavement. Satan searches for unsympathetic people he can use. I have seen this on several occasions. Here is a wonderful opportunity for us to prove that we really *are* the caring church we profess to be. May the Lord anoint our vision and give us tender hearts!

The Need of Support Groups

There is a desperate need in all our churches for a strong support group. We need compassionate people who will make themselves available to encourage and pray for those who have recently been freed from demonic harassment, control, and possession. There will be a growing need for such support groups. As time goes on, the attacks of Satan will become more varied and vicious. God can use such groups to save souls who might otherwise return to captivity. Jesus Himself felt the need of just such support. Remember, He took Peter, James, and John with Him in His Gethsemane battle against the powers of darkness. If He needed human support, how much greater is our need!

Our spiritual glasses need cleaning. Few of our members, either ministers or laity, recognize the reality of the great controversy on the personal level. Few realize that every human mind is an important battlefield. Few understand that Spiritual Warfare is a Christ-given, but neglected, part of the Gospel (Mk.3:15). We must take great care lest we ignorantly refuse to do Christ's appointed work. We are in a true crisis of faith. Happily, an increasingly large number of both ministry and laity are becoming alert to the urgency of this need.

Satan uses Friends and Relatives

It was Peter—Jesus' intimate companion—whom Satan used in an attempt to discourage Jesus. When Jesus told His disciples that He was soon to be crucified, Peter instantly rejected the very idea. "Peter began to rebuke Him" (Matt. 16:22). We are further told that "Satan was trying to discourage Jesus and turn Him from His mission. Peter, in his blind love, was giving voice to the tempter" (DA 416). Satan was speaking through Peter in an effort to discourage Jesus. Peter was Satan's agent.

Satan still uses this effective device. Evil angels try to use those we love and trust the most to destroy us. He frequently uses family members to dishearten the one who has experienced Deliverance. He used Peter. He will use anybody.

I have found that every criticism Jesus had to deal with is still being used effectively today. The best informed and most dedicated people of His time objected to Him. With the passage of time the faces have changed, but somehow the objections remain the same.

Cathy's Amazing Freedom

To close this chapter, I want to tell you an amazing, yet tragic story. It is the story of a Baptist lady who became an Adventist. She was delivered from a health-destroying bondage. Her healing brought her into the church, but the same church took away her healing. She was destroyed by criticism.

I received a phone call from a pastor, whom I shall call Smith. He was a dedicated man who saw the need of bringing Spiritual Warfare back into the arsenal of the church. When I first met him, Pastor Smith was retired, although he was still active. He had been a well-known evangelist. Many of my readers would recognize his name. Pastor Smith asked me to join him in praying for Cathy (not her real name).

Total Allergy: Cathy's was a violent case of nearly total allergy. She could tolerate almost nothing that is found in today's normal environment. Automobile fumes, paint, carpets, curtains, plastics—all these things, plus almost everything else we find in the average home—caused her to become violently ill. In addition to this, she was allergic to most foods we normally eat. Most of what she could eat had to be eaten raw. Since she was allergic to printer's ink, she put her reading material in a box with a glass top and read through the glass. In order to turn the pages she had to wear gloves.

Captive: Cathy could not shop for groceries or for any other of her personal needs. Others shopped for her. Odors and fumes associated with any kind of store brought on such violent reactions that she sometimes "passed out." Cathy was a prisoner to allergy.

Her Trailer: Cathy lived in a small travel trailer. There were no carpets, no curtains, no pictures. There was nothing that makes a house a home. Literally every square inch of the trailer's interior was covered with aluminum foil with the exception of the windows. The floor, the walls, the ceiling, even the simple furniture—which consisted of a table, a chair, and a built-in bed—all were covered with the same aluminum foil. This foil functioned as a barrier against foreign substances and odors. Cathy's auto-immune system had a limited tolerance for almost everything in her environment. Living inside that trailer was like being inside a giant tin can.

Odors: The stove on which Cathy did her limited cooking was outside. If she had cooked inside her trailer, the fumes from the stove and the odor of food would have made Cathy ill. This was only a small part of her problem. To put it mildly, Cathy's life was certainly not a normal or pleasant one.

The reason I have detailed Cathy's situation is that I want you to be aware of the severity of her problem; only then can you appreciate what God did for her in answer to our prayers. I do not know how Cathy first contacted Pastor Smith. I do remember riding the forty or so miles from Pastor Smith's home to Cathy's trailer. After a short season of prayer there, the three of us drove back to Pastor Smith's home. During that ride Cathy was amazed by the fact that she could stay in the car that long without becoming ill. This in itself was a miracle and an answer to our prayers.

Her Early Life: Cathy shared with us some information about her early life. In several ways her life was characteristic of many who later find themselves severely harassed by the enemy. As a child she was rejected by her father. Before Cathy was born, he kicked her mother in the abdomen in an unsuccessful attempt to cause an abortion. Her childhood had never been a happy one. Many times she was forced to witness her father beat her mother. She felt totally rejected. In her teen years she attempted suicide. She later became involved in spiritualism and numerology.

A True Miracle: On arrival at Pastor Smith's home, we spent several hours in special prayer for Cathy. That evening Cathy did something she had not done for years. She ate a normal meal, including whole wheat bread, strawberries, and buttermilk. These were foods she previously could not tolerate; yet there was no negative reaction. Later that evening she went to the local market. She walked up and down the aisles, doing what she had not done in years. Before, the variety of fumes would have made her deathly sick. Now she was enjoying some of the simple pleasures which we all take for granted.

Continued Victory: While Pastor and Mrs. Smith were on vacation, Cathy "house-sat" for them. One day I invited Cathy to go with me as a "prayer warrior" to do spiritual battle in another home in the community. We were in that home for almost six hours. In spite of the presence of two dogs, a gas stove with its pilot light, and the usual carpets, drapes, pictures, books, and other items found in a normal home, Cathy experienced no ill effects, for which we both thanked God. On our way back to the Smith's home Cathy said, "Before this I would have had to be carried out of that home." Cathy was enjoying the fruit of Christian freedom.

Her Baptism: When the Smiths returned from their vacation, Cathy continued to live with them for a few weeks while she was making necessary adjustments to her new life. During that time Pastor Smith studied the Bible with Cathy. The Smiths supported and nurtured her spiritually. Cathy soon moved into an apartment of her own. She began to attend the local Seventh-day Adventist church, and a few months later she, a former Baptist, became a baptized Seventh-day Adventist.

The Enemy Renews His Attack

We could wish that once a significant battle has been won that nothing but bliss would prevail. We cautioned Cathy that such would not be the case. We told her that there would be more battles to be fought. One of the greatest dangers is thinking that the war is over. This false expectancy has sometimes resulted in a re-enslavement. When the tempter renews his attack, a person can become discouraged and began to question the reality and validity of his Deliverance. For Cathy the surprising thing was the source of the attack. It came from within the church. It makes me sad to have to tell you about it, but we have been forewarned:

> "Never is one received into the family of God without exciting the determined resistance of the enemy" (PK 585).

> "The spirits of darkness will battle for the soul once under their dominion" (DA 259).

When Satan sees a soul escape from his control, he will work to recapture his one-time victim. For a time temptations may even multiply. The enemy may modify his approach. He may become more subtle and lay different snares; but he will never surrender voluntarily. Be certain—the tempter will come.

Doubts Appeared: My home was several hundred miles from Cathy's. Because of the distance that separated us, I do not know the details of what happened during the next few weeks or months. But I later learned that her symptoms reappeared.

She began to doubt the validity of her Deliverance. I do not know which came first, the doubt or the return of the problem.

Her Letter: I will never forget the day I received a letter from Cathy. I have it in front of me now. In this letter she expressed serious doubt regarding her Deliverance. She wrote in part: "Through Bible study and prayer I came to realize that exorcism or 'Deliverance' as some refer to it, does not have a scriptural basis. I do not believe that exorcism, at least as I and others personally know it, is of God. It is not scripturally sound" Elsewhere in her letter Cathy refers to Spiritual Warfare as "spiritualism." I fear it was her own pastor who helped her come to this worst of all possible conclusions.

Her Pastor's Sermon: Cathy spoke in her letter about hearing one of her pastor's sermons. She said he talked about demons. I did not hear his sermon. I have no idea what he said. I hope that he did not equate Spiritual Warfare with Spiritualism.

Pray for Our Pastors: Regardless of the pastor's purpose or intentions, Cathy lost her freedom listening to a Sabbath morning sermon. This was a turning point in her life—not toward freedom—but back into bondage. By the hearing of one sermon Cathy lost her boundless joy—joy that she had not known in years. It is a very sad experience to see a person rejoice in freedom, then lose it. We need Holy Spirit-anointed pastors to help them keep their freedom. Pray for our pastors!

Pray for Our Church: In the ministry of Jesus, His work of Deliverance stirred up great opposition. We must not repeat their mistake. Tragically, the worst human enemies of those who have come out of bondage, are still the critics from within the body of God's people. Some church administrators and pastors fault Deliverance as being the work of Satan. But that contention is no more valid today than it was during the ministry of Christ. There is an increasing number of pastors and lay persons who are beginning to recognize the need of helping oppressed people. It is time for restoration. May the joy that came to the Seventy soon come to us (Luke 10:17).

CHAPTER
15
On Staying Free

Finally, my brethren, be strong in the Lord, and in the power of his might. Put on the whole armor of God, that ye may be able to stand against the wiles of the devil...For we wrestle not against flesh and blood, but against principalities, against powers, against the rulers of the darkness of this world, against spiritual wickedness in high places. Ephesians 6:10-12

In this chapter I shall explore practical and preventive measures which you can take to maintain the victory you have won. In other words—how to keep your freedom. There is not a Christian alive who will not profit by reading this chapter, but it will be especially helpful for those who have had an intimate experience with Deliverance.

The Military Mentality

You have had a fierce fight to get free. Now you have a whole new way of looking at life—a way foreign to the average Christian. You are now aware that there are unseen powers to contend with. Others have interceded for you. You know for sure that this world is a battlefield. You are a soldier. The enemy's cover has been blown. You have won a battle, but the war is not over. If you stop fighting, you will be recaptured.

"Have Seventh-day Adventists forgotten the warning given in the sixth chapter of Ephesians? We are engaged in a warfare against the hosts of darkness. Unless we follow our Leader closely, Satan will obtain the victory over us" (Letter 140, 1903).

I fear that many Christians are asleep on this battlefield. The watchmen on the walls of Zion are nodding. Almost no warning is being sounded against a vicious enemy. The church has largely laid down her arms and has settled for an uneasy truce. This world is full of booby traps. The enemy has scattered them around like children's toys, but inside are deadly explosives, craftily concealed. This chapter sounds a warning. Let's suit up for the battle! The blood-stained banner of Prince Emmanuel flies overhead. We lose only by default.

147

Which Enemy?

Before we can consider how to keep from being recaptured, there are some things that we must understand clearly. The Bible is conclusive that the Christian has *two* enemies, one *outside* of himself, and the other *inside*. We are under double attack. Understanding this fact prevents confusion. Let me explain:

The Enemy Outside: We have stressed that this world is a battlefield. We are surrounded by powerful forces of evil against which, in our own strength, we have no resistance. For sake of simplicity, let us say that this enemy is *outside* of us.

The Enemy Within: But there is *another* enemy. He is *inside* of us. The Bible calls this foe our carnal nature; the flesh; the body of this death; the old man of sin. (Read Romans 7 and 8). In a sense we are our own worst enemy. If there were no influence from Satan, we would still be inclined to sin. This is the nature with which we were born (Ps.51:5). We have built-in, natural propensities to evil. We are all part of a fallen human race.

Humanism: If in practice you believe that *all* your problems come from *within* yourself; if you believe that with a little more effort, a little more will-power, you can make the needed changes in your life; if you believe that applied psychology and a greater self-understanding will give you victory over your evil ways, then you have become your own god, your own savior. You don't need Christ. You may speak about Him now and then, but your relationship with Him is remote. You have become what is known as a humanist, a "do-it-yourself" Christian. It is easy to fall into this trap. It happens frequently.

Fanaticism: On the other hand, if you believe that all of your problems come from Satan, that you are only a puppet on a demonic string; that you can seek out your pastor and have him pray for you, and from that day on be forever free of every temptation and problem, then you are a fanatic, an extremist. Both of these approaches to the sin problem are wrong. Those who believe in either humanism or fanaticism play into the devil's hands and give him an awesome advantage.

Christianity: If you believe that the *inside* and *outside* enemies can collaborate; if you believe that the devil exploits our human carnality; that he can take control of people and force them into the most degrading sins, often against their will; if you believe that Satan drives people to fear, to self-destructive behavior, alcoholism, violence, and lust; if you believe that the devil depresses people and drives them to the brink of suicide; if you believe that the mission of Jesus was to set people free of satanic bondage (Mark 1:27; Luke 4:18); if you believe that this is a vital part of the work He assigned to the church (Luke 9:1); if you believe that by unconditional commitment to the will of God, and by the intercessory prayers of fellow Christians, oppressed people can be set free even today—this is the victory you can have in Christ.

A Vital Difference: One vital principle must be clearly understood: you can cast out the devils, but you cannot cast out the flesh. Self is to be crucified; self must be denied; but it cannot be cast out. We must forever distinguish between the enemy *inside* and the enemy *outside*. This is the two-fold nature of Spiritual Warfare. Self is the strongest foe we have to meet (MYP 134). Paul said, "I die *daily*" (1 Cor.15:31) If self is not surrendered daily, the enemy has an internal collaborator. He will exploit this fact to the fullest possible extent. This battle with self will go on *daily* until we are clothed with immortality and incorruptible flesh (I Cor. 15:53). There is no quick fix. The war will be over only when Jesus comes. There is another caution that I must give you. It is

The Danger of a False Expectancy

An anguished voice was on the telephone. "Pastor, I am still being tempted."

This young woman was in great distress. We had prayed for her only a few days before. She was terribly discouraged. What was the source of her problem? *She was expecting immunity from temptation—something God had never promised!* It is vital that every Christian understand this fact—especially those who have been in severe bondage. She was out of touch with the nature of the war on this Battlefield. Take note of the word of God on this matter:

"There hath no temptation taken you but such as is common to man: but God is faithful, who will not suffer you to be tempted above that ye are able; but will with the temptation also make a way to escape, that ye may be able to bear it" (1Cor. 10:13).

God has never promised immunity from temptation—what He has promised is strength to stand and a way of escape. A false expectancy opens the door to the terrible discouragement this young woman was experiencing. Temptation will continue to be an influence in our lives right up to the coming of Jesus. Our victory depends not on any immunity, but how we deal with it in the grace and power of the all-prevailing name of Jesus Christ.

We have all tried in our own strength and failed. God has told us that humanly we are no match for Satan (5T 293). Only in the Lord's Name we can contend successfully with the enemy. Few Christians know how to cast themselves fully on Christ.

"In the whole Satanic force there is not enough power to overcome one soul who in simple trust casts himself on Christ" (COL 157).

Without Christ we are helpless to face this treacherous foe. But with our hand in His nail-pierced hand we are invincible! He is our triumphant Lord and Savior.

What Is Temptation?

I would like to suggest two different definitions, each from a different point of view:

1. From Satan's point of view, temptation is the means he chooses to lead us to sin and thus to bring about our destruction. The Genesis picture of the first temptation was at the tree of the knowledge of *good* and evil. It would not be a temptation unless it were inviting. "Good" implies something attractive.

Satan's temptations almost invariably have the appearance of being good—something to our advantage—but underneath the surface is evil and death. Sin has its allurements, but underneath is regret, sorrow, bitterness and eventual destruction. This powerful appeal to sin we call temptation.

2. From God's point of view, temptation is a circumstance in which there is a strong opportunity for Christian growth. Nothing affords the opportunity for character growth like a temptation met and conquered. Only in this way can we be strengthened for greater trials to come. In addition we prove our loyalty to Him and enhance our relationship with Him.

James' Epistle makes what appears to be a strange statement. He says that God permits temptations because there is a hidden growth factor built into it for us. God wants us to grow. Spiritual growth comes with exercise. "My *brethren, count it all joy when ye fall into diverse temptations; knowing this, that the trying of your faith worketh patience*" (James 1: 2,3).

The word, "temptation" as it is used here has a broad application that includes trials of all kinds, such as, persecution, sickness or calamity. But it also includes enticement. The point is that all these circumstances which God permits to come, and which seem to work against us, really provide an opportunity to show our loyalty (or disloyalty) to God. They help us to develop endurance and steadfastness of character which James speaks of as "patience." These temptations or trials are really blessings in disguise.

Dealing with Temptation

Temptation always carries with it the possibility of a battle between right and wrong, between the forces of Christ and the forces of Satan. Without a battle there can be no victory. The length and severity of the battle depends upon how we relate to the temptation. I will explain this in the next page or two.

How does Satan chose his temptations? He studies each one of us. He notes the weak points in our natures. He detects the sins each of us is most inclined to commit, and then he brings his temptations to bear on those areas (GC 555). Just as there is no aspect of our lives in which God is not interested, so there is no area of human conduct which is untouched by Satan's influence.

The battle between Christ and Satan is manifest in every human being. We are all involved. Every facet of our lives is under scrutiny. There is no "time out" in this game. The battle goes on relentlessly, twenty-four hours each day, seven days a week, every year of our lives. "He (Satan) sleeps not; he does not abate his vigilance for one moment"(3T 456).

You can be sure that since the devil does not relax his efforts for a moment, you will have to keep your guard up at all times. In order to stay free, you may have to learn to deal with temptation in quite a different way than you have in the past. There are some helpful stories in the Bible that need to be studied carefully. There are some basics to be learned.

How Joseph Handled Temptation

After being sold as a slave, during his travel toward Egypt, Joseph decided how he would react to any temptations that would come to him there. His thoughts turned constantly to his father's God. *During his long lonely journey to Egypt, Joseph committed himself fully to the Lord.* For the rest of his life, every time Joseph was tempted, the teaching of his father came vividly to his mind. He resolved always to prove himself true to God. He decided to act under all circumstances as would befit a loyal subject of the king of heaven (See PP 213, 214). *His making of an early, uncompromising covenant with God was the source of his continued victories.*

Joseph's Acid Test

Satan tempted Joseph on a basic human weakness and under ideal conditions. The scripture described him as "a goodly person, and well favored." Today we would say that he was a handsome young man. He caught the eye of Mrs. Potiphar. In time she became infatuated with him. Several times she made improper suggestions and advances to him. One day when Mrs. Potiphar and Joseph were alone in the house, Mrs. Potiphar became very insistent in her demands upon Joseph. When Joseph would not cooperate, "she caught him by his garment." His response was "How then can I do this great wickedness and sin against God?" (Gen. 39:9).

There is an essential lesson that every Christian must learn from the temptation of Joseph. Many wait till the moment of crisis to resist. All too often, it is too late. We have noted that day by day, morning by morning, Joseph had committed himself to obey God no matter what temptation came. His mind was made up long before Potiphar's wife ever approached him. His coat was left in her hand (Gen. 39:12). The Covenant he made with God before he ever got to Egypt and his faithful practice of a daily, early morning devotion had won the Battle.

Joseph is one of the few Bible characters against whom no sin is recorded. The sustaining grace of our all-conquering Savior is constantly available. We only lose it if we compromise.

"To everyone who surrenders fully to God is given the privilege of living without sin in obedience to the law of heaven" (RH, Sept. 27, 1906).

Why David Yielded to Temptation

The way David dealt with temptation was entirely different from that of Joseph. The start of David's sin with Bathsheba is recorded in 2 Samuel 11:2-4:

"It came to pass in the eveningtide that David arose from off his bed and walked upon the roof of the king's house: and from the roof he saw a woman washing herself; and the woman was very beautiful to look upon. And David sent and inquired after the woman. And one said, Is not this Bathsheba, the daughter of Eliam, the wife of Uriah the Hittite? And David sent messengers and took her; and she came in unto him..."

How innocently it all began! Through no planning of his own, David found himself in a tempting situation. The king was relaxing in the roof-top patio of his home. As he casually glanced over the surrounding area, a movement caught his attention. Then his eyes fell upon a woman innocently bathing in the privacy of the courtyard of her home. Nothing about the situation had been planned either by David or Bathsheba.

Up to the time when David saw Bathsheba, neither of them was guilty of any wrong. Neither had sinned. It was merely a situation, a circumstance, a coincidence. But it was a circumstance heavy with the possibility for good or evil, depending upon how the participants, especially David, reacted to it. Temptation and sin are not the same, but they are closely related. We must always distinguish between the two. I would like to suggest that sin begins when we enjoy the temptation. David's sin was not that he coincidentally saw a beautiful woman bathing. His sin began when he lingered to enjoy the view.

As a consequence of his yielding, he brought tragedy upon himself and weakened his spiritual and moral influence with his people for the rest of his life. Except for the grace of God, he would have lost eternal life.

The Danger of Delay

Our sins often begin with an unexpected situation arranged by Satan to entice us. We could escape unscathed if every day we made a firm commitment to be faithful to God in all situations and then carried through on the commitment. It is true that many times instant and specific decisions must be made. However, there is in our human nature an inclination to delay making decisions. If we mentally inspect the temptation even though we know it to be wrong, we are in trouble. Altogether too often we fall.

"Consecrate yourself to God in the morning, Make this your very first work. Let your prayer be, 'take me O Lord, as wholly thine. I lay my plans at your feet. Use me today as thy servant. Abide with me and let my works be wrought in thee' " (SC 70).

In too many cases there is very little battle, or no battle at all, because we capitulate to the enemy before the battle starts. But if there is a battle, we either resist the temptation and win that round in the conflict, or we eventually yield to the temptation and lose the round. If we resist and win, it is because of God's presence and power, and not our own. We need always to remember that "Without Christ, we cannot subdue a single sin, or overcome the smallest temptation" (4T 355).

One thing is sure—we are on the witness stand twenty-four hours a day. We testify for the Savior or for the devil.

Putting on the Armor

The book of Ephesians is the Spiritual Warfare book of the Apostle Paul. It has an essential message that in order to stay free, the Christian must always be prepared to fight. On this battlefield God's armor is essential to survival (Eph 6:10-17). It is essential that we know the facts about this armor.

"Finally, my brethren, be strong in the Lord, and in the power of his might. Put on the whole armor of God, that ye may be able to stand against the wiles of the devil " (Eph. 6:10).

Take special note that it is *God's armor and it is God's power.*
Without Christ we are totally defenseless and powerless. This
is why "do-it-yourself" Christians continue in sin. The Bible
teaches that we have no strength or defense of our own. Did not
the Lord say, "Without me ye can do nothing?" (Jn. 15:5) We
must be strong in the Lord because Satan is attacking everyone
on all fronts—emotionally, morally, mentally, financially,
physically, maritally, and spiritually.

The devil has had six thousand years of experience studying,
beguiling, and destroying human beings. We cannot outwit,
outsmart, or outfox him. Only in God's armor and in God's power
can we survive. The scripture says to put on the *breastplate* of
Righteousness. We must face this enemy because *there is no
back-plate.* There is simply no way to avoid him. Remember,
we don't wear armor to go swimming. We wear it to fight! We
will always be at war till Jesus comes. Expect no truce!

What does it Mean to put on the Armor? Some have thought
that by mechanically going through the physical motions of
putting on each element of the armor they were following the
scriptural directive. Putting on the armor is a spiritual exercise,
not mechanical. Putting on the armor is surrendering your entire
self to God. Note these words of the Lord's special messenger:

> *"If you pray in sincerity, surrendering yourself, soul, body,
> and spirit, unto God, you put on the whole armor of God,* and
> open the soul to the righteousness of Christ; and this
> alone,—Christ's imputed righteousness, — makes you able
> to stand against the wiles of the devil" (SD 346).

Wearing the Helmet: We must wear God's helmet to protect our
thoughts. Never forget that your mind is a prime target—here
the first contact with the enemy takes place. Visual and
audible suggestions to sin enter the mind. But you must stand
guard. Never linger in situations that generate and stimulate
unholy thoughts and ideas. That was David's downfall. He
watched Bathsheba in a tempting situation. This brought on
lustful thoughts. *He began to enjoy the temptation, and that
was the origin of his sin. Entertainment television carries this
same virus.* Keep this in mind. Make wise choices! The mind
must not "run loose." Instantly reject every thought alien to the
character of Christ. Eternal life hangs on our choices!

"We are under obligation to control our thoughts and to bring them into subjection to the law of God. The noble powers of the mind have been given to us by the Lord that we may employ them in contemplating heavenly things" (MCP 658). "The mind should not be left to wander at random upon every subject that the adversary of souls may suggest" (PP 460).

Progressive Bondage: Bondage rarely occurs in a moment. It progresses. It begins with a single, sinful thought. If you play with it, imagination goes to work (how nice it would be). It progresses to a single act (just this once). Then it becomes a habit (you fall easily). It becomes an obsession (always on your mind). Then you cannot stop (it has become a possession—a demonic stronghold). Notice—the path into bondage begins with a *single thought*. This is why the Bible says to bring *"every thought"* into obedience to Christ. Do this and you can stay free. There is no other way!

Implanted Thoughts

Most Christians make a sad mistake of thinking that every thought that comes into their mind is their own. One lady remarked, "I never realized that the evil ideas I had in my head were put there by Satan."

"There are thoughts and feelings suggested and aroused by Satan that annoy even the best of men; but if they are not cherished, if they are repulsed as hateful, the soul is not contaminated with guilt, and no other is defiled by their influence" (MCP 432).

How do you resist an evil thought? Here is something I have found helpful. If you are alone, speak out loud. If in a crowd, cover your mouth and whisper: "I now resist this thought in the Name of Jesus Christ." Remember that the mind is the first line of attack and the first line of defense. Let this mind be in you that was also in Christ Jesus (Phil. 2:5). The word of God speaks of taking control of *every thought:*

"Casting down imaginations... and bringing into captivity *every thought* to the obedience of Christ" (2 Cor.10: 4-5).

A Demonic Mental Trick: Let me describe one of the devil's favorite tricks. (Few Christians are aware of this tactic.) The devil puts a dirty, sinful, or angry thought into your mind. This is instantly followed by, "If you were a Christian you would not be thinking this." In this way he tricks you into questioning your entire Christian experience. You wonder whether you are a Christian at all. It is important that you recognize this as a satanic trick. Otherwise you could become terribly discouraged. You could go back into bondage. Remember these "mind-games" happen to "the best of men" (and women). As long as you don't play with the thought, it will not contaminate you. Instantly resist and it will not defile you.

Our Weapons

Prayer: Few Christians understand why early morning prayer is so essential. All of God's universe operates on precise law. Do you realize that you must give God a "license" to care for you? There is the law of spiritual privacy. This license must be renewed daily (Matt. 6:11). Yesterday does not count. Only you can issue this license. The demons will continually dispute God's care for you. But if *every day* you will ask Him to take charge of your life, your thoughts, your feelings—then you have given Him a legal permit. For just *that day* the devil's plans to defeat you are frustrated. You have untied God's hands. His angels can then give you unlimited *legal* protection.

Every Christian must learn this! Make this commitment *out-loud* in a joyous voice so that it goes clearly on the eternal record. Ask God every morning; He will be with you through the day. This daily communion with your Commander is absolutely essential to your continued freedom.

> *"The first resistance to the Spirit's pleading prepares the way for the second resistance.* Thus the heart is hardened, and the conscience seared. . . On the other hand, every resistance to temptation makes resistance more easy. Every denial of self makes self-denial easier. *Every victory gained prepares the way for a fresh victory.* Each resistance to temptation, each self-denial, each triumph over sin, is a seed sown unto eternal life" (LHU 299).

"Beware how you neglect secret prayer and a study of God's Word. These are your weapons against him who is striving to hinder your progress heavenward. The first neglect of prayer and Bible study makes easier the second neglect" LHU 299).

The Bible is Your Sword

Sharpening Your Sword: The Bible says that the word of God is the sword of the Spirit. (Eph. 6:17). Before discussing the sword, it is essential that we consider something unusual about the Spirit. *He does not talk about Himself* (John 16:13). His special work is to remind you of the words of Jesus (John 14:26). There is one thing the all-powerful Holy Spirit cannot do—*He cannot bring to your memory what you have never bothered to store there.* The Spirit cannot operate in your life apart from the Word of God. Many people pray for the Holy Spirit and neglect the Word. This cannot be. The two are inseparable.

The Essential Word: Can you not see why familiarity with the Book is essential to your continued freedom? That is why the devil will do everything he can to distract you. Jesus repulsed Satan with, "It is written" (Matt. 4:4,7). You must do the same. Spend time with the Book! Jesus said, "The words that I speak unto you, they are spirit and they are life" (John 6:63). Feed your soul on His words and you will live. The psalmist wrote, "Thy word have I hid in my heart that I might not sin against thee" (Psa. 119:11). Live in the Word, and by the Word you will keep your freedom. It will insulate you against the power and temptations of the enemy.

Study the gospels: We have been counseled to spend a thoughtful hour each day meditating on the life of Christ (DA 83). What is the value of this? The answer is simple. If we daily renew our vision of Jesus, the things of this world lose their fatal attraction. Neglect Him and the world keeps looking better and better. The battle is easy when Jesus has first place in our thoughts. Neglect Him, and you lose your freedom. Look at Him daily and stay free.

Standing on the Promises: It is a wonderful fact that for every human need and emergency there is a promise from God to fill that very need. He has, in His love, given promises for our use. Having an inventory of those promises in the files of our memory is vital to victory. Make it a part of your Bible study-life to store these promises in your mind. Just when you need them, the Holy Spirit will bring them to the front of your thinking. Your specific need will be met. Contact the publishers of this book for recommendations on books of promises.

Never Be Without a Bible: Make the Bible your companion. Carry one in your car. It is surprising how many times you will use it. While waiting for an appointment you can make good use of your time. Let me share with you how to use your Bible as a sword. When the tempter comes and it seems you can take no more, instantly open your Bible. Turn to one of the gospels. Start reading out loud, if only in a whisper. This is not only for your personal benefit (and that it is), but the powers of evil hate the sound of God's Word. Indeed, it is sharper than any two-edged sword (Heb. 4:12). Keep reading—relief will come! The Bible is an essential weapon to staying free.

Dealing with False Guilt

There is another fiery dart (Eph 6:16) about which you must be warned—*Guilt*. If you have done something wrong, it is essential that you repent and confess it. I am not discussing that kind of guilt. I am writing about "false guilt" from which so many people suffer. The devil may torment you by putting the thought into your mind that God doesn't love you—not after the terrible things you have done. If you dwell on this thought, he may lead you to believe that you have committed the unpardonable sin. I have seen people weep in fear that they had committed this sin. I must tell you that people who commit this sin generally do not weep. They become indifferent. If you still fervently desire a relationship with Christ, remember His promise: "I will never leave you" (Heb. 13:5). Nothing that you are willing to confess and forsake is outside His forgiving love.

Watch Your Words: Jesus warned about "idle words" (Matt 12:36). Few Christians realize the importance of this counsel. The devils make note of everything we say. With our mouths, we dig the ditches into which we fall. Devils cannot read your mind, but they listen to your words. From them they know your thoughts and your allegiance. If you say, *"I have a weakness for that,"* you can be sure that the devil will test this weakness. Be careful what you say!

"Satan studies every indication of the frailty of human nature, he marks the sins which each individual is inclined to commit, and then he takes care that opportunities shall not be wanting to gratify the tendency of evil" (GC 555).

Other Spiritual Weapons

Praise: Honest praise for God is almost as important as prayer. Don't forget to praise the Lord. This is the Hallelujah factor. Someone has said that the devils hate to hear us praise God because it reminds them of the privilege they once had. They have vivid memories of heaven. They are painfully aware of what they gave up. They despise hearing your praise, and they scatter. There is freedom in praise. A caution here: *Praise must be genuine.* When used as an idle expression, God is offended. Praise must be real or not at all! Let your words be genuine.

Singing: The fallen angels once sang in the heavenly choir. They hate to hear us sing to the glory of God. Singing resurrects painful memories for them. When we sing, "There is power in the blood", they remember their defeat at Calvary. On several occasions, I have heard demons shout out of their victims, "Don't sing that song! I cannot stand those words."

"Let praise and thanksgiving be expressed in song. When tempted, instead of giving utterance to our feelings, let us by faith lift up a song of thanksgiving to God " (MH 254).

Give Your Testimony : Defeated members of the Lord's army are strewn all over the battlefield. When someone gives a shout of victory, these victims will listen. They are eager to hear how to win. People are tired of listening to theory. They are eager to listen to the testimony of those who are "more than conquerors" (Rom. 8:37). This is Christian witnessing, but you cannot witness to something that has never happened. Tell your story!

The Power of Witnessing: In chapter five of Mark's gospel Jesus tells how to witness—an excellent model. This chapter tells about a violent, angry man. These activities were the evidence of demonic possession. Jesus set him free. After his freedom the man requested to stay with Jesus, but Jesus kindly refused him. Jesus did not tell him to go and give Bible studies (important as this is). Rather, Jesus said, "Go home to thy friends, and tell them how great things the Lord has done for thee, and had compassion on thee" (Mark 5: 19).

The Nature of Christian Witness: From the Gadara story we learn that Christian witness contains a large element of praise. for God. *Tell what God did. Let your testimony be positive.* Do not magnify Satan, nor dwell on the sordid things that have happened in your life. Rather, glorify God! This is Christian witnessing.

As you witness to others of His grace and power in your own life, the benefit to you is greater than for your hearers. "He that watereth shall be watered also himself" (Prov. 11:25). Your words become a savor of life unto life—for you and for them. Let me warn you, your testimony will meet with resistance. Some will say you have lost your mind. Some may laugh at you. They jeered at Jesus on the cross. Don't expect any better. But others will receive your words as rain on a parched ground.

Some Booby Traps

"Lest Satan should get an advantage of us: for we are
not ignorant of his devices" (2 Cor. 2:11).

The Trap of Ignorance: Well-meaning people will advise you never to think about the devil. But the Bible teaches that ignorance of his work gives the devil a terrible advantage. Christ must always take first place in our thoughts; but to blindly walk through the devil's mine field is foolhardy. Ignorance is not a virtue. Ignorance is always a vice. It is dangerous, even deadly.

"Oh, that all could get a view of it as God revealed it to me, that they might *know more of the wiles of Satan* so as to be on their guard" (Ms. 1, 1849).

"*So long as we are ignorant of their wiles, they have almost inconceivable advantage;* many give heed to their suggestions while they *suppose* themselves to be following the dictates of their own wisdom" (GC 516).

"*His great success lies in keeping men's minds confused and ignorant* of his devices, for then he can lead the unwary, as it were, *blindfolded*" (Ms 34, 1897).

The Entertainment Trap: Never has seductive entertainment been so readily available. Never has the media ravaged our emotions with such force. Don't let the devil play games with your emotions through violent or sensual television, rock music, videos or novels. Your priorities must change. Eternal life depends on it. You must make a clean break with the past. This worldly stuff is sick. It is easy to give it up—if you have a spiritual mind. If sinful entertainment still looks appetizing to you, then seek for divine help until it becomes repulsive to you. Don't sell your soul for a video or a soap opera. Stand guard over the gates of your mind and emotions. We easily become fascinated. Entertainment is a sly seductress.

> "Amusements are doing more than anything else
> to counteract the working of the Holy Spirit and
> the Lord is grieved" (MYP 371).

The Habit Trap: We are all creatures of habit. Some of these are good, but many are bad. Bad habits make staying free very difficult. The Lord will provide power to break them—but He does not do it all for us. He will guide us and empower us, but the choice is always ours. Frequently a whole new set of habits must be formed—Bible study habits—prayer habits—turning to Him moment by moment for guidance. These changes are gradual. We might compare it to someone confined to bed in a prolonged illness who is now learning to walk again.

Helping Ellen to Mature

For example, let me tell you about Ellen (not her real name). She had been controlled by a demon of immaturity during all of her adult life. She had the body of a mature woman, but she thought like a little girl. She could not make adult decisions. She had never accepted adult responsibility. She was controlled by a demon—one of many—who called himself Peter Pan. He would not allow her to grow up emotionally. Speaking through Ellen, he said he had entered her when she was a child. She had become obsessed with a character called Peter Pan in a movie by that title.

After her deliverance, Ellen confirmed this to be true. She had gone to see that movie "at least fifteen times." The result was that she never thought of herself as a mature woman but always as a girl about eight or ten years of age. By beholding we become changed. These are not idle words!

The Time Factor: Ellen's deliverance freed her from this demonic domination. However, she was not instantly mature, but she was now *free to change* into a mature adult. It took time for her to develop new habits and attitudes. She had to build a whole new perspective on life. In order to help her "grow up," we arranged for Ellen to live for one year with an Adventist sister who knew about Ellen's past problems. She guided Ellen through various learning experiences to help her gain maturity. It required much patience and the ministry of the Holy Spirit for her to survive that year without becoming discouraged. She was tempted many times to return to the security she felt when in demonic captivity. Taking on adult responsibility was not easy. Habits and attitudes are not instantly or easily broken.

The Friendship Trap: This is one of Satan's most seductive traps. He exploits our God-given affection for family and friends in an effort to destroy us. Jesus said it this way: "And a man's foes shall be they of his own household" (Matt. 10:36).

In the centuries since Jesus spoke these words of warning, family influence has intensified. Everyone has a telephone. "Reach out and touch someone" is a sales pitch. Easy communication with worldly friends is both a convenience and a hazard. Much is at stake in your choice of friends:

> "When Christians choose the society of the ungodly and unbelieving, they expose themselves to temptation. Satan conceals himself from view and stealthily draws his deceptive covering over their eyes. They cannot see that such company is calculated to do them harm; and while all the time assimilating to the world in character, words, and actions, they are becoming more and more blinded" (GC 508).

Make Friends of God's children: There is a rule of thumb that I recommend to you: "Love those most who love God best." You may have to make a complete new circle of close friends. This may take time. You will have to work at it. Satan may try to use old friends to destroy you. What do you do about one very special old friend? Here is another rule of thumb—if you are leading him, *keep him;* but if he starts leading you, break it off—fast! Take no risks! This can be a deadly Booby Trap.

> "If you choose the society of those who are the enemies of Christ, do you expect God to work a miracle to keep you from yielding to Satan's power?" (5 T 511).

The devil may use members of your own family in an attempt to destroy you. Because they do not understand the spiritual battle as you do, they may cause you to doubt. They may laugh at your new Christian experience. They may say that it was all in your head—a psychological game. They may try to turn you against your Christian counselor and encourage you to hate him or her. Remember that Jesus warned, "And a man's foes shall be they of his own household" (Matt.10:36).

A Big Lie: Another one of the devil's most popular traps is "Christians don't have fun." Here are the facts: We are happier and more excited than anyone else in the world. It is simply that we have a different set of values that make us happy. The world doesn't look good to us. It is plastic. It is fiction. We work hand-in-hand with angels. We see answers to prayer before we finish sentences. Incredible!

The things of this world never satisfy. There will always be the search for a new and greater thrill; another drug, another fashion, another game, another dollar, another conquest—and in the end, a funeral without hope. The Christian escapes all this "joy." Face it—this world is a graveyard. The Christian is the happiest person in the world. He lives in the expectancy of the undiluted joy of life eternal—to behold the God who loved us—to see the Father and the Son with his own eyes! Then everlasting peace shall be ours when the war is over. Take courage, fellow warrior; there is Victory on the Battlefield.

CHAPTER
16
To the Praise of Jesus Christ

"For I have determined to know nothing among you save Jesus Christ and Him crucified" 1 Corinthians 2:2.

I must not close my book without a chapter of praise to the glory of Jesus Christ. His Name must be magnified. I cannot think of His cross without tears coming into my eyes and a choking feeling in my throat. My purpose is to portray the incredible victories of our Lord in a way that will reach your heart too.

In a special way I will emphasize those victories that He won in the closing days of His earthly ministry. In those final days there was an intense, all-out, moral and spiritual battle between good and evil— between Christ and Satan. The importance of those battles is beyond description. In every conflict He was fighting in our behalf. When we grasp the intensity of that struggle, and the sacrifice He made, we should have no difficulty giving Him our total devotion.

"Satan assailed Christ with his fiercest and most subtle temptations, but he was repulsed in every conflict. *Those battles were fought in our behalf; those victories make it possible for us to conquer"* (GC 510).

In this book I have exposed the reality and tactics of the Devil. He is unseen, but real. Ignorance of his workings gives him a terrible advantage. But warnings alone are not enough. We must learn how to meet him and overcome him. We cannot do this ourselves. He has six thousand years of experience and advantage over us. Without Christ we cannot win; with Him we cannot lose (1 Cor. 10:13). This chapter discusses the why and the how of victory in Christ. Through Him we can be more than conquerors.

In this last chapter I will focus on the brutal conflicts of our Lord with evil of every description. *Every struggle, every temptation, which either you or I will ever experience, was met and conquered by the Lord Jesus Christ.* I wish to point these out one by one. Lastly, I want to make some suggestions on how we can claim His victories as our own. This chapter can change your life. Keep reading!

A Return to Calvary

It is not my purpose here to attempt to portray *all* the events of Calvary. However, there is one particular aspect of Calvary whose importance is frequently overlooked—I refer to the darkness—the Egyptian kind of darkness that completely surrounded Him (Mk. 15:33). This has awesome importance.

The First Source of Darkness: First, there was the absence of the Father; darkness is the absence of light (1 Jn.1:5). When the Father turned His back on His Son, everything at Calvary became dark (Matt. 27:46). While Jesus bore the sins of the world (1 Pet. 2:24), the Father veiled His glory in the darkness. *Nothing shows the abhorrence of God for sin so much as the fact that He would conceal Himself from His only Son to bring about its destruction.*

The Second Source of Darkness: When the Father of lights withdrew, the powers of evil moved in and encompassed Him. Satan is the ruler of the darkness of this world (Eph 6:12). From Gethsemane onward Jesus stated that this was the hour and power of darkness (Luke 22: 53).

> "The principalities and powers of darkness were assembled around the cross, casting the hellish shadow of unbelief into the hearts of men" (DA 760).

> "Christ was nailed to the cross, but He gained the victory. *The whole force of evil* gathered itself together in an effort to destroy Him who was the light of the world..." (7 ABC 924).

> "And having disarmed the powers and authorities, He made a public spectacle of them, triumphing over them in the Cross" (Col. 2:15).

Not One Was Missing: Day by day Satan's every effort to overcome Jesus had met with nothing but failure. Now at the Cross he would make his last desperate effort to overwhelm Him. Every fallen angel was on Calvary's hill. Not one was missing. If one fallen angel were absent, he would have been in dereliction of duty. If only *one* had been missing, there would be one undefeated demon left in the world. They were *all* there turning on their hellish power.

Incredible Victory: The wondrous greatness of Jesus' victory can be understood only as we see one lone Man withstand and defeat *simultaneously* all the combined forces of evil. Remember, He had no help from His Father. Not one angel was permitted to help him. Our Lord *single-handedly* defeated the combined legions of hell. This was total victory! Physically, mentally, emotionally and spiritually, He was victor. *Because of His sweeping victory, we can have total victory.* Calvary was the decisive battle of the war with evil.

The Unseen Victory: To the natural eye of men, Calvary was an ignominious *defeat* for this Galilean carpenter who went about talking as though He were God. Exactly the opposite is the truth. It was a *glorious victory.* This one lone Man had defeated all the unseen billions of the forces of evil. Earthly victories by men pale into insignificance compared to Calvary.

At Calvary He defeated all the collective forces of evil;
Jesus Christ is Lord over all evil.

Loneliness: Jesus Christ was fighting this last battle at Calvary alone. We will never comprehend the anguish of His loneliness. The eternal, perfect fellowship between Him and His Father was broken because of sin. The human mind and heart can never fully grasp the suffering this rupture caused both the Father and the Son. Remember—Jesus never uttered one complaint about what *men* did to Him. The only thing that drew a cry of complaint from His lips was being forsaken by His Father. This was the great suffering and agony of Calvary.

You and I can have confidence that we will never be left alone. We will never be called upon to endure what He endured. Never believe the devil's lie that God has abandoned you. He never will. "I will be with you always, even unto the end of the world" (Matt 28:20). "I will never leave you, nor forsake you" (Heb. 13:5).

Jesus Christ is Lord over loneliness and abandonment.

Rejection and Depression: The devil had a field day at Calvary. Minute by minute he talked to Jesus. "Where are the five thousand who wanted to make you king? Nobody wants you! Where are your twelve friends? Even they have lost confidence in you. One betrayed you, another denied you. Look at the three women and the one man who stand by. Can't you see they are totally disillusioned?"

There is a time in almost everyone's life when it may seem that no one really cares whether he lives or dies. When that happens it is easy for self-pity to take over. The depression that comes at such a time is almost unbearable. Jesus experienced all of this. He was despised and rejected of men, a man of sorrows and acquainted with grief (Isa. 53:3). Look at the Cross again—no matter how bad your circumstances may be, they can never equal His. Satan fiercely and continuously tempted Jesus to be discouraged, but by faith Jesus defeated Satan's every attack.

Jesus Christ is Lord over rejection. He is Lord over depression. Jesus Christ is Lord over discouragement and sorrow.

Victory Over Pride

Pride is a satanic trait. It was an important aspect of Lucifer's fall (Eze. 28:17). It, too, had to be met and overcome. From the very beginning of His earthly pilgrimage, He met Pride and conquered him. The Lord's victory over pride began in a stable in Bethlehem, in the stench of animal manure. There was no more humble place to begin. Again, when He washed His disciples' feet He was rebuking pride (John 13:5). His last and most decisive defeat of pride was on the cross. Out of respect for our Lord, great artists have always portrayed him as wearing a loin cloth. There is no evidence that this was true. The Apostle Paul speaks of Him as despising the shame (Heb. 12:2). The scriptures define "shame" as nakedness (Gen. 2:25; Rev. 16:15). The people who carried out a crucifixion maximized the humiliation. No doubt he was naked. Now we can understand why the adorning of the body for purpose of self-display is so offensive to the Lord of Calvary.

"There is nothing so offensive to God or so dangerous to the human soul as pride and self-sufficiency. Of all sins it is the most hopeless, the most incurable " (COL 154).

Jesus Christ is Lord over pride, vanity, and fashion.

His Victory Over Hatred and Anger

The victory of our Lord over selfish Hate and Anger may well have been His greatest triumph of the Passion week. We shall reverently look at His incredible victory.

His Teaching about Anger: At the very beginning of His ministry our Lord preached what we call the Sermon on the Mount. In this sermon He endorsed the whole of the law of ten commandments (Matt. 5:17). Then He targeted two of them. He pointed out the two most destructive and prevalent sins of the human family—hate and lust. In effect He was warning that the devil would make a special attack on these two areas of human weakness. I wish reverently to point out the Lord's own victories over these two cardinal sins and how by His grace we can have victory.

Jesus taught that Anger is a Cardinal Sin: We don't think of anger as sin, but that is what it is—a great, uncontrolled sin. We do not think of ourselves as murderers, but Jesus equated anger with murder (Matt. 5:22; 1 Jn. 3:15). Anger is a sin—it is the seed of murder. Anger is deceptive because we constantly justify it. The devil persuades us that we have the right to be angry—"if you only knew what he did to me.." or "if you knew what she said..." "I am a Choleric." These are excuses borrowed from the devil's notebook. We justify our anger. This must be stopped. Victory must be gained over anger. Eternal life is at stake, but praise God, there is victory in Christ. (1 Cor. 15:57).

> "A man cannot be a Christian and allow his *temper to fire up at any little accident* or annoyance that he may meet, and show that *Satan is in him* in the place of Jesus Christ" (Ms 166).

In the final hours before His death the devil made an all-out effort to make the Lord angry; to persuade Him to abandon the human race to its well-deserved fate. The violence of the devil's attack never let up for a moment. Watch His victories!

Jesus' Victory Over Anger

Victory in Gethsemane: His betrayal by Judas Iscariot was a Satanic scheme. Judas led the mob out to Jesus' special place of prayer in the garden of Gethsemane. Can you not see the devil putting this thought in Jesus' mind, "Judas, after all the kindness I have shown you, how could you do this to me?" How did our Lord respond? He called him, "Friend." Why is this scene told in such detail? Can we not see that it was to let us know the magnitude of His grace? Here was perfect victory over anger. There was no rancor. There was no bitterness; —only kindness and forgiving love.

Victory before Caiaphas and Pilate: Notice His composure before Pilate. His unearthly character and bearing in the face of injustice and death unnerved even a hardened Roman Governor. How did He react to the injustice of Caiaphas and Annas? Always with patience and kindness! By His patient love Jesus was saying: "You can lash me with stripes; you can pluck my beard; you can strike my face; you can laugh at me and jeer; you can mock me with a purple robe; you can ridicule me with a crown of thorns. There is one thing you cannot do—you cannot make me angry at you."

Victory at Calvary: The last and greatest victory came at the Cross. There Jesus gained His greatest and most incredible victory over anger. What was He saying? "You can nail my feet that have day and night gone on missions of mercy for you; you can nail my hands that have healed your sick, opened your blind eyes and straightened your twisted limbs. There is one thing you cannot do—you cannot make me angry at you —because I love you! I love you!"

Can you not see that Jesus is Lord over tirades, anger and rage? He conquered it for you and me. He wants to set us free of these displays of evil spirit.

Total Victory: Jesus gained the victory over hate and anger under all of these circumstances. These situations were much more difficult than any of us will ever face. Everything done to Him was totally unjustified, yet He did not retaliate. *Jesus Christ is Lord over evil temper.* We have no excuse for being angry—not since Calvary. Jesus provides all the power necessary for total victory. The Holy Spirit ministers His grace to us. Open your heart and ask Him in. You can have His meek spirit. Cry out-loud in His Name and ask, not only for forgiveness for your evil temper; ask for deliverance. The Christ of Calvary will set you free. "And if the Son shall make you free, you shall be free indeed" (Jn. 8:36).

> "We can overcome. Yes, fully, entirely. Jesus died to make a way of escape for us that we might overcome *every evil temper*, every sin, every temptation, and sit down at last with Him "(1T144).

Jesus Christ is Lord over hate. He is Lord over anger. and bitterness. This was His monumental Calvary victory.

Forgiveness—the Source of Victory: How did Jesus conquer anger? *He did it through forgiveness.* He prayed, "Father, forgive them." He manifested no resentment for the people who nailed Him to the Cross. He forgave them! If Jesus had snarled; if His eyes had narrowed; if His jaw had tensed for even a moment, the whole human race would have been lost. Satan would have triumphed. The character of Christ would have become satanic. But the love of Christ for you and me is greater than Satan's hate and Satan's anger. Jesus is not a stoic. He is victor!

Accepting Jesus

What does it mean to accept Jesus? We hear these words frequently. It means more than accepting His forgiveness—it means living as He lived. It means forgiving those who have unjustly treated us. It won't be difficult to do—if you have seen Jesus.

Victory in Christ: How does this apply to us? Many people go through life full of bitterness. Their tempers flair at the slightest provocation. Many people "trying" to be Christians are consumed by hate. Freedom from anger can never be separated from forgiveness. We must, from our hearts, forgive the people who have unjustly treated us (Matt. 18:35). Everyone who has ever done us an injustice must be forgiven. This is eternally serious. Those who do not forgive as Christ forgave cannot enter the kingdom of God. By the grace of Christ we can and must forgive everyone who has ever abused or hurt us in any way. We have freedom in Christ only as we give unconditional forgiveness. We can get this forgiving spirit only from Him. Jesus is the only source of supply. Victory can be had over this controlling angry spirit. This must be our all-prevailing prayer:

"It is impossible for man to be tempted above what he is able to bear while he relies upon Jesus, the infinite conqueror" (Conf. 31).

"Lord, Give me your forgiving spirit. Take this bitterness, this desire for revenge, this grudge, this anger, this hatred, out of me." Again I say—Jesus Christ is Lord over anger.

Lust

Another Cardinal Sin—Lust: In His Sermon on the Mount, Jesus also focused on the second cardinal sin of humanity—Lust. His teaching went far beyond the physical act of adultery. He spoke of the desires, the thoughts. To Him, entertaining lustful thoughts was sin. In speaking of the signs of His second coming He referred to the conditions in Noah's day. He said they were marrying and giving in marriage (Matt. 24: 37). He was certainly not criticizing a loving family relationship. Lust was the consuming obsession of Noah's day. History is being repeated. Today lust is worshipped. Lust is an almost universally accepted and welcomed obsession. It has taken on the form of entertainment which people cultivate and enjoy.

Sign of Our Times: It is not my purpose to dwell here on today's lustful climate. Advertising today is filled with lust. Automobile manufacturers have a half-clothed beauty sitting on the fender. Porno shops, racy novels and magazines abound. Television soap-operas are saturated with lust. These are the devil's means of seduction. These satanic hooks must become repulsive to us if we would have Jesus' victory.

Jesus Victory over Lust: Here we are walking on sacred ground; But if Jesus is to be our Savior in all things, He must have met this siren temptation. Did He conquer lust? If He is to give us victory, He must have a victory to share. Why is Mary Magdalene mentioned so many times in the gospels? This seductive, vulnerable, pretty woman might have been Satan's tempting foil. Jesus gave no response, not even by a thought.

In Mary's House: When in Bethany, Jesus always stayed at the home of Mary, Martha, and Lazarus. Many have wondered why Jesus would do this. It did not seem like good judgment on His part to stay overnight in the same house with Mary, a lady of easy virtue. Why would He risk His reputation in this way? One answer is apparent: *No one can say that Jesus was never exposed. He was exposed to lust in a most advantageous situation.* He conquered! If one has a problem with lust—call aloud on His mighty name. His victory in Mary's house is ours for the asking. Will you ask Him? Call on Him. You will not fall! The tempter is already defeated.

Jesus Christ is Lord over lust.

Materialism

A Satanic Possession: When our Lord discussed the signs of His second coming, He compared end-times with the days before the flood. There is a warning here. He said they were buying and selling. The Lord was not speaking of normal commerce. He was speaking of the love of *things*—materialism. This was a prevailing sin before the flood. It prevails now even among God's people. It is a subtle form of demonic possession. Materialism is the worship of things. It is a violation of the second commandment—Idolatry.

A few years ago Pastor Glen Maxson, then President of the Inter-American Division of Seventh-day Adventists, was asked why demon possession was not seen in the United States as it was in his mission field. He gave an insightful answer:

> "It is very simple; the devil does not need to show his power in demon possession. He has most of the people in North America under his possession already through the love of *materialism*. The devil little cares whether individuals believe in his power as long as they don't become active, aware Christians preparing for the coming of Christ" (*Insight*, July 11, 1972).

Jesus Overcame Materialism: Shortly after His baptism, the Lord had three encounters with Satan in the wilderness (Matt. 4). In the last temptation Satan offered Him all the kingdoms of this world if Jesus would just worship him. Satan's choice was clever. He still seduces by offering us the world. The love of things is universal; it may be money, a car, a house, clothing, or a diamond ring. It may be only a trinket about which we tell a lie in order to possess. It is a widely-accepted phrase that every man has his price—everyone except Jesus. We, too, must overcome. As soon as our involvement with the things of this life takes priority over eternal things we are possessed by a spirit of materialism—the deadly sin of idolatry.

Jesus Christ is Lord over materialism and the love of money,
both of which are a form of idolatry.

Appetite

This is another essential victory that Jesus gained. It is of immediate and eternal importance. We must discuss it. People today do not think of unbridled appetite as a sin. Remember that the fall of the human race centered around food.

Jesus taught that one of the reasons for the judgment of God on the human race in the days of Noah was perverted "eating and drinking" (Matt 24:38). How people eat and drink is a serious matter in the eyes of God. Like Noah's day, perverted appetite has become a major god in our culture. We worship at his altar. The result is that the human family is paying a high price in poor health and in shortened life. Health care providers everywhere are warning about foods high in cholesterol, salt and sugar. Our society is literally digging its graves with its teeth. Appetite has become a murderer. "Thou shalt not kill" (Ex. 20:13).

> "Satan is constantly on the alert to bring the race fully under his control. *His strongest hold on man is through the appetite*, and this he seeks to stimulate in every possible way" (CD 150).

> "Christ withstood the fiercest temptation upon appetite, which has had such a great influence upon the human family; so that whatever may be the habits and practices of men, they may overcome them in His name and through His merits... Divine power may combine with human effort, that through Jesus man may stand free, a conqueror. *Man may conquer perverted appetite*" (RH June 30, 1890).

> "Through no class of temptation does Satan achieve greater success than through those addressed to the appetite. *If he can control the appetite he can control the whole man*" (Te 276).

In this end-time, God is calling for a reformation at the dining table. For our own good He wants us to return to the original dietary of fruits, nuts and grains (Gen. 1:29). Nutritionists everywhere are urging this change. Our appetites are so perverted that everything we eat must be either fatty, spicy, salty, or sweet; or a combination of these. In addition to that, we are a generation of "over-eaters." The taste buds of the entire western world are corrupted. Can we return to the "low key" taste of natural foods and be happy? It will be a difficult adjustment. It will take a miracle from the Lord. He can do it.

Jesus' Victory over Appetite: Every Bible-reading Christian is aware that the devil tempted Jesus to turn stones into bread and feed himself. You will remember the Lord's reply, "Man shall not live by bread alone..." In other words Jesus refused to yield to appetite. We must remember that He did this after being without food for forty days and forty nights (Matt. 4:1-4). Jesus overcame appetite under circumstances greater than you and I can possibly face. Kneel at His feet. He will set you free.

Jesus is Lord over perverted appetite.

Fear

One of the plagues of mankind is fear. Many are controlled by it. Fear comes in many degrees from simple timidity, shyness, to absolute terror. Those who live in fear are tormented (1 Jn. 4:18). Fear in any form —in any degree is destructive. It is of the enemy. The Lord has not given us the spirit of fear (2 Tim.1:7).

Jesus Overcame Fear: He had a showdown with fear in a degree that you and I will never know. There is no fear greater than the fear of death (Heb. 2:15). It was at the door of death that the Lord met and overcame fear. We often say that the Lord died the "second death." He took the place of lost man—the man who will be told to depart from God—never again enter His presence (Matt. 25:41). We say that Jesus died the "second death" altogether too casually. When our Lord committed Himself to the redemption of man, He felt that He was going out of existence forever—*like a lost man.* This is why He sweat blood in the garden of Gethsemane. He was meeting Fear. He conquered it. His perfect love for man and His trust in His Father's love cast out the fear (1 Jn. 4:18).

We cannot grasp the price of our redemption until we realize that in His mind and heart He was permanently and willingly giving up His unity with His father—a unity unbroken from all the ages of eternity. The eternal bonding of the Godhead was fractured so that an eternal bonding might be forged between man and God. He did this that we might have the privilege of eternal fellowship. I have good news for you, dear reader; none need live in bondage to fear (Rom. 8:15).

Jesus Christ is Lord over the tormenting spirit of fear.

Two More Victories

Alcohol: There are two more precious victories that the Lord won at Calvary which are often overlooked. Let us go back to Calvary and see Him there. The silence was broken as He said, "I thirst." There was offered to him vinegar mingled with gall (Matt. 27:34). Unfortunately the King James version covers up the meaning of this temptation. Vinegar is composed of two old French words—"Vin" is our English word—wine. "Aigre" is a French word for bitter. In other words, they were offering alcohol to Jesus. *Jesus refused it.* If anyone could justify the use of alcohol, it would be Jesus under these circumstances. Alcohol is an anesthetic. As an act of kindness, He was offered alcohol to help Him bear the pain. He turned it down. One of the last things our Lord did before He died was to gain a victory over alcohol for every alcoholic.

Jesus is Lord over the spirits of alcohol.

Drugs: There is yet another victory at Calvary that we must not overlook. There was gall mixed in the vinegar. Gall was a drug. It was an opiate to dull the pain. Offering Him the gall was, once again, an act of kindness on the part of the donors. *Jesus refused it.* One of the last things our Lord did before He died was to gain a victory over drugs for every drug addict.

Jesus Christ is Lord over every drug addiction.

His Victory Over Death

Jesus gained for us a glorious victory over every sordid, sensual and vicious trait in our characters. One more enemy needed to be met and defeated. That enemy was Death. This was the last and ultimate enemy. His victory at Calvary would not be complete without His resurrection.

A massive stone was rolled before the door in an attempt to keep him in. A Roman seal was placed upon the stone. A hundred Roman soldiers were stationed to guard the grave. Their assignment was to prevent fraud and violence. In a blaze of glory an angel came, broke the seal, and rolled away the stone (Matt. 28:2). When Jesus arose, the keepers fell as dead men. The Gentile guards stationed to keep Him in the tomb now were the first unbiased, unprejudiced witnesses of His triumph. They saw Him rise. He had forever proved his claim to be "the resurrection and the life" (Jn. 11:25).

Now He is alive forevermore (Rev. 1:18). The gates of hell did not prevail (Matt. 16:18). He had tasted death for every man (Heb. 2:9). Death had been conquered. The purpose of His coming to this world to break the bondage of sin and death over man had been accomplished. Because He lives, we too shall live. We have nothing to fear—not even death itself.

Jesus Christ is Lord over death.

Jesus, The Complete Redeemer

Deliverance from the *penalty* of sin is the beginning of redemption. Deliverance from the *power* of sin is the next essential step. The Lord does not forgive the drunk to let him go on drinking. He sets him free! The Lord does not forgive the murderer to let him go on killing. He sets him free! The Lord does not forgive the adulteress to continue in sin. He sets her free! The Lord does not forgive anger to let a person go on being angry. He sets him free! The Lord does not forgive the violent to let him go on abusing. He sets him free! The Lord can do more with sin than merely forgive it. He conquered sin in the flesh (Rom. 8:3). That fact is the fullness of the Gospel of Christ.

He Came to set the Captives Free!

The good news of the Gospel is that Jesus Christ is Lord over every evil human propensity, both acquired and inherited. "Jesus was in all points tempted like as we are and yet without sin"(Heb. 4:15). If we yield to temptation, it is because we have failed to call on Him who alone can give us victory. He alone can and has made a way of escape. Everything we need for deliverance from sin is found in the person of Jesus Christ. He came to set the captives free.

Claiming His Victory

One of the greatest needs of the church today is to bring His victories out of the realm of theology and discussion, and into our practical daily lives. How seldom is the cry of victory heard! The forces of evil are all around us. We are engaged in a conflict that cannot be avoided. We are not wrestling with flesh and blood, but against wicked spirits in high places (Eph 6:12). Satan has blinded our eyes to this unseen reality. The more we know about the triumph of Christ, the more sure we are that victory over sin can be ours. This experience can be ours if He is truly Lord of our lives. We shall eternally give glory to Him who has redeemed us. When the gates of pearl are opened, we shall enter in and magnify His Name. We will joyfully shout, "The war is over! The war is over!" We will join the heavenly chorus and sing His praises forever. We will cast our crowns at His nail-pierced feet. By His grace the liberated Captives out of every nation, kindred, tongue and people will enter His Holy City—there to give Him glory forever, and ever, and ever, and ever.

HE BLED FROM HIS HANDS:

To atone for the things we have done, we should never have

DONE.

******

HE BLED FROM HIS FEET:

To atone for the places we have gone, we should never have

GONE.

******

HE BLED FROM HIS BACK:

To atone for the burdens we have carried, we should have never

CARRIED.

****

HE BLED FROM HIS HEAD:

To atone for the thoughts which we should have never

THOUGHT.

****

HE BLED FROM HIS SIDE:

To atone for the feelings which we should never have

FELT.

*****

JESUS CHRIST IS VICTOR
AND LORD OF ALL.

Appendices

A Word to the Serious Reader

The last portion of this book consists of an
unusually large appendix. It contains much
information which many will find interesting
and informative. We recognize that not every
reader will be intrigued by this supplemental
material. However, we trust that many will
find the Appendices to be very rewarding.
We encourage you to invest some time
in this portion of the book.

We solicit your questions, and comments.
Please address them to me in
care of the publisher.

Vaughn Allen

Compiler's Observations

In my efforts to help the oppressed, the Bible has been my primary source of guidance. I have also found the writings of Ellen White to be a veritable gold mine of help and insights. This appendix contains selected quotations from her writings. In no way do they represent a complete study of her material of this nature. In fact, they merely scratch the surface. I have carefully compared my fifteen years of experience with what I have found on the subject from her writings. Nowhere have I discovered any incompatibility between God's leading in my ministry with the information given in the Spirit of Prophecy.

"In sending out the twelve, Christ sent none alone. They were to go forth two and two, invested with power from himself to heal the sick and rebuke Satanic agencies as proof of their mission" (RH March 23, 1897).

"Satan takes possession of the minds of men today. In my labors in the cause of God, I have again and again met those who have been possessed, and in the name of the Lord I have rebuked the evil spirits" (2 SM 353).

"Satan is Christ's personal enemy.... If our eyes could be opened to discern the fallen angels at work with those who feel at ease and consider themselves safe, we would not feel so secure. Evil angels are upon our track every moment" (1 T 302).

"Have Seventh-day Adventists forgotten the warning given in the sixth chapter of Ephesians? We are engaged in a warfare against the hosts of darkness. Unless we follow our Leader closely, Satan will obtain the victory over us" (Let. 140, 1903).

"The fact that men have been possessed with demons, is clearly stated in the New Testament. The persons thus afflicted were not merely suffering with disease from natural causes...He recognized the direct presence and agency of evil spirits" (GC 514).

In the interest of brevity, I have selected and italicized some sentences that make the point to be emphasized. I would suggest that the serious reader study each of these quotations in its context. I would also encourage the reading of chapters 31 and 32 of "The Great Controversy" by Ellen White.

Vaughn Allen

The Unseen Battle.

"Could our eyes be opened and could each see the conflict of angelic agencies with the Satanic confederacy what astonishment would come upon the soul. The holy angels are working with terrible intensity for the salvation of men, because the destroyer of souls is seeking to make of no effect the salvation which has been purchased at infinite cost. Could our spiritual vision be opened we should see that which would never be effaced from the memory as long as life should last... We would see angels flying swiftly to aid the tempted ones who stand as on the brink of a precipice. These tempted ones are unable to help themselves and avoid the ruin which threatens them; but the angels of God are forcing back the evil angels, and guiding souls away from the dangerous places, to plant their feet on a sure foundation. *We should see battles going on between the two armies, as real as those fought by opposing forces on earth*" ST October 10, 1894.

Evil forces are involved in all human activity.

"...He is intruding his presence *in every department of the household, in every street of our cities, in the churches, in the national councils, in the courts of justice,* perplexing, deceiving, seducing, everywhere ruining the souls and bodies of men, women, and children, breaking up families, sowing hatred, emulation, strife, sedition, murder. And the Christian world seem to regard these things as though God had appointed them and they must exist" GC 508.

Satan is gathering thousands under his control.

"He (Satan) flatters men with the pleasing fable that there is no rebellious foe, no deadly enemy that they need to guard against, and that the existence of a personal devil is all fiction; and while he thus hides his existence, *he is gathering thousands under his control.*" Conf.35,36 .

"The condition of things in the world shows that troublous times are right upon us.... *Men possessed of demons* are taking the lives of men, women, and little children. Men have become infatuated with vice, and every species of evil prevails." 9 T 11.

Satan hates every human being.

"We have a powerful enemy, and not only does he hate every human being made in the image of God, but with bitterest enmity he hates God and His only begotten Son Jesus Christ." FCE 299.

The battle with Satan is very real.

"Satan is Christ's personal enemy.... If our eyes could be opened to discern the fallen angels at work with those who feel at ease and consider themselves safe, we would not feel so secure. *Evil angels are upon our track every moment.*" 1 T 302.

"It is not a mimic battle in which we are engaged. We are waging a warfare upon which hang eternal results. We have unseen enemies to meet. Evil angels are striving for the dominion of every being." MH 128.

"Satan and his angels are unwilling to lose their prey. They contend and battle with holy angels, and the conflict is severe." MYP 60.   *Isa 49:25*

Demons are struggling for control of every human being.

"He (Jesus) knows that *a demon power is struggling in every soul*, striving for the mastery, but Jesus came to break the power of Satan and to set the captives free." MLT 300.

"We should ever keep in mind that unseen agencies are at work, both evil and good, to take control of the mind. They act with unseen yet effectual power.... The great adversary of souls, the devil, and his angels are continually laboring to accomplish our destruction." AH 405.

"Satan is busy every moment, going to and fro, walking up and down in the earth, seeking whom he may devour." 5 T 294.

Satan will have his greatest success as we near the end of time.

"*As we near the close of time*, the human mind is more readily affected by Satan's devices." 1 T 293.

"None are in greater danger from the influence of evil spirits than those who, notwithstanding the direct and simple testimony of the Scriptures, deny the existence and agency of the devil and his angels...*This is why, as we approach the close of time, when Satan is to work with greatest power to deceive and destroy,* he spreads everywhere the belief that he does not exist. It is his policy to conceal himself and his manner of working." GC 516.

Every one of us is controlled either by God or by Satan.

"We must be daily controlled by the Spirit of God or we are controlled by Satan." 5 T 102.

"We are co-workers together with Christ, or co-workers with the enemy. We either gather with Christ, or scatter abroad. *We are decided wholehearted Christians, or none at all.* 1 T 15

"Every man, woman and child that is not under control of the Spirit of God is under the influence of Satan's sorcery." MYP 278.

Ignorance of demonic working is a false protection.

"If God has granted to His children promise of grace and protection, it is because there are mighty agencies of evil to be met—agencies numerous, determined, and untiring, of whose malignity and power *none can safely be ignorant or unheeding.*" GC 513.

"So long as we are ignorant of their (the devil and his angels) wiles, *they have almost inconceivable advantage.*" GC 516.

"Satan is well aware that the weakest soul who abides in Christ is more than a match for the hosts of darkness, and that, should he reveal himself openly, he would be met and resisted." GC 530.

"There is nothing that the great deceiver fears so much as that we shall become acquainted with his devices." GC 516.

"There are evil angels at work all around us, but because we do not discern their presence with our natural vision *we do not consider as we should the reality of their existence as set forth in the Word of* God." 5 T 533.

Satan is a master workman with much experience.

"He (Satan) has been growing more artful, and has learned the most successful manner in which to come to the children of men with his temptations." 1T 342.

"Satan has the same power and the same control over minds now, only it has *increased a hundred fold* by exercise and experience. Men and women today are deceived, blinded by his insinuations and devices, and know it not." 3 T 328.

"Satan is a master workman. His infernal wisdom he employs with good success.... Our adversary, the devil, is not void of wisdom or strength." 2 T 172.

Satan does not always come as a roaring lion.

"He (Satan) does not always wear the ferocious look of the lion, but when he can work to better effect, he transforms himself into an angel of light. *He can readily exchange the roar of the lion for the most persuasive arguments or for the softest whisper.*" 2 T 287.

"The enemy does not always come as a roaring lion; he frequently appears *as an angel of light,* assuming friendly airs, presenting peculiar temptations which it is difficult for the inexperienced to withstand." 4 T 407.

Satan studies every individual's weaknesses.

"Satan studies every indication of the frailty of human nature, he marks the sins which each individual is inclined to commit, and then he takes care that opportunities shall not be wanting to gratify the tendency of evil." GC 555.

"*Satan is at your side when you least suspect it,* watching to find a weak spot in your armor, where he can introduce his darts, and wound your soul by betraying you into sin. He has access to minds that are open to receive his suggestions, and by long experience he has learned how to apply his temptations to the best advantage." ST May 8, 1884

Evil forces are frequently undetected.

"When Christ revealed to Peter the time of trial and suffering that was just before Him, and Peter replied, 'Be it far from thee, Lord, this shall not be unto thee' (Matt. 16:22). The Savior commanded, 'Get thee behind me, Satan' (Matt. 16:23). Satan was speaking through Peter, making him act the part of the tempter. *Satan's presence was unsuspected by Peter,* but Christ could detect the presence of the deceiver, and His rebuke to Peter He addressed the real foe." 2 SM 353; DA 416.

In our own strength we have no defense against Satan.

"The power and malice of Satan and his host might justly alarm us were it not that we may find shelter and deliverance in the superior power of our Redeemer. We carefully secure our houses with bolts and locks to protect our property and our lives from evil men; but we seldom think of the evil angels who are constantly seeking access to us, and *against whose attacks we have, in our own strength, no method of defense.*" GC 517.

"Man is Satan's captive and is naturally inclined to follow his suggestions and do his bidding. He has in himself no power to oppose effectual resistance to evil. It is only as Christ abides in him by living faith, influencing his desires and strengthening him with strength from above, that many may venture to face so terrible a foe. Every other means of defense is utterly vain. *It is only through Christ that Satan's power is limited.*" 5 T 294.

"Good people" can be harassed by demons.

"There were hours when the whisperings of demons tortured his (John the Baptist) spirit, and the shadow of a terrible fear crept over him." DA 216.

We have the Right to Rebuke Them.

"Satan takes possession of the minds of men today. In my labors in the cause of God, I have again and again met those who have been possessed, and *in the name of the Lord I have rebuked the evil spirits.*" 2 SM 353.

Lack of Knowledge of their Working is Blindness.

"Satan summons all his forces and throws his whole power into the combat. Why is it that he meets with no greater resistance? Why are the soldiers of Christ so sleepy and indifferent? Because they have so little real connection with Christ; because they are so destitute of His Spirit. Sin is not to them repulsive and abhorrent, as it was to their Master. They do not meet it, as did Christ with decisive and determined resistance. They do not realize the exceeding evil and malignity of sin, and they are blinded both to the character and the power of the prince of darkness. There is little enmity against Satan and his works, *because there is so great ignorance concerning his power and malice, and the vast extent of his warfare against Christ and His church....* Among professed Christians, and even among ministers of the gospel, there is heard scarcely a reference to Satan, except perhaps an incidental mention in the pulpit. They overlook the evidences of his continual activity and success; they neglect the many warnings of his subtlety; they seem to ignore his very existence." GC 507-508.

Satan enters through uncontrolled thoughts and feelings.

"You should keep off from Satan's enchanted ground and not allow your minds to be swayed from allegiance to God.... When you decide that as Christians you are not required to restrain your thoughts and feelings *you are brought under the influence of evil angels* and invite their presence and their control." 5 T 310.

We can come under Satan's control in many ways.

"Satan has summoned the hosts of darkness to war against the saints. We can not afford to be indifferent to his attacks. *He comes in many ways,* and we must have clear spiritual discernment that we may be able to discern when he is seeking to gain possession of our minds." OHC 19.

The demons that possessed Mary were cast out seven times.

"Mary had been looked upon as a great sinner, but Christ knew the circumstances that had shaped her life....It was He who had lifted her from despair and ruin. *Seven times* she had heard His strong cries to the Father on her behalf." DA 568.

Satan may gain entrance when we knowingly disregard God's commandments.

"There are multitudes today as truly under the power of evil spirits as was the demoniac of Capernaum. *All who willfully depart from God's commandments are placing themselves under the control of Satan.* Many a man tampers with evil, thinking that he can break away at pleasure; but he is lured on and on, until he finds himself controlled by a will stronger than his own. He cannot escape its mysterious power. Secret sin or master passion may hold him a captive as helpless as was the demoniac of Capernaum." MH 92, 93.

Un-Christlike behavior opens doors to possession.

"When men reveal the opposite traits (from the Christian), when they are *proud, vain, frivolous, worldly-minded, avaricious, unkind, censorious,* we need not be told with whom they are associating, who is their most intimate friend. They may not believe in witchcraft; but, notwithstanding this, *they are holding communion with an evil spirit.*" 5T 225

Satan may gain entrance through intemperance and frivolity.

"The cause of this (demon-possessed) man's affliction...was in his own life. (See Luke 4:31-37). He had been fascinated with the pleasure of sin and thought to make life a grand carnival. *Intemperance and frivolity perverted the noble attributes of his nature, and Satan took entire control of him.*" MH 91.

We often tempt Satan to control us.

"In this degenerate age, Satan holds control over those who depart from the right and venture upon his ground. He exercises his power upon such in an alarming manner.... Some, I was shown, gratify their curiosity and tamper with the devil. They have no real faith in spiritualism and would start back with horror at the idea of being mediums. *Yet they venture and place themselves in a position where Satan can exercise his power upon them.* Such do not mean to enter deep into this work, but they know not what they are doing. *They are venturing on the devil's ground and tempting him to control them.* This powerful destroyer considers them his lawful prey and exercises his power upon them, and that against their will. When they wish to control themselves they cannot. They yielded their minds to Satan, and he will not release his claims, but holds them captive. *No power can deliver the ensnared soul but the power of God in answer to the earnest prayers of His followers.*" 1 T 299.

Unpleasant words in the home open the door for evil angels.

"Parents, let the words you speak to your children be kind and pleasant, that angels may have your help in drawing them to Christ. A thorough reformation is needed in the home church. Let it begin at once. Let all grumbling and fretting and scolding cease. *Those who fret and scold shut out the angels of heaven and open the door to evil angels.*" AH 441.

Unconverted children are an easy prey for Satan.

"*Children who have not experienced the cleansing power of Jesus are the lawful prey of the enemy, and the evil angels have easy access to them....* By faithful and untiring efforts of the parents, and the blessing and grace bestowed upon the children in response to the prayers of the parents, the power of the evil angels may be broken and a sanctifying influence shed upon the children. Thus the powers of darkness will be driven back." CT 118.

We may fall prey to Satan when we cherish known sins.

"All who indulge sinful traits of character, or *willfully cherish a known sin,* are inviting the temptations of Satan. They separate themselves from God and from the watchcare of His angels; as the evil one presents his deceptions, *they are without defense and fall an easy prey.*" GC 558-559.

****

DETAILS OF DEMONIC ORGANIZATION

Editors Note. From our years of experience we have learned that the forces of evil are highly organized. The following quotations are not psychological metaphors. Ellen White gave clear insight into the complexity and details of demonic organization.

Satan assigns a specific work to each of his angels.

"*Satan assigns to each of his angels a part to act.* He enjoins upon them all to be sly, artful, cunning." EW 90.

Demon of Unkindness.

"Some who profess to be servants of Christ have so long cherished the *demon of unkindness* that they seem to love the unhallowed element and to take pleasure in speaking words that displease and irritate." SL 16.

Demon of intemperance.

"*The demon of intemperance* is of giant strength, and is not easily conquered." Te 176.

"Indulgence in intoxicating liquor places a man wholly under the control of the demon who devised this stimulant in order to deface and destroy the moral image of God." Te 32.

"He (Christ) can give us help to conquer even this *demon of intemperance.*" CG 401.

Demon of Strife.

"If the law of God is obeyed, the *demon of strife* will be kept out of the family." AH 106.

Demon of Ambition.

"Christ came to a people who were deceived and deluded by the *demon of ambition.*" LHU 135

Demon of nicotine.

"Men professing godliness offer their bodies upon Satan's altar and burn the incense of tobacco to his satanic majesty. Does this statement seem severe? Certainly, the offering is presented to some deity. As God is pure and holy, and will accept nothing defiling in its character, He must refuse this expensive, filthy and unholy sacrifice; therefore, we conclude that Satan is the one who claims the honor." SL 31.

Demon of selfishness.

"If he (Judas) would open his heart to Christ, divine grace would banish *the demon of selfishness*, and even Judas might become a subject of the kingdom of God." DA 294.

Demon of jealousy.

"*The demon of jealousy* entered the heart of the king Saul when David received praise for victory in battle." PP 650.

Evil thoughts give them entrance and control.

"It is not safe for you to trust to your impressions and feelings.... Your imagination and nerves have been under the control of demons.... You may, and frequently do, let down the bars and *invite the enemy in*, and he controls your thoughts and actions, while you are really deceived and flatter yourself that you are in favor with God." 3 T 418.

Demon of passion (Anger).

"The intelligence (knowledge of David's whereabouts) aroused the *demon of passion* that had been slumbering in Saul's breast." PP 668.

Demons take delight in misery and destruction.

"The ruin of souls is his (Satan's) only delight, their destruction his only employment; and shall we act as though we were paralyzed?" 5 T 384.

"Their (evil angels) only delight is in misery and destruction." GC 517.

Demon of affliction.

"Satan will go to the extent of his power to harass, tempt, and mislead God's people. In a marvelous manner will he *affect the bodies* of those who are naturally inclined to do his bidding." 1 T 340-341.

"Satan's influence is constantly exerted upon men to distract the senses, control the mind for evil, and incite to violence and crime. *He weakens the body,* darkens the intellect, and debases the soul." DS 341.

Christ spoke to demons as intelligent beings.

"The daughter of the Syrophenician woman was grievously vexed with a devil, whom Jesus cast out by His word. (Mark 7:26-30). 'One possessed with a devil, blind, and dumb' (Matthew 12:22) ; a youth who had a dumb spirit, that oftentimes 'cast him into the fire, and into the waters, to destroy him,' (Mark 9:17-27); the maniac who, tormented by 'a spirit of an unclean devil' (Luke 4:33-36), disturbed the Sabbath quiet of the synagogue at Capernaum—all were healed by the compassionate Saviour. In nearly every instance, *Christ addressed the demon as an intelligent entity,* commanding him to come out of his victim and to torment him no more." GC 515, 516.

Satan works to retain his captives.

"The spirits of darkness will battle for the soul *once under their dominion.*" DA 259.

"He (Satan) will not hesitate to engage all his energies and call to his aid all his evil host to wrest a single human being from the hand of Christ.... *Satan and his angels are unwilling to lose their prey. They contend and battle with holy angels, and the conflict is severe.*" 1 T 301.

"Satan will not yield one inch of ground except as he is driven back by the power of heavenly messengers." GC 559.

Christ cast out demons by the power of His word.

"It was by His word that Jesus healed disease and cast out demons." GW 250.

The casting out of demons is a miracle.

"'Master,' he (John) said, 'we saw one casting out devils in Thy name, and he followeth not us; and we forbade him, because he followeth not us.' James and John had thought that in checking this man they had in view their Lord's honor; they began to see that they were jealous of their own. They acknowledged their error, and accepted the reproof of Jesus, 'Forbid him not: for there is no man which *shall do a miracle in My name,* that can lightly speak evil of Me.'" DA 437.

Satan cannot force us to sin against our wills.

"While we should be keenly alive to our exposure to the assaults of unseen and invisible foes, we are to be sure that they cannot harm us *without gaining our consent.*" AH 405.

"I was shown that Satan cannot control minds *unless they are yielded to his control.*" 1 T 301.

"No man without his own consent can be overcome by Satan. The tempter has no power to control the will or to force the soul to sin. He may distress, but he cannot contaminate. He can cause agony, but not defilement." GC 510.

"In no case can Satan obtain dominion over the thoughts, words, and actions, *unless we voluntarily open the door and invite him to enter.*" AH 402.

Either God or Satan controls the Mind.

"Either God or Satan controls the mind; and the life shows so clearly that none need mistake to which power you yield allegiance. Every one has an influence either for good or for evil." FE 89.

"*Either the evil angels or the angels of God are controlling the minds of men.* Our minds are given to the control of God or to the control of the powers of darkness; and it would be well for us to inquire where we are standing today..." 6BC 1120

"*If permitted* the evil angels will work (captivate and control) the minds of men until they have no mind or will of their own." MS 64, 1904

We can keep Satan from gaining entrance.

"Fearful is the condition of those who resist the divine claims and yield to Satan's temptations, until God gives them up to the control of evil spirits. But those who follow Christ are ever safe under His watchcare. Angels that excel in strength are sent from heaven to protect them. *The wicked one cannot break through the guard which God has stationed about His people.*" GC 517.

God never ignores a cry for help.

"God does not control our minds without our consent; but every man is free to choose what power he will have to rule over him. None have fallen so low, none are so vile, but that they may find deliverance in Christ.... *No cry from a soul in need, though it fail of utterance in words, will be unheeded.*" MH 93.

"Satan and his angels are unwilling to lose their prey. They contend and battle with holy angels, and the conflict is severe. And if those who have erred continue to plead, and in deep humility confess their wrongs, *angels who excel in strength will prevail and wrench them from the power of the evil angels.*" MYP 60.

"Nothing is apparently more helpless, yet really more invincible, than the soul that feels its nothingness and relies wholly on the merits of the Saviour. *God would send every angel in heaven to the aid of such a one, rather than allow him to be overcome.*" 7 T 17.

Satan a Defeated Foe

"...Henceforth Christ's followers are to *look upon Satan as a conquered foe.* Upon the cross Jesus was to gain the victory for them; that victory He desired them to accept as their own." MH 94.

We may have all the help that Christ had.

"The life that Christ lived in this world, men and women can live through His power and under His instruction. *In their conflict with Satan they may have all the help that He had.* They may be more than conquerors through Him who loved them and gave Himself for them." 9 T 22.

It was God's plan that the healing gifts be continued.

"Souls possessed with evil spirits will present themselves before us. We must cultivate the spirit of earnest prayer mingled with genuine faith to save them from ruin, and this will confirm our faith. *God designs that the sick, the unfortunate, and those possessed of evil spirits shall hear His voice through us* " Spaulding-Magan Collection, p. 89.

"The church is not now the separate and peculiar people she was when the fires of persecution were kindled against her. How is the gold become dim! how is the most fine gold changed! I saw that if the church had always retained her peculiar, holy character, the power of the Holy Spirit which was imparted to the disciples would still be with her. *The sick would be healed, devils would be rebuked and cast out, and she would be mighty, and a terror to her enemies.*" EW 227.

"We are to feed the hungry, clothe the naked, and comfort the suffering and afflicted...through His servants God designs that *the sick*, the unfortunate, and *those possessed of evil spirits shall hear His voice.* Through His human agencies He desires to be a comforter such as the world knows not." MH 106.

Evil Angels Cause Accidents

"I saw that in our journeying from place to place, Satan has frequently placed his evil angels in our path *to cause accidents* which would destroy our lives; but holy angels were sent upon the ground to deliver. Several accidents have placed my husband and myself in great peril, and our preservation has been wonderful. I saw that we were the special objects of Satans attacks, because of our interest in and connection with the work of God." 1T 347

APPENDIX B

ELLEN WHITE AND DEMONIC HARASSMENT

There is one almost universally held misconception that must be forever trashed. Many people believe that Christians have total immunity from demonic attack. The opposite is true—we are the *special* objects of satanic wrath. The following experiences of Ellen G. White uphold the latter view. In addition, she predicted that "many of God's people will be overcome." We feel keenly that if God's people were protected by the truth of demonic workings, much of this loss would be prevented.

Demonic Pain and Ellen White

"Since coming to this meeting, I have passed through a strange experience. One day, after appearing before the conference to read some matters to you, the burden that was upon my soul continued to press upon me after I returned to my room. *I was in distress of mind.* That night I could not seem to lose myself in sleep. It seemed as if evil angels were right in the room where I was. And while I was suffering in mind, it seemed as if I was suffering *great bodily pain.* My right arm, which through the years has nearly always been preserved from disease and suffering, seemed powerless. I could not lift it. Then I had a most severe, *excruciating pain in the ear; then most terrible suffering in the jaw.* It seemed as if I must scream. But I kept saying, 'Lord you know all about it.'

"I was in perfect agony. It seemed that *my brain and every part of my body was suffering.* At times I would rise up and think, 'I will not lie here another moment.' Then I would think, 'You will only arouse those that are in the house, and they cannot do anything for you.' And so I kept looking to the Lord, and saying, 'You know all about this pain.' The suffering continued, *at times in the jaw, and then in the brain,* and then in *other members of the body,* until nearly daylight. Just before the break of day I fell asleep for about an hour.

"My arm is all right this morning. *Legions of evil angels were in that room,* and if I had not clung by faith to the Lord, I do not know what might have become of me.

*"I shall never be able to give you a description of the satanic forces that were in that room,...*but since standing before you the next morning, I have had no suffering.

"Light has been coming to me that unless we have more evident movings of the Spirit of God, and greater manifestations of divine power working in our midst, *many of God's people will be overcome. Satanic agencies will come in as they came to me. But we cannot afford to yield to the power of the enemy"* (TDWG 36).

Note: Ellen White used her own painful experience to predict that direct satanic attacks on God's people would become more common. Like hers, these attacks might come in the form of pain—mysterious, irrational, undiagnosable pain. Pain that is organic generally can be localized. Our experience has taught us that if a pain moves from one part of the body to another in an unpredictable pattern, as described in the experience of Ellen White, it is suspiciously demonic. In these cases when the demon leaves the pain he has caused is gone.

(See Page 246 for further information about demonic pain)

Allergy

"The first of October, 1858, Mrs. White was given a vision in which she was shown that at some place in our contemplated journey *Satan was going to make a powerful attack upon her...*

"While journeying by train Mrs. White's face became inflamed just under the eyes...she was obliged to take to her bed. The inflammation increased for two days, depriving her of sleep, as well as preventing her from taking any part in the meetings. Her head was swollen so that both eyes were closed, and her face was so disfigured that it no longer looked like that of a human being...the enemy was striving hard to cause her to murmur against God. Thus things continued till the end of the meetings.

"After the meetings had closed Elder White said to me, *"Brother John, this is the very attack upon my wife of which we were warned in Rochester.* You remember the promise was there made that if we would take hold together and hold her up by faith, not letting go for a moment when the struggle came, *the power of the enemy would be broken, and she would be delivered.* Let us go in at once and have a praying season."

"We went into the room where Mrs. White was confined to her bed, and engaged in earnest prayer. In about ten minutes after we began to pray the power of the Lord came down and filled the room. Mrs. White was instantly relieved of all pain...This was about five o'clock in the afternoon. By seven o'clock the swelling had all disappeared upon her face, and she attended the meeting that evening, to all appearances as well as ever." (GSAM 335-337).

Note: Not all allergy is demonic, but in certain difficult cases that possibility ought not to be ignored.

Strokes

"In the vision at Lovett's Grove, most of the matter I had seen twelve years before concerning the great controversy of the ages between Christ and Satan was repeated, and I was instructed to write it out. I was shown that while *I should have to contend with the powers of darkness, for Satan would make strong efforts to hinder me,* yet I must put my trust in God, and angels would not leave me in the conflict" (LS 162).

"Little did they realize the anger of Satan because of this revelation of his character and wiles, or the intensity of his determination to defeat the plans for the writing and publishing of the proposed book. Arriving at Jackson, Michigan, en route to Battle Creek, they visited their old friends at the home of Daniel R. Palmer. At this time Mrs. White was in usual health, and the following experience, as given in her own words came as a complete surprise" (4 SP 508, 509).

"As I was conversing with Sister Palmer, my tongue refused to utter what I wished to say, and seemed large and numb. A strange cold sensation struck my heart, passed over my head, and down my right side. For a time I was insensible (unconscious) but was aroused by the voice of earnest prayer. I tried to use my left limbs, but they were perfectly useless.

"I was shown in vision that in the sudden attack at Jackson, *Satan intended to take my life, in order to hinder the work I was about to write, but angels of God were sent to my rescue"* (LS 162).

Note: At this time Ellen White was 31 years old—very young for a "real Stroke." Can a demonic attack of this nature occur and perhaps cause death? Ellen White's answer is "Yes."

Ellen White in Depression

"On our way home it seemed to me that *Satan had stepped in* and was troubling Edson. We found the child at the point of death...Satan had wanted to hinder the work of God, so he afflicted the child, but he was beaten back by faith in God, and His Name shall have the glory.

"When Satan found that he could not take the life of the child, he tempted me that God had left me or the child would have been healed when we first prayed for him. I sank under this temptation in despair...*My heart seemed within me like lead, but God delivered me that eve, and Satan's power was broken*" (Biography, Vol.1 Pg. 182).

Note: Ellen White, for the moment, believed Satan's lie. He told her that God had forsaken her. When she accepted this lie as truth she went into depression. It is of interest to notice that she knew exactly when Satan's power was broken. She spoke of this break in his power as "Deliverance."

Conclusion

Contrary to popular opinion, God's people are the special objects of Satan's attacks. Our ignorance of this fact gives him a special advantage over us. It is the prayer of the author that this book will give you wisdom.

"I was shown that Satan's power is *especially exercised upon the people of God*. Many were presented before me in a doubting despairing condition. The infirmities of the body affect the mind. A cunning and powerful enemy attends our steps and employs his strength and skill in trying to turn us out of the right way. And it is too often the case that *the people of God are not on their watch, therefore are ignorant of his devices*. He works which will best conceal himself from view, and he often gains his object." 1T 304

Does Satan harass God's consecrated people? Does he take human life? Does he afflict the human body? Can he cause disease? Does He cause allergies? Can he bring depression and other emotional ills? Does he cause pain which defies medical diagnosis? Indeed he does all these things; often to the bewilderment and consternation of the finest of medical professionals. The answer to all of these is unquestionably, Yes!

A Warfare Prayer

The following "Warfare Prayer" has proved to be powerful in spiritual battle. Satan hates this prayer. In essence, this is the prayer which the demons controlling Paula Green would not let her read. Others have been able to read it only with great difficulty and effort.

This prayer was originally written by a Dr. Matthews. It lays claim to the great Bible truths which Satan cannot deny; It holds out the Bible promises which the true believer can claim. However, we must remember that this prayer is not a magic formula or an Aladdin's lamp. It has meaning only as it expresses the sincere heart-cry of the one who prays it. The power is not in the prayer, but in God and His Word and the faith of the one who prays.

Occasionally, I use this prayer in Spiritual Warfare. I ask the one for whom we are interceding to read the prayer silently. If he or she finds himself or herself in harmony with the prayer, then I ask that person to read it orally, as a personal prayer coming from the heart. It is at that point that some persons have experienced extreme difficulty in reading the prayer because of interference by the enemy. This interference may come in the form of blurred vision, inability to speak, or extreme mental confusion. In some cases the enemy, working through the victim, has attempted to destroy the paper on which the prayer was typed. I suggest that this prayer be read privately and aloud.

Heavenly Father,

I bow in worship and praise before you. I ask for a covering of your holy angels for my protection during this time of prayer. I surrender myself to you unreservedly in every area of my life. I take a stand against all the workings of Satan that would hinder my prayers. I address myself only to the true and living God and refuse any interference from Satan or his agents during my devotions.

Satan, I command you, in the name of the Lord Jesus Christ, to leave my presence with all your demons. I bring the blood of the Lord Jesus Christ between us.

Heavenly Father, You are worthy to receive all glory, praise, and honor. I now renew my allegiance to you and ask that the blessed Holy Spirit would teach me how to pray as I ought. I thank you, Heavenly Father, that you loved me so much that you sent your only Son into the world to die in my place. I am thankful that the Lord Jesus Christ stands at your right hand to intercede for me. I praise you that my sins are forgiven and I am washed in the blood of the Lamb. I rejoice in the hope of eternal life; I thank you for the robe of perfect righteousness which your Son has provided me. I thank you for His free gift of justification. I rejoice that I have been accounted worthy to be called your child. I accept your offer to be my guide, my daily helper and my strength.

Heavenly Father, come and open my eyes that I might see how great you are and how complete has been your provision for my salvation. In the name of the Lord Jesus Christ, I take my place with Him in the heavenlies with all principalities and power of darkness and wicked spirits under my feet.

I am thankful for the victory that Lord Jesus Christ won for me on the Cross. I renew my faith in the power of His resurrection to give me overcoming grace. Because I am seated with the Lord Jesus Christ in heavenly places; I now declare that all principalities and powers and all wicked spirits are subject to me in the name of the Lord Jesus Christ.

Heavenly Father, I am thankful for the complete armor you have provided. I put on the girdle of truth, the breastplate of righteousness, the sandals of peace, the helmet of salvation. I lift up the shield of faith against all the fiery darts of the enemy. I take in my hand the sword of the Spirit, the Word of God. Guide me today through your Word against all the forces of evil. I wear your whole armor in full assurance of your total protection.

I am grateful, Heavenly Father, that the Lord Jesus Christ spoiled all principalities and powers and made a show of them openly and triumphed over them. I claim the merits of His victory in my daily life. I now reject all the insinuations, the accusations, and the temptations of Satan. I know that your Word is truth. I commit myself, Heavenly Father, to live my life in the joy of obedience to your word. I want above all things to have sweet fellowship with you. Open my eyes and show me anything in my life that interferes with our fellowship. Occupy my life that there be no place for Satan to gain an advantage over me. Show me my hidden weaknesses. I want a full measure of the ministry of the Holy Spirit in my life.

I surrender myself that the old man of sin might die. I desire to live as a new person in Christ in the glory of His resurrection power. I give up my old way of living and ask that the new man in Christ be made alive in me. I now put off the old nature with its selfishness, and I put on the new nature with its love. I put off the old nature with its fear and I put on the new nature with its courage. I put off the old nature with its weakness and I put on the new nature with its strength. I put off today the old nature with all its deceitful lusts and I put on the new nature with all its righteousness and purity.

I choose to live in the certainty of His ascension and the glorification of the Son of God where all principalities and powers were made subject to Him. I claim my place in Christ, victorious with Him, over all the enemies of my soul.

Blessed Holy Spirit, I pray that you would fill me. Come into my life, tread down every idol and cast out every foe.

I am thankful, Heavenly Father, for the guidance of your Word. Make me humble to accept its correction, and strong to believe its promises. I am thankful that your word assures me of every spiritual blessing in heavenly places in Christ Jesus.

I praise you that you have given me a new and living hope by the resurrection of Jesus Christ from the dead. I am thankful that you have made provision for me to live filled with the Spirit of God. May love, joy and self-control fill my life. I recognize that this is your will for me, and I therefore reject and resist all the endeavors of Satan and of his demons to rob me of the peace of God. I hold up the shield of faith against all the doubts, accusations and insinuations that Satan would put in my mind. I claim the fullness of the joy of living within the revealed will of God.

I am thankful, Heavenly Father, for your assurance that the weapons of my warfare are able to pull down even the greatest of the enemy's strongholds. I ask that every imagination and every high thing that exalts itself against my relationship with you be cast down. I desire that every thought of my mind be brought into obedience to the Lord Jesus Christ. I pray that even the silent meditations of my heart will be acceptable to you. I smash every plan of Satan which he has formed against me.

I thank you, Heavenly Father, that you have not given me the spirit of fear, but of power and of love and peace in a sound mind. I break every stronghold that Satan has formed against my doing your will. I choose to make my every decision and choice in harmony with your holy will as revealed in your word. I smash the strongholds of Satan formed against my body today. I give my body to you, recognizing that it is your temple; I invite your Holy Spirit to dwell within me.

Heavenly Father, I pray that at all times you would quicken me; show me the way that Satan is hindering and tempting and lying and counterfeiting and distorting the truth in my life. Make me aggressive in prayer and constant in seeking your will. Make me alert mentally to think only your thoughts after you. O' Heavenly King, sit on the throne of my heart and make my mind and my life as your own this day and always.

Again, I now cover myself with the blood of the Lord Jesus Christ. I invite your Holy Spirit to sanctify my entire life— spirit, soul and body. I completely surrender myself to you. I reject all discouragement. You are the God of all hope. You have proven your power over all Satanic forces by the victory of Calvary. I claim this victory as my own through the all-prevailing name of the Lord Jesus Christ.

Amen.

Understanding Matthew Seven

A passage of Scripture in Matthew Seven, previously given little notice, has of recent years become a focus of attention. One passage is believed by many to teach that God's church should studiously avoid any belief in or practice of a Deliverance Ministry. I refer to Matthew 7:22, 23.

> "Many will say to me in that day, Lord, Lord, have we not prophesied in thy name? and in thy name have cast out devils? and in thy name done many wonderful works? And then will I profess unto them, I never knew you: depart from me, ye that work iniquity" (Matt. 7:22, 23).

Eternal destinies hang on the correct interpretation of this passage. A people are described who are an abhorrence to the Lord, yet working in His name. The context shows that this is an end-time, judgment-day event. It carries an atmosphere of urgency. The seriousness of the Lord's warning is beyond any doubt. Souls are in the balance—souls for whom Christ died.

Three Possible Interpretations

There are at least three possible conclusions and interpretations of this passage—all of them worthy of our close attention

1) That the Lord disapproves of *all* Deliverance Ministry; that there is little place or need for it in God's end-time church.

2) That evil men in the End-time will take a valid, scriptural ministry and prostitute it into a form of show-business. The Lord condemns this in no uncertain terms.

3) While the Lord disapproves of unholy ministers, there are times when God will honor His name above the character of the men who speak His name.

The First Interpretation Examined

Does Matthew 7:21-23 delete or dilute the Deliverance Ministry from the end-time work of the Gospel Commission? We think not. We submit five scriptural reasons:

1. **The Harmony of Scripture:** The Word of God is always in harmony with itself. Jesus would not *condemn* the Deliverance Ministry in chapter seven of Matthew, and then in chapter ten *authorize* and *empower* His disciples to do what He had earlier condemned. The problem is with men—not a ministry.

"When he had called unto him his twelve disciples, he gave them power against unclean spirits, to cast them out, and to heal all manner of sicknesses and all manner of disease" (Matt.10:1).

Our righteous Lord would never give His disciples the power to perform a "work of iniquity." We believe this passage censures evil men—not an evil ministry. These must not be confused.

2. The Ordination of the Ministry:

"And he ordained twelve that they should be with Him, and that He might send them forth to preach, and to have power to heal sicknesses and to cast out devils" (Mk 3:14,15)

We should fear to alter or dilute in any way this original Ministerial ordination. There is real danger in that officially we may accept the entire ordination in principle and deny it in policy or practice. We know that the world still needs the preaching of the gospel; we are very positive that sick people have need of healing; yet helping those oppressed by Satan meets with subtle opposition. The Lord wants us to carefully and intelligently carry out the full ordination. This is a demon-ridden world and it is dying before our eyes. May God help us!

3. The Model Ministry of our Lord:

"How God anointed Jesus of Nazareth with the Holy Spirit and power, and how He went about doing good and healing all that were under the power of the devil, because God was with Him" (Acts 10:38 NIV).

The gospels portray Jesus as busy helping the oppressed. The violent men of Gadara and the lustful Mary Magdalene come to mind. Has the sinful behavior of mankind changed? Is the world less violent now? Is this a less lustful world now? Might the ministry that Jesus applied to these problems be equally valid now? Have we become so sophisticated that this ministry does not enter our minds? He did this kind of work because "God was with Him." Might God be with us if we did not labor to discount a proper ministry? We need to think about it. If we compare the model ministry of the Lord with that of the contemporary church, there is little resemblance. An intelligent, Biblically oriented restoration is long overdue.

4. His Parting legacy to His church:

"And he said unto them, Go into all the world and preach the gospel to every creature... *And these signs shall follow them that believe. In my name they shall cast out devils;* they shall speak with new tongues; they shall take up serpents; and if they drink any deadly thing, it shall not hurt them; and they shall lay hands on the sick, and they shall recover" (Mark 16:17, 18).

In these parting words He emphasized what was uppermost on his mind. His burden was that the work of His church include the whole of the original commission. He specifically included the Deliverance Ministry. To Him, this was a matter of prime importance. It should be no less to us. We must not diminish or detract from what we know to be the express will of our Lord!

5. The Comments of Ellen White on Mark 16:

"They shall lay hands on the sick and they shall recover... Christ came to heal the sick, to proclaim deliverance to the captives of Satan... He imparted His life to the sick, the afflicted, *those possessed of demons. He turned none away who came to receive His healing power...* When virtue from Christ entered into those poor souls, they were convicted of sin, and many were healed of their spiritual diseases, as well as their physical maladies. *The gospel still possesses the same power and why should we not today witness the same results?"* (DA 823).

What is the answer to this rhetorical question, "Why not today?" We are assured that the same result is still available. This passage also speaks of *belief*. Might *unbelief* be our problem? Might we have some of the form of Godliness but unconsciously deny the power? (2 Tim. 3:5). Might we be turning oppressed people away? Is it possible that we do not recognize possession when we see it? Possession can easily be interpreted as a psychosis or a "behavior problem."

In summary, we find no internal evidence in either the Bible or the Writings that the Deliverance Ministry has been omitted or diminished in the work of God's end-time church. The commission stands exactly as given by our Lord. The needs of the human race are the same and increasing. There is a work to be done that must not be neglected. We must be cautious, but also careful not to curtail the commission as authorized by the Lord.

Examining the Second Interpretation

I will here refresh your mind that the matter under discussion is how to interpret Matthew 7:21-23.

> "Many will say to me in that day, Lord, Lord, have we not prophesied in thy name? and in thy name have cast out devils? and in thy name done many wonderful works? And then will I profess unto them, I never knew you: depart from me, ye that work iniquity" (Matt. 7:22, 23).

In 1983 the Biblical Research Institute released a Report on Deliverance Ministry and Spiritual Warfare. It issued a number of strong cautions based on Matthew 7:22, 23.

Page 58 of the Report sounds the following warning:

> "The church is also highly conscious of the fact that our Lord foretold false (and apparently successful) efforts at casting out demons, by professing Christians, just prior to His second coming to this earth; and He emphatically disassociates Himself from such activity in the strongest terms."

There is no doubt that Matthew Seven delivers one of the strongest warnings ever given to man. This warning applies now! Day and night on American television is displayed what is called Deliverance Ministry and Healing. These manifestations are nothing short of horrifying and blasphemous. Large halls and theaters are seen, filled with people who have come to "watch the show." Indeed it is "show-business." Evil men have taken a valid, scriptural ministry and have prostituted the provisions of the gospel to their own gain. The Lord condemns this in no uncertain terms. The Report has made a correct judgment— but failed in its legitimate application.

The people described in this text are professedly Christian. Because everything is done in the name of the Lord the laity are disarmed. They feel totally secure. But the power manifested in these demonstrations is satanic. The devil is a counterfeiter. Both the people and the ministers are in a deception. The Adventist church has a mandate from God to sound an alarm. Are we doing it? If we were to adequately warn the people of Protestant America about this massive deception—overnight we would be a very unpopular people. We must tactfully and judiciously take that risk. The Cross of our Lord is proof that God's work cannot be done without pain and risk. We must not let our interest in public relations mute our testimony. If we fail perhaps the rocks will cry out. We have a responsibility. Let us not shrink from our duty!

A Word Study

The BRI Report has correctly chosen the word "disassociation" to express the utter revulsion of the Lord toward this spectacle. However, in that connection, there is a crucial question. From what did the Lord disassociate himself? A careful reading of the gospels make exceedingly clear that the Lord was "disassociating" himself from *evil men—not a proper ministry.* It is *men* whom He told to depart from Him.

A point of danger: There is obviously a close relationship between these reprobate men and the doctrine of Deliverance. The Lord rejects these men. We must take extreme care not to use this passage to oppose a Deliverance Ministry. People who need help are more numerous now than at any time in world history. Regretfully the Report is interpreted almost universally as a virtual "stop-order" against helping the oppressed. I must believe that this impression is unintentional. If this were intentional it would be a serious matter. God has commissioned His church and ordained its ministry to rescue people from the control of Satan. This is the purpose of salvation. The conservative approach of the Report appears to interfere with our duty to carry out this part of His three-fold plan to save mankind. This is more than a technical question. It is extremely serious. Jesus died to set the captives free (Luke 4:18). To diminish the benefits of His death on the Cross in even the smallest degree is indeed a major matter.

The Lord refused to "disassociate." The scriptural record shows that the Apostle John tried to lead Jesus to disavow the Deliverance Ministry of an unknown stranger. Jesus strongly refused.

> "Teacher," said John, "we saw a man driving out demons in your name and we told him to stop, because he was not one of us. Do not stop him, Jesus said, no one who does a miracle in my name can in the next moment say anything bad about me" (Mark 9:38, 39 NIV).

Jesus refused to "disassociate" Himself from this ministry even when it was done by an unknown stranger. He took that position then. He would take the same position today.

In Conclusion: Did the Lord in Matthew Seven intend to restrict the work of helping oppressed people? Did Jesus repudiate the casting out of demons—the Deliverance Ministry—if you please—at any time? Has he "disassociated" himself from a valid ministry? We surely believe not.

The world wide effect of the Report has been that any Adventist pastor or layman who prays with or for "those possessed with evil spirits" (to use the words of Ellen White in MH 106) almost immediately becomes suspect. World-wide, opposition to any and all Deliverance has been instantaneous and vigorous. We must be careful lest we tamper with the express will of Christ and as a result souls are lost.

Application Number Three

In the Scriptures and in the Writings, there are a few examples of God using unconverted men to do a sacred work. In such cases, we must differentiate between the men and their ministry.

Jonah: God saved Nineveh through the ministry of this racially bigoted and reluctant preacher. God's love for the people of Nineveh was stronger than the character of His prophet. To the despair of Jonah, this wicked city repented. The story of Jonah is not a study in whale anatomy. It is a picture of a marvelous God who manifests His love and deliverance through an unconsecrated minister.

Judas Iscariot: "The Savior did not repulse Judas. He gave him a place among the twelve. He trusted him to do the work of an evangelist. He endowed him with power to heal the sick and *to cast out devils*. But Judas did not come to the point of surrendering himself fully to Christ" (DA 717).

A Vile Adventist Minister: "A case was held up before me of a minister who was sent to pray for a sick woman... He went and prayed in earnest and she prayed; she believed the minister to be a man of God. Physicians had given her up to die of consumption. She was immediately healed. She arose and prepared supper, a thing that she had not done for ten years. Now the minister was vile, his life was corrupt, and yet here was a great work" (2 SM 347).

It was this woman's faith that brought about her healing, but *not* until a *vile and corrupt minister* came did God heal her. It is impossible to say whether there might be an element of this included in the Lord's warning in Matthew Seven.

Conclusion

1) We find that both the Bible and the Writings affirm the gospel commission as originally given by our Lord. It stands unmodified, undiluted, and in full force till the work of God is done. Two thousand years ago the leaders of Israel fiercely opposed the Deliverance Ministry of the Lord Jesus Christ. He called their opposition the greatest of all sins (Matt. 12:32). The scene has changed; faces have changed; but in our effort to prevent fanaticism, we must take extreme care not to repeat their mistake. The consequences are eternal.

> "In the days of Christ the leaders of Israel were powerless to resist the work of Satan....They disputed over insignificant technicalities, and practically denied the most essential truths. *Thus infidelity was sown broadcast. God's word was robbed of its power, and evil spirits worked their will*" (DA 257).

2) We feel that the voice of the church should properly be raised against the prostitution of the Deliverance Ministry as currently seen in much of evangelical Protestantism. This is the emphatic and authoritative warning that we should declare in harmony with Matthew seven. As a church we ought not to avoid this unpleasant responsibility.

3) How much and how often the Lord honors his Name above the character of certain ministers is difficult to determine. Perhaps there are two tests —the test of fruit and the test of time in the lives of those who are benefited.

Rejoice! Rejoice!

The Lord is coming. The final battle of Armageddon will soon be fought. The hostages of planet Earth will soon be safely within the walls of the New Jerusalem. There we shall eternally praise Him who fought a victorious battle and has set every unwilling captive free.

APPENDIX D

THE MACKIN CASE

There is little in the extensive ministry of Ellen White that is more misunderstood than her counsel given in 1908 to a Brother and Sister Ralph Mackin. There are three sources for the Mackin story — 3 *Selected Messages* Pp. 363-378; the *Review and Herald* , August 10, 17, 24, 1972; and Volume 6 of the E. G. White biography, Pages 171-174. We must consider this case in some detail. A misinterpretation of her interview with the Mackins has had a destructive effect on the thinking of many on whether or not to intervene in behalf of oppressed people. The following sentence is often quoted:

> "The work of *declaring* persons possessed of the devil, and then praying with them and *pretending* to cast out the evil spirits, is *fanaticism* which will bring into disrepute any church which sanctions such work" (3SM 378).

An isolated reading of the above sentence could easily be understood as forbidding anyone to help the oppressed; that *any* effort to help the oppressed is nothing but "pretense" and deception. Is this the message that Ellen White was conveying? I don't think so. What were the Mackins doing that, if it were continued, would bring disrepute upon the church? Here is the record:

The Mackins Were Fanatics

A careful consideration of their activity reveals that Ellen White's counsel had nothing to do with the legitimate "casting out of demons." What they were doing would gain the disapproval of any rational mind. Bear in mind the Mackins openly identified themselves as Adventists. Without question the reputation of Adventism was at stake! What they were doing had to be stopped! Here is a brief description:

1) They were preaching on the streets and were put in jail as a public nuisance.

> They were preaching on a street corner in Toledo, Ohio. Mrs. Mackin was talking in tongues. The *police came and locked them up*. They felt that they were suffering for the sake of the gospel (See RH 8/10/1972).

2) They were *talking in tongues* on the city streets of Mansfield, Ohio.

Under dateline of August 22, 1908 in the Mansfield, Ohio, Newspaper called the *"Daily Shield"* there appeared the following item:

> "Gift of tongues causes trouble, Mackin claims to be master of *Chinese Jargon,* which he says came to him from God. Dissension at camp meeting results in arrest of Mackin, wife and daughter, and two lady companions; they hold services behind prison bars and seem quite proud of the distinction." (RH 8/10/1972).

3) They caused confusion at an Adventist Camp meeting.

> Mrs. Mackin stood out of doors at the camp meeting in Ohio and sang the following words over and over, "He is coming, He is coming, Get ready, Get ready, Receive ye the Holy Ghost." She would sing the word, "Glory," over and over and over again. She could be heard all over the camp grounds." (RH 8/17/1972; 3SM 366).

4) They put on theatrical displays.

> "Satan will come in with bewitching power, through these exhibitions. It is high time you called a halt. If God had given you a special message for his people, you would walk and work with all humility not as though you were on the stage of a theater" (3 SM 377).

> "Your wife, in speech, in song, and in strange exhibitions that are not in accordance with the genuine work of the Holy Spirit, is helping to bring in a phase of fanaticism that would do great injury to the cause of God, if allowed any place in our churches" (3 SM 376).

5 They were openly telling people that they were possessed.

> "The work of *declaring* persons possessed of the devil, and then praying with them and *pretending* to cast out the evil spirits, is fanaticism which will bring into disrepute any church which sanctions such work" (3SM 378).

The circumstances in which they were declaring people to be possessed is not clear. In view of their other antics, it is possible that they were telling people on the city streets that they were possessed. Indeed this would bring disrepute on the church!

6 Mrs. Mackin claimed that she had the gift of Prophecy.

Mrs. Mackin predicted some terrible calamity soon to take place in Toledo (3 SM 365). Nothing took place.

7. They disappeared and left the church.

After the interview with Ellen White at Elmshaven, they disappeared and were never heard from again. (*Biography*, Vol. 6, Page 174) .

We concur completely with the position set forth by Ellen White. This behavior was fanaticism in its most obvious form. We believe that her counsel to them was sound and is still good advice. *However, none of the antics of the Mackins in any way describes the Deliverance Ministry as seen in the Bible or in helping oppressed people today.*

The *pretense and antics* of the Makins is falsely used as proof that Adventists should have nothing to do with helping oppressed people. We believe that this is a defective application. This demands:

Some Further Thinking

Ellen White's counsel to the Makins is widely being interpreted as a blanket cancellation of any ministry for the oppressed. If this were true, it would set up the following contradiction:

1. This interpretation would contradict the Gospel commission.

"In His record of the giving of the commission Mark says, 'He said unto them. Go ye into all the world and preach the gospel to every creature.... And these signs shall follow them that believe; In my name *they shall cast out devils;*...they shall lay hands on the sick, and they shall recover.' *These words are to be literally fulfilled. This is the work the Lord Jesus Christ will do through his appointed agencies*" (Kress Collection 126).

2. This interpretation would condemn her own ministry:

"In my labors in the cause of God, I have *again and again* met those who have been thus possessed and *in the name of the Lord, I have rebuked the evil spirit*" (2SM 353).

3. This interpretation would destroy the example of the Lord.

Our Lord's ministry was full of multiple examples of Deliverance from demonic possession. The need of this ministry is greater now than ever before. The need will grow and intensify as we approach the final conflict.

"The period of Christ's personal ministry among men was the time of greatest activity for the forces of the kingdom of darkness... Satan summoned all his forces, and at every step contested the work of Christ...*So it will be in the great final conflict of the controversy between righteousness and sin*. While new life and light and power are descending from on high upon the disciples of Christ, a new life is springing up from beneath, and energizing the agencies of Satan" (DA 257).

4. This interpretation of the Mackin case builds a wall of doubt and unbelief between human need and the power of God.

"And he called his twelve disciples together, and gave them *power* and authority over all devils and to cure diseases" (Luke 9:1; DA 823).

There is no scriptural evidence that this power and authority have ever been withdrawn. It is our unbelief that has held God away from meeting human need. The position of the Spirit of Prophecy is that we may still work in His power—power that would be seen in the healing of the sick and delivering those possessed of evil spirits. Read this quotation carefully.

"God designs that the *sick*, the unfortunate, *those possessed with evil spirits*, shall hear His voice through us.... There are needy close by us; the suffering are in our very borders. We must try to help them. By the grace of Christ, *the sealed fountains of earnest, Christ-like work are to be unsealed*... The time of need and of necessity makes plain our great need of a present, all powerful God, in whom is everlasting strength and in whose power we may work." (Ms 65b, 1898, Spaulding-Magan, page 89).

5. This interpretation creates incompatible testimony.

In the package of Mackin errors was one of their *pretending* to cast out demons. Ellen White's displeasure is unmistakable. Her disapproval of them has been almost universally accepted as a blanket cancellation of Deliverance Ministry. This is an unwarranted assumption. I will explain why. Balanced scholarship assembles and considers all available information on a given subject before reaching a conclusion. When this is done, it will be found that Ellen White is not an opponent of Deliverance—She was a careful advocate. Consider this statement that needs little interpretation:

> "Souls possessed of evil spirits will present themselves before us. We must *cultivate* the spirit of earnest prayer mingled with genuine faith to save them from ruin, and this will *confirm our faith*. God designs that the sick, the unfortunate, *those possessed with evil spirits shall hear His voice through us*. Through His human agents He desires to be a comforter *such as the world has never before seen*" (Spaulding-Magan, p. 89, 1898).

This quotation says that we should "cultivate" the spirit of prayer to help the possessed. The words—*cultivate* and *cancel* carry diametrically opposite meanings. What the Mackins were doing had to be canceled. But the true ministry must be "cultivated." In its final phase this ministry would take on a character "such as the world had never before seen." We believe that time has come.

It is high-time that we cast away our fears of a defeated foe. The enemy is attacking on all fronts. God's people are being hurt and even destroyed. The church must now renew its God-given authority. The "sealed fountains" must now be "unsealed." As needs arise, we must do the work the Lord appointed and set the captives free (Luke 4:18). We must not allow a misunderstanding of the Mackin experience to prevent the will of God being done in helping the oppressed to go free (Isa. 58:6).

APPENDIX E

APPENDIX F

"BEWARE OF DELIVERANCE MINISTRIES"

An article with the above title recently appeared in one of our widely-circulated denominational magazines. The writer--one of my fellow pastors--took a strong stand against all Deliverance Ministry. I feel that I must make a kind, but vigorous rebuttal.

The author referred to the counsel of Ellen White to a Brother and Sister Ralph Mackin. In 1908 this couple came to her for guidance. The author interprets her counsel to them as forever opposing any ministry for oppressed people. I agree that this couple were truly fanatics. They needed correction; but to build this unjustifiable conclusion from her counsel to the Mackins is, in my opinion, a serious misinterpretation of her writings, beyond this it does violence to the Bible itself. (See App. F).

I have carefully read all of Ellen White's counsel to the Mackins. Contrary to the conclusions in the magazine article, I find many implications from Ellen White that a legitimate Deliverance Ministry would be restored at the end of time. It would come as a much needed work of the Holy Spirit. This is Ellen White's statement:

> "There will be things that will transpire at the very close of this earth's history, it has been presented to me, similar to some of the things that you have presented; but I cannot say anything on these things now" (3 SM 367).

Is it possible that God was telling us that "at the very close of this earth's history"--during the time in which you and I are living--there would be a genuine deliverance ministry in contrast to the false and pretended ministry of the Mackins?

It seems to me that this is a valid conclusion, especially in light of three other statements Ellen White made to them.

Work of the Holy Spirit will be Declared Fanaticism.

During the course of their interview , Ralph Mackin asked her,

> "But is it true that *when the Holy Spirit does come,* as stated in your works, that *many will turn against it, and declare that it is fanaticism?*"

217

Notice Ellen White's answer:

> *"Of course they will; and for this reason we ought to be very guarded"* (3 SM 375 Emphasis supplied).

One other thing she said to them:

> "In the future we shall have special tokens of the influence of the Spirit of God—especially at time when our enemies are strongest against us. The time will come when we shall see some strange things; but just in what way—whether similar to some of the experiences of the disciples after they received the Holy Spirit following the ascension of Christ—I cannot say" (3SM 369).

In view of this counsel, we must stand guard lest a departure from what we consider "normal" be tagged as fanaticism. Things we may consider "strange" will really be a token of the influence of the Spirit of God. Israel did not recognize the miracle working power of the Second Person of the Godhead. We are in equal danger of not recognizing the Third Person.

Earlier Information

Ellen White's reply to Ralph Mackin's question is in perfect harmony with statements she had made earlier:

> "There is to be in the churches *a wonderful manifestation of the power of God*...In the manifestation of that power which lightens the earth with the Glory of God, they will see only something that *will arouse their fears*, and they will brace themselves to *resist it. Because the Lord does not work according to their expectations and ideals, they will oppose the work,* 'Why' they say, 'should we not know the Spirit of God since we have been in the church so many years?" (RH 12/23/1890, Emphasis supplied).

Admittedly, Ellen White does not give a detailed description of how that power will lighten the earth with the glory of God. However, we must not rule out the possibility that the coming of the Holy Spirit in power might include the restoration of Spiritual Warfare with its remarkable physical, spiritual, and emotional healing. This possibility cannot be dismissed. I will tell you why. Consider carefully the words of the Savior:

"But if I cast out devils *by the Spirit of God*, then the kingdom of God is come unto you" (Matt 12:28).

We are in extremely dangerous territory when we pass judgment on the Deliverance Ministry, because Jesus linked it so tightly to the work of the Holy Spirit.

This magazine article might well be a fulfillment of what Ellen White predicted as a time of "blindness;" of "resisting;" of "fear;" of "considered to be dangerous." I must confess I trembled at this possibility as I read this magazine article.

Whether or not Ellen White was referring to the Deliverance Ministry when she wrote the paragraph quoted above (RH Dec. 23, 1890), I cannot prove. One thing I can say, I have had 15 years experience ministering to those who were demonically oppressed. During these years I have had much opposition. Her word "blindness" fits many a person's negative reaction like the proverbial glove fits the hand.

It is not my desire to embarrass anyone, to attack or to be critical of any of our publications. But I believe we are dealing here with life-and-death issues. These matters must be discussed openly. Human destinies--eternal destinies--are at stake. So I am going to carefully analize this current article. I do so because it appears to fulfill Ellen White's prediction of blind opposition to the work of the Holy Spirit. This is a ministry that leaves no room for error.

Contradictory Conclusions

The author begins his article with an eloquent statement of Biblical truth with which I could not be more in agreement:

> "Jesus gave His church power over all evil, and there is no record of it (sic) being withdrawn. Our failure to conquer evil is not attributable to a divine power shortage, but rather to human negligence, as is evidenced in Matt. 17:14-18. There are many instances recorded in which Satan and his hosts suffered total defeat from Christ's followers exercising faith in His name. *This can and should be the experience of the church today.*" (Emphasis supplied.)

I wholeheartedly agree with every word of the above paragraph, especially his concluding sentence. It is in complete harmony with the teaching of the Bible and the Spirit of Prophecy. *His first paragraph beautifully and accurately summarizes what I have endeavored to say in this entire book.*

The Contradiction: Then an astonishing thing occurs—after this eloquent defense of biblical and historic Deliverance, I was amazed to read only a few paragraphs later, in the same article, by the same author, the following words:

> "The casting out of demons is just another form of this *fanaticism* that now threatens the Adventist church" (Emphasis supplied).

His conclusions in the above two quotations are in total conflict. They contradict each other. The casting out of demons (by whatever name we may choose to call it) can not be an activity which "can and should be the experience of the church today," and at the same time be "just another form of this fanaticism that now threatens the Adventist church." These two concepts are hostile to each other. Both cannot be held as truth at the same time in a rational mind.

The deliverance ministry, conducted in harmony with the Bible, must be either from God or from Satan. It must originate with one or the other, but it cannot come from both. We must stop talking out of both sides of our denominational mouth.

Divisiveness

The writer of the article faults the Deliverance Ministry on the basis of its being a divisive issue. He states that "Every church under its influence has been adversely affected, some to the point of being split."

I wish to make two comments on his observation. Page 357 of the Desire of Ages comes to mind:

> "The Savior bade his disciples not to hope that the world's enmity to the Gospel would be overcome and that after a time its opposition would cease. He said, 'I am not come to send peace but a sword.' *This creating of strife is not the effect of the Gospel, but the result of opposition to it.*"

I heartily agree with these inspired words. Unless I misread the facts, it was pastoral opposition in Michigan not the Deliverance that caused the strife referred to in the magazine.

There is a second point of disagreement. I have yet to see a church "split" over this matter. While this may be true in some cases, my experience has been that church members who are involved in real Spiritual Warfare are led to a more serious study of the Bible and a deeper heart searching. The unity of the church depends upon the outlook of its leadership. Much of what Christ did and taught split the church of His day, but this did not discount His ministry.

We must always remember that *Scripture--not congregational or even denominational approval or acceptance--is the test of truth.* Isaiah 8:20 still gives us the standard by which truth must be measured.

The article goes on to tell how a few months after the "Deliverance," "the church family" disfellowshipped Mike and Debbie (not their real names) for "apostasy into *spiritualism*." I believe that disfellowshipping this Adventist family was a far-reaching mistake. It was a tragedy for Mike and Debbie, but very possibly it was even more tragic for the church. There may have been other members in that church needing help. After the uproar created by leadership, other members would not dare ask for help. The result is that they remain in bondage. The door was not only shut on Mike and Debbie; worse, much worse—it was shut on the Holy Spirit; and it was shut to the needs of people whose names we will not know till the day of judgment.

In response to this article, I have a counter question. I reverse the challenge. Why does the Deliverance Ministry, in which the Lord Jesus Christ was so deeply involved, have no place in our church today? Is it for want of need, or a case of blindness on our part? Why are our ministers not being trained to diagnose this problem? This is a question of utmost importance. It concerns a vital part of the mission of the church. Why are we doing little or nothing? Indeed why are we not investigating without prejudice how to relieve the burdens of oppressed souls? We were told years ago that a great need of this ministry would arise:

"Souls *possessed with evil spirits* will present themselves before us," and "God designs that the sick, the unfortunate, *those possessed with evil spirits* shall hear his voice through us" (MS 65B, 1898).

God has told us not only that those who are demon possessed will come to us for help, but that we are to pray with them and for them; and that "*this will confirm our faith*" (MS 65 B, 1898). But how can our faith be confirmed by this act of the Holy Spirit when we

- refuse to become involved in the experience
- deny that such an experience is needed
- attribute the experience to spiritualism
- consider the experience a form of fanaticism, and
- disfellowship those who are delivered, because of their part in the experience?

May God open our eyes to the reality of a war raging around each of us. Eternal loss of souls is the price of blindness.

Another Look at the Unpardonable Sin

It is customary that we think of individuals committing this sin of all sins. Those of us in the ministry have shuddered as we have seen individuals turn away from transparent truth and call it error simply because the truth did not fit their wishes.

There is yet another aspect to this sin that goes far beyond the individual soul. The leaders of Israel in Christ's day told the people that the work of Christ was satanic. The rank and file of Israel completely trusted the religious judgment of their leaders. Their leaders were wrong. The result was that the entire nation was blindly led to its destruction. In 70 AD there was starvation, cannibalism, and a massacre in Jerusalem—the bitter fruit of unquestioning trust. Trust—but investigate! "Prove all things..." is still God's counsel. (I Thess 5:21).

"Whosoever speaketh a word against the Son of Man," said Christ, " it shall be forgiven him: but whosoever speaketh against the Holy Ghost, it shall not be forgiven him"(Matt 12:32). These words were spoken by our savior when *the gracious works which he had performed through the power of God were attributed by the Jews to Beelzebub*" (PP 405).

"They [the Pharisees] attributed to Satanic agencies the Holy power of God, manifested in the works of Christ. Thus the Pharisees sinned against the Holy Ghost. Stubborn, sullen, iron hearted, they determined to close their eyes to all evidence, and thus they committed the unpardonable sin" (RH Jan. 18, 1898).

"To speak against Christ, charging His work to Satanic agencies and attributing the manifestations of the Spirit to fanaticism is not of itself a damning sin, but the spirit that leads men to make those assertions places them in a position of stubborn resistance where they cannot see spiritual light" (5BC 1092).

A Solemn Statement

"Those who will not act when the Lord calls upon them, but wait for more certain evidence and more favorable opportunities, will walk in darkness, for the light will be withdrawn. *The evidence given one day may never be repeated*" (3T 258).

Will We Repeat Their Mistake?

Dear Reader, you must understand me. As I write these words, I do not stand in a place of judgment—but this article has caused me the deepest kind of concern. The day may come, and even now may be here, when we shall approach the same fork in the road reached by ancient Israel. That place was reached when they criticized and rejected Jesus' ministry for the oppressed. This was a crisis turning point.

Perhaps we too will have to decide whether it is of God or is it of Satan. Two thousand years ago the answer to that question had painful and eternal consequences. Because they were the chosen people of God they thought themselves beyond making a mistake. We must not think ourselves beyond making that same fatal error. I pray God that it will not be so.

If this article which appeared in an official publication of the denomination expresses our official teaching and practice on this part of the Gospel ministry, we are in deep trouble.

A Former Captive Speaks

AUTHOR'S NOTE: In Appendix F, I made an extended reply to a magazine article entitled: "Beware of Deliverance Ministries," written by a fellow minister. If you have not read this Appendix, please do so. I disagree vigorously with his position. His thoughts are contradictory, non-biblical, and at times irrational. He wrote about the Deliverance of a member of his church. His first conviction was that God had intervened to bring freedom to a badly oppressed lady. But within four weeks or less he changed his mind completely. He avoided the family. He had nothing more to do with them. He took the position that the whole experience was a demonic deception. Under his direction the husband, wife, and two children were disfellowshipped.

Her Testimony: This appendix is the first hand testimony of this former captive written about in the article. She became free and is still free. You will see that her testimony is quite different from his. Hers is one of joy and freedom. For purposes of privacy I shall call her Debbie. This is not her real name. The serious reader may secure her real name and the validation of her experience by writing to the publishers of this book. Please enclose a stamped and self-addressed envelope.

Similarities: I was not involved in Debbie's deliverance. But I can say that the description of the events is similar to scores of others which I have witnessed in the last fifteen years. When we pray in the all-powerful name of Jesus Christ, it is not unusual for demons to speak out, object, boast, and beg just as they did in the Lord's own ministry. This does not always happen by any means; but when it does we are not surprised. Our experiences have been comparable to the many found in the biblical record. Debbie's symptoms listed here are not at all unusual.

- Mysterious health problems,
- Childhood abuse,
- Involvement in the occult,
- Fears and Voices,
- Threats,
- Nightmares,
- Inability to pray or to praise God in song,
- Filthy and vulgar language,
- Thoughts of suicide
- Facial Distortion.

Commonality: Before you read Debbie's personal story I am going to reveal a surprising fact: In my fifteen and more years of helping oppressed people, with very few exceptions, these experiences have been those of your spiritual brothers and sisters. They have been members, like Debbie and her husband, of the Seventh-day Adventist Church. They are the people who sit next to you in the pew on Sabbath morning. They may include your doctor, your dentist, your nurse, or even your pastor. I know, for I have witnessed the deliverance of persons in each of these categories. They are people who have become tangled in Satan's web, but who by the grace and power of God have been delivered.

My deeper concerns: As I studied into the relationship between the pastor, his church, and Debbie's family my concerns went far beyond the pastor's article. I was worried about the damage done to this family. Where *are* they now? What was their response to being shunned and treated as they were? Did they leave the Adventist Christian faith? Did they become disillusioned and angry? Did Debbie return to the bondage from which she had been delivered? I wanted to inspect the fruit of this deliverance. This to me would be the critical test of the ministry and the Christian commitment of the family!

Contact: Through information provided by friends I made contact with the family by telephone. Debbie told me that she had read the magazine article. She said it contained many inaccuracies. She totally disagreed with the writer's conclusions. Debbie had already begun to write her version of what had occurred in Michigan. She gave me permission to included a copy of her personal experience in this book.

Her Viewpoint: The way Debbie saw what happened is quite different from that depicted in the article. In addition I can say that I have talked to three other adults who witnessed her Deliverance and the events that followed, and they support Debbie's version of the story.

She is still free: The best news is that Debbie is still rejoicing in her freedom in Christ after those years of terrible bondage. In the next ten pages Debbie's tells of the joy of her liberty. She tells her side of the story of what God did for her and her family in Michigan.

Debbie Tells Her Story

My Childhood Abuse: It is important for you to know a little about my background. I grew up in a home that was physically and sexually abusive. What I am trying to put in words does not do justice to the horrible reality of the abuse that went on.

My dad always had a violent temper. It was worse when he drank. Beatings, verbal abuse, and sexual abuse were normal in the climate in which I grew up. My mom always worked nights. This opened the door for my dad to drink and run around.

I could not look to Mom for protection. That "protection" was not possible anyway because Dad beat Mom also. In your wildest imagination you cannot picture the situation as it really was. I was held at gun point, sexually abused by my father, his friends, and my brothers (although they were abused also!).

Although my brothers were abusive toward me, we were close in many ways. I "raised" my brothers, since Mom and Dad were almost always at work.

As we got older and were more able to defend ourselves, the abuses subsided somewhat. I dreamed of escaping to a different and better life. I wanted to put even the thoughts of my abusive childhood behind me. As I got older and able to make my own decisions, things did not turn out as well as I had hoped. I found myself involved in drugs and alcohol, and dabbling with the occult.

I had no Religious Training: At that point in my life I had no understanding of the reality of either Christ or Satan. Now I am sure that Satan was very active in my childhood home. He was the unseen agent in my years of abuse. One of my brothers died at age 17. My first baby died at birth. I had a battle with cancer (all by the time I was 19). Satan had worked in so many ways.

Growing up, I had known very little about God. Those few times when I did turn to Him, it seemed to me that He never "came through." Since my own father did not love me, I was convinced that this "Father in heaven," this "male image," did not love me either. "Use and abuse"—that was my mother's motto for men, and it became my motto.

My Marriages: After a disastrous first marriage that ended in divorce, I did meet a man with whom I fell in love and whom I eventually married. Lyle (not his real name) is still my husband.

Drug Involvement: Soon after we were married, what seemed to be a perfect dream became a nightmare. We were both involved in drugs, heavy rock music, and concerned only with ourselves—not each other. I now had two children, a son from my first marriage and a daughter by Lyle. He and I clashed on everything. There was a complete lack of harmony in our home.

Seeking something that would make us a happier family, we began to attend a church. As a teenager, Lyle had learned something of Jesus and His love from his grandmother. Eventually we became actively involved in that church as youth advisers. I guess you could say that we thought our good works would make us happy. But it was not long before we left that church. The "friends" we thought we had made at the church no longer called or visited. We were still searching for truth that would help our troubled life-style.

We Become Adventists: My best friend's husband was attending a local university near our home town. They received in the mail a flyer telling about a "Revelation Seminar" to be held on the university campus. We were unsure about going to the meetings at first, but after seeing how excited our friends were, we decided to attend. Largely as a result of these meetings we became members of the Seventh-day Adventist church in August of 1982, and we have remained faithful to its message ever since.

Looking to Jesus: I remember the advice one of the older sisters gave us when we first became members of the church. "Debbie," she said, "always remember that we have a perfect message, but we are not a perfect people. Always keep your eyes on Jesus, not on people." The counsel of this precious sister has helped us to hold fast to our pews many times. I felt more at peace in this church than in any we had attended, but this peace was not to last for long. Satan hates to lose even one soul to Christ. It wasn't long before he went to work. We had been taught that there is victory in Christ, but we were not taught how to obtain that victory until we had been six years in the church.

Employment Problems: When we joined the church, my husband had not had steady work for three years. Our employment problem was doubled when we became Sabbath keepers. He was turned down time after time because of the Sabbath. Lyle finally got a job at an automobile agency in Berrien Springs, Michigan.

Lyle later found work as a machinist in a small town in central Michigan. It was a great job with no Sabbath problems and with full health, dental, and optical insurance. The man who hired Lyle told him that he had once lived next door to a Seventh-day Adventist family, and that he would employ Lyle because of the good impression left by that neighbor. Thank God for Adventist families and neighbors who witness by living their faith!

But about six weeks later—just as we had become nicely settled into our home and job—another "opportunity" opened up. A wood mill at one of our academies offered both Lyle and me work. The move would mean a cut in pay and loss of some benefits. However, there would be one big advantage—we could keep our children in church school. Our son would be ready for the academy the next year. We did not want to have to send him away. So, we moved forty miles further north.

One day while I was working I noticed what I called a blood bubble forming on my right index finger. It grew rather large, so I showed it to my husband who was working nearby. We showed it to my supervisor. He immediately sent me to see an Adventist doctor. He referred me to a specialist who treated my finger and put me on a two-week leave from work. When I returned to work, the same thing happened again. This time my finger required surgery. I was off work for six weeks.

Harassment: The only reason I tell you about my finger is that the enemy took advantage of being alone in the house for six weeks. I had time to reflect about my troubled past. There were memories that did not enter my mind while I was on the job. I began to have spells in which I would black out and feel as though I were dying. It was an awful feeling. Later I learned that these were panic attacks. There were times that I would be awakened—by hands choking me, or being smothered by my pillow. Then the opposite would occur. I would go into such a deep sleep it seemed that I could never wake up. I was being molested by Satan himself.

A Retired Pastor saw the problem: I mentioned these painful experiences to a retired Adventist pastor. His wife was my son's sixth and seventh grade teacher. He asked me if we had ever asked the elders to pray for us. He thought we were being demonically harassed. We told him we had never thought about having special prayer and the matter was dropped. In the meantime, these strange experiences made me think that I was going insane. I must be crazy. Things like this just did not happen to Christians. What was going on? I needed help.

My Friend's Testimony: I called my closest girl friend in Ohio to confide in her and ask her advice. She told me that her family just had a beautiful experience. They had attended a seminar in Bowling Green where they heard a couple explain the reality of the great controversy on the personal level. They were told how victory over demonic oppression is still possible today through Jesus Christ. They told me that their son had terrible things happening to him, but through the power and grace of God he had been set free. This visiting couple named Nelson taught them how to pray and go to Jesus for help. We decided to visit our friends in Ohio and learn more about what had happened.

When we arrived at our friends' home, they explained to us about their son's deliverance from satanic oppression. We could certainly see a big difference in the son. He could now pray and praise the Lord, which he had never done before. The entire family was different. I could see the peace in their home. After much discussion and many tears I knew that I also wanted that same peace in my family. My heart cried out for it, but something in my mind kept saying, "No."

My Need for Help: I knew that these attacks while in my sleep were not normal. These irrational panic attacks were destroying me. I could not go on. I needed help; yet something kept me from making a decision to seek help. Finally our friends and my family prayed that the Lord would not allow Satan to block my mind, that I would have freedom to choose. I prayed that if it was the Lord's will I would be able to make contact with the couple who had prayed with my friend's son. We trusted Jesus to do this for me, and He did. I told my husband to make a phone call to Michigan. The Nelson were located and were soon on the line.

I Talk to Nelsons: My situation was explained to them; then they asked to speak to me. It was all I could do to converse with them. It seemed as though another power was trying to control me. I know now that this was not my imagination. The couple said they would counsel and pray for me if it was God's will. We were to pray the same. After my husband hung up the telephone, we had a season of prayer, but I could not pray. After an hour or so the Nelsons called and said they would meet with us. We told them we would be returning home to Michigan on Sunday. They agreed to come to our home.

Nightmares: That Friday night was a very restless one for me. I had horrible nightmares of my body being contorted in various ways, and of being thrown out of my bed. In the morning we were all preparing to go to church. But I did not want to go. I did not know why, but I felt rebellious about the whole idea. When I went into the bathroom I discovered that I was hemorrhaging very badly. It frightened me as I had just had my period two weeks earlier. I called my girl friend into the bathroom and told her what was happening.

She went into the living room and returned with a copy of *Ministry of Healing* and began to read about the woman with the issue of blood, and what Jesus did for her. But my bleeding did not stop! She told me that Satan was probably furious because of what we planned to do. She prayed for God to give us strength not to become discouraged, but to hold on. I "held on" all right; I held on to that copy of *Ministry of Healing*, even though my bleeding did not stop. At times my whole body shook and trembled, and I found it very difficult to concentrate. I felt as though I wanted to leave—to go somewhere where no one would ever find me.

Suicide Thoughts: We did attend church, although I did not want to be there. The entire day was awful. Thoughts of suicide were never as powerful as they were on that day. I was sure that this would be my last Sabbath on earth. But it finally came to an end.

On Sunday morning we packed, said good-bye, and headed home. It took about four hours to get there. I held *Ministry of Healing* on my lap all the way. I had a queer, jittery feeling which I cannot explain.

I Meet the Nelsons: They arrived a few hours after we did. I did not feel like being involved in any introductions, or even having them in my home. We went into the living room and talked for a while; and then they had a Bible study with us. All I could do was cry. Then Donna suggested that we have some music. Bert took out his guitar and we began to sing hymns of praise to the Lord. I found out that Satan hates Christian music. As we were singing, my eight-year-old daughter looked at Bert and said, "Satan won't let me sing." She and my twelve-year-old son both started crying uncontrollably. Bert and Donna looked at each other and at us and Bert said, "We have never prayed for two people at the same time before."

But the Lord kept everything under control. Steven and June, our son and daughter, were both crying and asking Jesus to help them and telling Him that they loved Him. Suddenly our daughter's eyes opened wide and she looked up at the ceiling. Donna said, "Look at June, she is not breathing." And she wasn't. "She is seeing something we can't see," Bert said to Donna. "Ask her what it is." June said she was by a stream. She saw a rabbit and a fox in the same hole, and a lion and a lamb together. Then she saw a man come to feed the animals. She recognized the man as Jesus. This went on for about fifteen minutes, and during that time we could not see her take a breath. I know because I was holding her hand and leaning over her to check her breathing.

Then June sat up; she blinked; then she said, "Oh, Mamma, Jesus is real! Jesus is real!" Steven kept saying, "June, I'm happy for you." They were both calm and able to sing again. We sang "All to Jesus I Surrender," but I could not sing. I love that song, but all I could do was cry.

After we put the kids to bed, Bert and Donna explained to us how much Satan hates to lose even one soul to Jesus and how he will go to any lengths to prevent it. They asked if I would like to have a season of prayer. I nodded Yes, because at that time I could not speak. Then Donna asked me to lie down so that I would be comfortable.

The Battle Began: I no sooner lay on the couch when a horrible, hideous male-sounding voice screamed out of me, "Hate! Hate!" Bert commanded them in the name of Jesus to be quiet. Then he asked me to repeat a beautiful prayer after him. I tried but I could not complete it. Then Bert and Donna asked me if it was if it was my desire to let them intercede for me. I nodded and said, "Yes." At that instant all hell seemed to break loose. I could not believe the voice or the words that came out of my mouth, but I could not stop it. Bert prayed, asking God if it was His will and to my benefit to hear these voices, if so my ears would be open; and if not, to close them. I heard everything.

I could not Pray: I would try to pray, but my prayer was continually interrupted by this voice. It would scream and yell, threatening Bert, "I'd kill you if I could." My arms were forced to try to grab him; and under satanic control I spit at him. Bert would hold up the Bible and repeat Scripture, but Satan forced me to turn my head. I could not look at that Book. Vile things were coming out of my mouth——filthy words I would never have used, even before I became an Adventist. Our friends in Ohio had told us about their experience, but to go through the experience myself was something entirely different.

Another Voice: I would try to speak, but that hideous voice would cut in, bringing things out of the past——trying to justify Satan's right to me. My husband told me later that even my green eyes turned cold-looking and piercing. My face became contorted. Intermittently I would strike out with my arms. I had begun to believe I was going to die when all of a sudden I saw this huge bright form of a man. He had blue eyes and long blonde hair. He was pointing a sword at the dark form which seemed to be cowering over me, and which now seemed small and powerless compared to the other form which I sensed was Gabriel. Once more I had hope! I wanted more than anything else to get this evil dominance out of my life. The cause of the oppression that had plagued my life was now clear to me.

I saw Christian Love: I had heard about demons—Satan's troops—during the six years I had been an Adventist. However, no one ever told me that I could gain the victory through prayer the way it was happening. These two people, Bert and Donna, had exercised their faith on my behalf. They had interceded for me. For the first time I felt and saw true Christian love in action. After about three hours, I suddenly sat up. I did not feel a complete release. God in His mercy knew we were very tired from traveling and from the experience we were having. We went to bed, but we did not get much sleep. My husband and my children had never seen or heard anything like this. But we did get some rest, which we badly needed.

Voices Again: The next morning, on arising, as I walked from the bedroom into the hall, those voices started again. I knew they were speaking out of me, but I could not help it. I had no control over them. I just could not let the children go off to school seeing me like that. So I knocked on Bert and Donna's door and asked to come in. Donna prayed with me while Bert and my husband got the children ready for school. They prayed for the holy angels to be with them that day, and sent them on their way.

As soon as the children left, I walked from the bedroom into the kitchen. As I passed my husband, I growled at him—a low, animal-like growl. I knew when it happened, but it was a voice I could not control. I was not the one who did it, but it came from my throat.

Identification: I went into the living room and lay down on the couch. Before anyone had a chance to get dressed or do anything else, the voices were screaming and yelling, just as they had the day before. Then the demonic voices began to identify themselves. "Drugs." "Cancer." On and on the list went until more than one hundred identifications had been made.

But good angels were there also. A war was being fought right in our home. I could feel the presence of Jesus and I knew that victory would come, but not without a battle. Satan repeatedly screamed his name out of my mouth. I was totally aware of what was happening. I could not help it, but I was no longer afraid.

Pastor Gregory Was Called: The battle had continued for quite a while when I cried out to Bert, "Call Pastor Gregory! Call Pastor Gregory!" (not his real name). Bert told my husband that many pastors preferred not to become involved in this kind of ministry; but that he would pray, and if God opened the door it would be done. Then Bert went into the bedroom to pray, and when he came out he asked my husband to call the pastor.

My husband called the church and Pastor Gregory answered. When Lyle asked him if he could come immediately to our home, he said he did not have a car at his disposal at that time. So Lyle made the quarter-mile trip and picked him up. There was very little time to explain to the pastor what was happening. My husband did tell Pastor Gregory that he was about to witness something he had probably never seen before, and that I was being prayed for, and that I had requested that he be there.

Pastor Gregory came: As soon as Pastor Gregory walked into our living room I sat up on the couch, pointed at him and yelled, "What are you doing here? You may lose your job over this." You understand that it was not really I who said it. It was a demon, speaking through me. He was using my voice.

Pastor Gregory ran to my side, grabbed my hand, and claimed the promise, "Where two or three are gathered together in my name, there am I in the midst of them." (Matt.18:20). It appeared that he thought I would be set free instantly, but this was not to be. Donna explained that demons do not leave willingly. They have to be commanded to leave. That is why Jesus gave His disciples and us authority over them. Demons are not subject to reason, but to the authority of Jesus Christ.

I don't know how long the battle lasted, but I remember that in the afternoon everyone read from the Scriptures. Even I was able to read the Bible. When Bert read, "Jesus is Lord," there was a definite reaction. Satan's voice yelled, "Never! Never!" This was repeated over and over. But then the words changed. The voice said, "Yes, yes, Jesus is Lord. Jesus is Lord. I had her for thirty-six years, but now I have to go."

Born Again: I remember sitting up suddenly and saying, "I'm OK, I'm OK!" The darkness that had dominated and controlled my life was gone. We rejoiced and thanked God. I am sure the angels of heaven were rejoicing too. I felt totally clean. I will never forget the date: March 29, 1988. That is my spiritual birthday. I had been born again, thank God. I had been set free.

Pastor Gregory's Testimony: One week later I heard from Pastor Gregory again. He called me on the telephone and said, "After much prayer and study I feel that what I witnessed was a true deliverance from demonic spirits." During the next three or four weeks we had sweet fellowship together. Friends from everywhere came to see us. Pastor Gregory was there. It was good.

Pastor Gregory asks me to give my testimony: He asked me how long I thought it would take for me to give my testimony in church. I told him I did not know since I had never done it before. He said he wanted to get with me to discuss it and to set up a time. But He never called again. I was never permitted to give my testimony. The entire climate of our previously warm and happy relationship suddenly chilled and became cold. I feel that church politics made the sudden change.

Pastor Gregory Rejects Us: He never came to visit us again. If he walked by our house, he turned his head so as not to face our home. We did not stop going to his church until later. Things were not the same at church either. When Pastor Gregory would see us coming toward him, he would avoid us—using another aisle if necessary. I could not see Jesus doing this.

We were asked to give up our positions in the Pathfinder club. Our children were made fun of and tormented by other children at school. Other children drew pentagrams and other demonic signs and symbols on the chalk board. Several times other children shouted, "We are going to put a curse on you." In order to place our children in a better environment, we moved to another area.

Fruitless Hope: In the hope of reconciliation we gave our testimony to two local elders. Shortly after that we received a letter warning us that if we did not deny our experience and say that it was not of God, we would be disfellowshipped. In good conscience we could not deny what God had done for us. We began to be shunned in different ways. We were ignored in Sabbath School, given the "cold shoulder" treatment. My husband's work was criticized. This was a new experience.

We were Disfellowshipped: Eventually the local church disfellowshipped us on the grounds that we had apostatized into spiritualism. In order to escape from the unpleasant situation, we moved to northern Michigan. Our reputation went before us. But, as the pastor and elders heard our testimony and saw the fruits of the experience in our lives, they said they saw no reason for our being treated the way we had been treated. We were re-baptized as proof of our complete dedication to the Lord.

With the help of Jesus we remain faithful. There are still challenges; we are not yet perfect. But we recognize the reality of the war, and we know that Jesus has already won the victory. We praise Him daily.

The Lord is good!

Deliverance Ministry in the Early Christian Church

It is well known that in spite of bitter persecution, the church had a remarkable growth in the first three centuries. The faith of the martyrs in the face of death brought multitudes to conviction. However, few people, even among ministers, know that Deliverance Ministry was a powerful tool of the Holy Spirit in that early explosive growth. Jesus statement that signs would follow the ministry of the church was specifically fulfilled.

"Go ye into all the world, and preach the Gospel to every creature," Jesus said. "And these *signs* shall follow them that believe; *In my name shall they cast out devils* ..." Then He said that their words would be *confirmed by signs* (Mk. 16:15, 16,20).

Why the Early Church Grew

Dr. Ramsey MacMullen, a Yale University historian, did a massive research into early church history. His findings were published in his book, 'Christianizing the Roman Empire—AD. 100-400. 1984, Yale University Press.

His research showed that Deliverance Ministry went on almost unabated for *three hundred or more years* into church history. This show of supernatural authority in the Name of Christ opened the minds of the people of the Greek and Roman world to receive the gospel. It was a strong influence in the growth of the church. When the people saw the power of God, they asked, "Who is this Jesus Christ in whose Name you work? Tell us about Him." Casting out devils gave proof to the preaching. The same evidence that was seen in the Lord's ministry. The same proofs that accompanied the ministry of the Apostles.

MacMullen found much historical data about demons being cast out of possessed people. He notes the tremendous effect of this miracle on the society of the times. These deliverances were frequently done in public. These displays of the power of the Holy Spirit caused the people to cry out, "What shall we do to be saved?" (Acts 2:37). As in the story of the man in the synagogue in Capernaum, demons would openly confess that Jesus Christ was Lord (Mark 1:24).

With such open demonstrations of supernatural power the pagan religions lost their credibility. Christianity spread like fire in the stubble. This summarizes Ramsey MacMullen's historical findings. We also include a few quotations from Jesse Penn Lewis' book, "War on the Saints" (WOS). Page numbers are for MacMullen's book unless otherwise specified.

The Power of the New Testament Church

The Gospels are an accurate record of the miraculous power seen in the ministry of our Lord. He healed the sick, raised the dead, and gave freedom to the captives of Satan (Acts 10:38). The book of Acts tells that these same remarkable powers continued into the ministry of the Apostles. A man who had never walked—Walked! (Acts 3:2-8). A dead woman—Rose! (Acts 9:40). Unclean spirits—Cast out! (Acts 5:16). All of these facts are fairly well known. Church growth was phenomenal under these manifestations of divine power.

Ellen White Confirms

"The church is not now the separate and peculiar people she was when the fires of persecution were kindled against her. How is the gold become dim! How is the most fine gold changed! I saw that if the church had always retained her peculiar, holy character, the power of the Holy Spirit which was imparted to the disciples would still be with her. The sick would be healed, devils would be rebuked and cast out, and she would be mighty, and a terror to her enemies." (EW 227).

As long as the church did not compromise with the world, the Holy Spirit and His power remained. When the church lost its holy character, the healing ceased and the deliverances stopped. The manifest power of Holy Spirit power departed. The church went into apostasy.

Early Christian Historical Record

The following historical records give profound insights into early church life and progress. They will be worth your careful reading. You will have knowledge about the early church known only by the few. Unless otherwise noted the references are to page numbers in the MacMullen book. I am also including some historical references taken from the appendix of the book "War on the Saints." (WOS) by Jesse Penn-Lewis.

TERTULLIAN (B. circa 160 AD.) had full understanding of the continuity of the entire Gospel commission, and confirmed that it was visibly in force in his own time.

"Jesus' authority over the fiercest infestations of satanic power, making them do whatever he wished by a mere word of command, he passed on to his disciples, with instructions to use it" (p. 27, see Luke 9:1).

"The manhandling of demons, humiliating them, making them howl, beg for mercy, tell their secrets, and depart in a hurry-- served a purpose quite essential to the Christian definition of monotheism: *it made physically (or dramatically) visible the superiority of the Christian's patron power over all others.* One and only one was God. The rest were *daimones* demonstrably, and therefore already familiar to the audience as nasty, lower powers that no one would want to worship anyway...Christian converts, by contrast, denied the name and even the very existence of all those gods, from the moment of believing" (p. 28).

Tertullian's Challenge

"... Let a person be brought before your tribunals who is plainly under demoniacal possession. The wicked spirit, *bidden to speak by a follower of Christ,* will as readily make the truthful confession that he is a demon, as elsewhere he has falsely asserted that he is a god. Or, if you will, let there be produced one of the god-possessed, as they are supposed -- if they do not confess, *in their fear of lying to a Christian,* that they are demons, then and there shed the blood of that most impudent follower of Christ.

"All the authority and power we have over them is from our naming the name of Christ, and recalling to their memory the woes with which God threatens them at the hand of Christ their judge, and which they expect one day to over take them. Fearing Christ in God and God in Christ, they become subject to the servants of God and Christ, so at one touch and breathing, overwhelmed by the thought and realization of those judgment fires, *they leave at our command the bodies they have entered, unwilling and distressed, and before your very eyes, put to shame....*" (WOS 140).

JUSTIN MARTYR, (ca. 100-165) in his second Apology addressed to the Roman Senate, says: "Numberless demoniacs throughout the whole world and in your city, many of our Christian men—exorcising them in the name of Jesus Christ Who was crucified under Pontius Pilate --have healed and do heal, rendering helpless, and driving the possessing demon out of the men, though they could not be cured by all other exorcists, and those who use incantations and drugs" (WOS 140, p 27).

CYPRIAN (ca. 200) expressed himself with equal confidence. After having said that they are evil spirits that inspire the false prophets of the Gentiles, and deliver oracles by always mixing truth with falsehood to prove what they say, he adds:

"Nevertheless these evil spirits adjured by the living God immediately obey us, submit to us, own our power, and are forced to come out of the bodies they possess (WOS 140).

"At Ephesus, so told the Acts of John, the Apostle encountered unbelievers but, with miracles of healing, won them over. More effectively yet, in the very temple of Artemis himself, he prayed, "'O God... at whose name every idol takes flight and every demon and every unclean power: now let the demon that is here take flight at thy name...' And while John was saying this, of a sudden the altar of Artemis split in many pieces... and half the temple fell down. Then the assembled Ephesians cried out, '(There is but) one God, (the God) of John!...We *are converted, now that we have seen thy marvelous works!* Have mercy on us, O God, according to thy will, and save us from our great error!' And some of them lay on their faces and made supplication, others bent their knees and prayed; some tore their clothes and wept, and others tried to take flight" (p. 26).

"At such a sign it could be seen how God 'threatened all men with terrible wrath,' and before it the whole town 'confessed the one and only God of the Christians.' That is, they were converted" (p. 26).

"Driving all competition from the field head-on was crucial. The world, after all, held many dozens and hundreds of gods. Choice was open to everybody. It could thus be only a most exceptional force that would actually displace alternatives and compel allegiance..." (p. 27).

"In so doing, they have declared the study of exorcism, possibly the most highly rated activity of the early Christian church, a historiographical 'no-go' era. But we have Justin boasting 'how many persons possessed by demons, everywhere in the world *and in our own city,* have been exorcised by many of our Christian men; *Irenaeus asserting that 'some people incontestably and truly drive out demons, so that those very persons often become believers"* (p. 27).

Then the Yale historian comments on Cyprian's statements:

"I don't think the explanatory force of this scene should be discounted on the grounds that it cannot have really happened, that it is fiction, that no one was meant to believe it. I suppose instead that *it was quite widely believed in the second and third centuries* with which we are concerned at the moment" (p.26)

"SAINT ATHANASIUS : (in the 350's) writing the Life of Saint Anthony, depicted the old man demonstrating the superiority of Christianity. He had been visited and challenged by 'persons counted as wise among pagans' (74). In answer to them, he undertook to offer proof (80) that 'believing, *pistis,* in Christ is the only true religiousness,' derived not by 'seeking logical conclusions through reasoning' but rather through that believing in itself. 'We convince,' he says, *'because people first trust in what they can actually see, and then in reasoned argument'*" (p. 112).

"Look now: here are some folk suffering from daimones' (for there were present some who were troubled by demons and had come to him; so he brought them forward, and went on). 'Either cleanse these men by your logic-chopping or by any other skill or magic you wish, and calling on your idols, or otherwise, if you can't, lay down your quarrel with us and witness the power of Christ's cross.' And with these words he called on Christ, sealed the sufferers with the sign of the cross twice and a third time, and straightway the men stood forth all healed" (p. 112).

"In one private house a sick man, thought by his family to be in extremis, was converted through an exorcist. Later he was to become Bishop of Rome. In that sort of discreet setting it is easy to imagine much spreading of familiarity with Christianity, if not precisely evangelical conversions. I sketched such a scene in an earlier chapter. " (p. 111).

Summary

The growth and progress of the early church was not entirely the result of anointed and persuasive preaching. The Apostle Paul specifically denies this to be the case. He stated that his converts were not won by his skill as a preacher. He attributed his success to a visible evidence of the power of God which accompanied his ministry.

"And I ,brethren, when I came to you, came not with excellency of speech or of wisdom, declaring unto you the testimony of God....And my speech and my preaching was not in enticing words of man's wisdom, but in *demonstration* of the *Spirit and of Power*. That your faith should not stand in the wisdom of men, but in the *power of God* (I Cor. 2:1-5).

Ellen White commented that the preaching of the early church was validated by evidences of visible power.

"In sending out the twelve, Christ sent none alone. They were to go forth two and two, invested with a power from Himself to heal the sick and rebuke Satanic agencies *as a proof of their mission*" (RH 03-23-97).

Paul's personal testimony and the above statement by Ellen White are fully supported by MacMullen's historical research.

"Miracles further served as a proof, not only as divine authority behind Christian teachings, but of God's unique claim to His title, whereas other supernatural beings deserved only to be called demons" (p. 108).

MacMullen does not say what happened after 400 AD. It was outside the scope of his research. However, there seems to be a direct relationship between the politicizing of the church under Constantine and the withdrawal of the Holy Spirit. The Holy Spirit would not share the governance of the church with politicians. The Holy Spirit withdrew and the slow decline and corruption of the church began. The manifest signs of the presence of the Holy Spirit were no more.

May the presence of the Holy Spirit soon be seen among us again to the glory and praise of Jesus Christ, the mighty Deliverer.

AMEN

The Deliverance of Nathaniel Davis

During Ellen White's ministry in Australia, (1891-1900) she had a very close working relationship with Elder A. G Daniells, then President of the Australasian Union Conference. The Lord revealed to Ellen White that a Literature Evangelist named Nathaniel Davis was possessed by an evil spirit. Daniells, in turn, was drafted as God's reluctant human instrument to set him free.

In brief this is what we know about Davis. He had been converted to Adventism only two or three years before (Circa 1894). Ellen White describes him as a pleasant person, very intelligent, and a good communicator. His excellent command of language is reflected in his letters to her. He had a practice of borrowing money from people and not repaying. In other words, he was a liar and a thief. It was also revealed to Ellen White that he was immoral.

Davis Wrote to Ellen White

On September 9, 1896 , he wrote an eloquent and repentant letter to her, confessing his mistakes and pleading for help:

> I have dishonored my Lord, disgraced my profession, made shipwreck of faith, and am now in despair, for I see only the blankest ruin and the direst need confronting me and have no one to blame but myself.
>
> I cannot pray; it chokes me to attempt to sing. I am a living lie, and am ready to sink into utter despair. Yet in spite of all, and as base as I am, I love the truth; I love the Saviour. I desire to do right, God knows I do; and yet I wonder myself how I can, for my life is full of wrongdoing and contemptible motives.
>
> I am willing to do anything that the Lord may direct, to follow in any course He may open up. But he seems not to hear me and I dread His wrath. Pray for me; beseech a testimony from the Lord regarding my case. I will submit to His word, only direct me, and I will follow (ND to EGW 9/9/1896).

Davis wrote several other letters to Ellen White in which he revealed that he was suffering greatly from guilt. In spite of his deplorable life-style, he was genuinely seeking help. By August, 1897, he had reached the breaking point.

> We cannot go on as we are at present....The difficulty is that I am perfectly nonplused. I want to do right and to honorably discharge all my liabilities....I want to overcome my vile traits of character and honor my Savior by my life. But how I am to do it, what course I ought to pursue and what step I ought to take now, I cannot see....I am a failure and I fear lest that fact will lead me to utter ruin. (Nathaniel Davis to Ellen G. White, Aug. 23, 1897, pp. 1, 2)

Ellen White Wrote to A. G. Daniells

On August 31, 1897, Ellen White wrote Daniells and described Davis' condition in clear-cut language:

> *Evil angels are all about him, and at times have control of him in a strange, revolting way....I have the word from the Lord that he is possessed of an evil spirit, and 'has no power from the snare to go.' His case is like the cases of ancient times.* At times, he thinks, speaks, and acts under the influence of satanic agencies, and does revolting things. This casts him into despair. *His only hope is to present his case before his brethren who have a living connection with God.* The spell will be broken only by the most earnest wrestling with God, and this I present to you...As soon as possible, this demon tempter's power must be broken...*Satan must be rebuked as in olden times, in the name of Jesus Christ of Nazareth.* This in faith we must ask the Lord to do, and He will fulfill His word. The Lord will hear prayer....Labor we must to have the man dispossessed. (Letter 39, Aug. 31, 1897, pp. 6, 7) (Italics supplied)

Daniells Seeks More Guidance

Daniells in his letters to Ellen indicated that he was hesitant to address the problem. Indeed he would not do so without her guidance. He wrote to her as follows: "I feel that I must have more counsel from you before I can take another step in his case" (Letter AGD to EGW August 30, 1897).

Daniells received the specific counsel he asked for. Ellen sent a letter to Davis in care of Daniells. He was told to read the letter to Davis. Sensing the great urgency in her letter Daniells stopped at Ballarat on his return from Adelaide. A meeting was arranged at Davis' home.

Daniells Reads the Letter to Davis

When I began reading it to him, he became very much excited. After a little, I heard some sort of disturbance, and looking up, saw him with an open knife in his raised hand. I asked, 'What is the matter?' He grated his teeth and glared at me like a madman.

His wife and I appealed to him to put the knife down, but he was menacing us so wildly that I did not dare to go on reading. I did not know whether he would thrust it into me or his wife or himself. I said, 'Let us kneel down and pray to God. There is a God in Israel who can help us, and we must have His help."

We knelt down, and I may tell you that I was never in a more perplexing place. I knew that demons were in the room and I knew that we must have the power of that same Christ who subdued demons and cast out devils while among men.

The first thing I said was 'O Lord, we come to Thee in the all-prevailing name of Jesus.' At the mention of the name Jesus, that man hurled his knife across the room with terrible violence. At the mention of the all-powerful name of Jesus he broke into sobs and the violence disappeared. After his wife and I had prayed, he prayed most earnestly to God to deliver him from those tormenting devils.

"When we arose I asked him to tell us what he knew about the truthfulness of this message.

Davis' Astounding Confession

He said, 'Brother Daniells, every word of it is true. For weeks I have been tormented by these evil spirits. I have been thrown out of my bed, and I have been hammered on the floor by those demons; it has wrecked my nerves, and I was about to give up to them and become their obedient slave again. " (Ministerial Institute address, June 25, 1928; transcript in Australasian Record, Aug. 13, 1928)

Daniells Further Description

About twelve o'clock we reached the place where it seemed we could all bow together with one heart, and ask the Lord to give him deliverance. We bowed down, and the moment I mentioned the name of Christ, the room seemed flooded with the presence of the divine Being. I have a few times when alone felt the wonderful presence of God as I did that night, but I do not remember ever having done so in company with anyone else. We all realized in a moment that Christ was in the room, and that Satan's power was broken....We began to praise God, not in any noisy, boisterous way, but quietly and calmly. We could do nothing but praise the Lord...we knew that Jesus was there, and that Satan had left us.... (AGD to EGW 9/12/97, p. 2)

Davis' Extraordinary Testimony

Davis described the spirit that had followed him....It purports to be the spirit of an Oriental from Tibet. This spirit has appeared to Brother Davis over and over again. He has a white beard and wears a turban. Many times this spirit has taken hold of Brother Davis body. Whenever he has done this, *it has left a pain in the part that was touched.* The last time this spirit appeared...Brother Davis had just gone to bed when it approached him with a terrible countenance. On reaching the bedside, it laid one hand upon him, and raised the other hand and swore that he would kill him. Brother Davis cried out in agony, and it left. He says that the awful visage of that spirit remained in his mind so that he could hardly sleep that night. It seemed to him that if it appeared to him again, it would surely end his life." (Ibid. p. 3)

Daniells' Gratitude for Her Guidance

I am very glad for the instruction you gave me to deal very kindly and patiently with him. I am glad you referred me to Jude 21-25. The experience was of great value to me. I have always shrunk from meeting the devil in that form, and have dreaded the idea of having to rebuke Satan. But when I saw how the mention of the name of Christ in living faith broke the power of the enemy, scattered his darkness, and filled our hearts with light and joy and peace, I received new impressions in regard to meeting the power of the enemy." (Ibid. p. 3)

Davis Testifies of His New Freedom

Now I have a continual experience of the presence and communion of heavenly intelligences stimulating my love for truth and righteousness and cheering me in the blessed hope of present victory and future rapture. Both my wife and I are rejoicing in this liberty" (Nathaniel Davis to Ellen White, Oct. 10, 1897, p. 1).

Postscript

We are grateful to God for the details about the Deliverance of Nathaniel Davis. It has given many insights.

1) Why did he not pray and set himself free? Notice that Davis could not pray. This is often true of person in a serious bondage. A key word in Deliverance is Intercession. The man of Gadara and Mary Magdalene could not free themselves—Jesus intervened. He left us a perfect example. Intercession is more needed now than at any previous time in human history.

2) The experience of Nathaniel Davis has given yet another blessing. It confirms what we have seen and experienced on many occasions. People have come to us telling of being thrown on the floor and beaten by unseen hands. Finding someone who will listen and believe their story is a source of indescribable relief to them. Altogether too frequently inexperienced people have turned them away in disbelief or told them that they were fantasizing or having mental problems.

3) The unusual pain Davis experienced is typical of what we have discovered in many suffering people. These mysterious pains do not generally yield to drugs (See EGW experience on page 195).

4) Daniells gave some important counsel to those who would be free:

> The Lord has shown Himself ready to give the man complete deliverance. *It rests altogether with Brother Davis himself. If he will believe God and abide in Him, he will be a free man.* I shall write to him at once, urging him to *be very careful not to lose the Savior a single day.* If he does, he will lose the blessing he has received. If you have any further light on his case I shall be very glad to receive it (AGD to EGW 9/12/97, Ibid. p. 4).

5) It is noteworthy that both Daniells and Ellen White called the new freedom of Davis a "Deliverance." We have chosen to use this same word.

6) Daniells predicted a growing need of this ministry:

> I have many times feared that his hellish shadow would sometime destroy me, but I believe that Jesus is a refuge for His people. *There is no doubt but what the enemy is exerting a terrific power over people at the present time, and there is no doubt that before the end comes, we shall have to meet him in human beings.* O, how glad I am that we have a refuge. How glad I am that we have a Saviour, who has met Satan and conquered him. In Christ we need not fear. But severed from Him, we are lost. (Ibid. p. 3)

7) Like Daniells, we have learned that there is no freedom without a total commitment to Christ. This decision Davis was willing to make. Freedom can be had under no other terms. There can be no benefits apart from surrender. Demons are not cast out so much as they are crowded out by the Holy Spirit. He brings this precious freedom only with the total consent of the human will.

Summary

The same Lord who set Davis free is still alive and willing to work for his people today. There are multitudes of precious people all about us whose lives are out of management. Like Davis they struggle and reach the point of despair and sometimes suicide. Can we not see the need and plead the victory of Christ in their behalf? This is part of the Lord's appointed ministry and the third element of the commission. There are many Nathaniel Davis's all around us seeking help. May the Lord guide us in helping them to find peace in Christ.

Freedom is a gift of the Lord Jesus Christ. He purchased it for you and me at awesome cost at Calvary. May you, Dear Reader, wear God's armor and be strong in the Lord until the final victory on this battlefield is won. To those who prevail the gates of the New Jerusalem, the city of Peace, will be opened, never to be shut.

The Oppression of Mrs. Riggs

J. N. Loughborough tells of an unusual experience on pages 173 and 174 of his book, *The Rise and Progress of Seventh-day Adventists*. He tells of Ellen White being given a special message for a lady member of the church who was being oppressed. Her torment was unknown by even her closest friends. Here is the record as told by Loughborough:

"There was in our company a sister, Mrs. Riggs, who seemed to be in deep trial of mind, but by the closest questioning she could not be induced to disclose the cause of her grief. Mrs. White told her the Lord had revealed to her the cause of all this sadness.

Ellen White's Vision

"She said, 'I was shown that after you retire for the night, and extinguish the light, there appears to you what looks like an old woman dressed in black, and it terrifies you. This apparition tells you that if you tell anybody she will choke you to death. When you are in the presence of your sisters, you think you will tell them all about it, and have them join you in a season of prayer that the Lord may rebuke this, which you regard as the work of Satan, as it really is. It is from the same source as the rapping spirits. The cause of your distress and staring into vacancy in the presence of your sisters is that you fear to tell them of your trial, lest this spirit carry out its threat, and take your life. Continuing, Mrs. White said, Sister Riggs, I have been shown that if you take your position against this power, *and have the brethren pray for you, it will be rebuked, and you will never be troubled with it again.*'

"Mrs. Riggs did not at that time say whether this was so or not, but a few days after, as Mrs. White called at the house of Mr. Orton, she found several of the brethren present, and also this Mrs. Riggs. Mrs. White said to her, 'Now, Sister Riggs, this is a good time for you to take your position against that spirit which is troubling you, and we will unite in prayer for you.'

The Battle Was Real

"The sister began to say, 'It is so,' but only succeeded in saying the words, 'It is,' when she began to struggle as though trying to extricate herself from the grasp of some strong person. She turned black in the face, as though indeed she was choking to death.

"Finally she cried out, 'Pray.' Those present immediately engaged in a season of prayer for her, and as they prayed, victory came. *Mrs. Riggs rebuked this evil spirit in the name of the Lord*, and was very happy. My first wife was present and witnessed the scene, and took part in the praying season.

Mrs. Riggs' Testimony

"When Sister White began to talk with me, I thought I would own up to the truthfulness of what she had told me of my case; but the moment I formed the resolution, the apparition was in the corner of the room, shaking her head at me, and saying, 'If you do tell, I will choke you to death.' I thought, I will say, It is so, so quickly that she cannot choke me; but the moment I spoke a word, as it seemed to me, she had me tightly grasped about my throat, and I was struggling for life. All Sister White said about the case is true. Thank the Lord; he has given me the victory.

The Results of Prayer

"Mrs. Riggs lived some twelve years after the above circumstance, but never had any more trouble of that kind. So the testimony that she would be relieved in answer to prayer was fulfilled, as also the promise that she would "never be troubled that way any more." With those then composing the Rochester church, the pointing out of this unknown difficulty, and the fulfillment of the promised relief, were indubitable proofs that these testimonies were the work of God, a true manifestation of the gift of prophecy. "

The Author's Final Question

With the experience of Nathaniel Davis, Sister Riggs and others on record, how can we fail to recognize the reality of the war on the personal level? How can we deny the need of the Deliverance Ministry in today's demon-saturated culture? With the endorsement of Scripture, the personal experience and counsel of Ellen White, how can we seriously question the need to restore an appropriate Deliverance Ministry?

With this is mind, we raise a vital question: Is it not time for us to re-evaluate our position in regard to Spiritual Warfare?

We believe that time has arrived.

Amen!

Index

A

B

C

V

W

Y